AFRICAN AMERICAN BIOGRAPHY

AFRICAN AMERICAN REFERENCE LIBRARY

AFRICAN AMERICAN BIOGRAPHY

VOLUME 1
A–D

U·X·L

An Imprint of Gale Research Inc.

AFRICAN AMERICAN BIOGRAPHY

STAFF

Carol DeKane Nagel, *U•X•L Developmental Editor*
Thomas L. Romig, *U•X•L Publisher*

Amy Marcaccio, *Acquisitions Editor*

Barbara A. Wallace, *Permissions Assistant (Pictures)*
Shanna P. Heilveil, *Production Assistant*
Evi Seoud, *Assistant Production Manager*
Mary Beth Trimper, *Production Director*

Cynthia Baldwin, *Art Director*

Weigl Educational Publishers Limited, *Page and Cover Design and Typesetting*

Library of Congress Cataloging-in-Publication Data

African American biography.
     p. cm. -- (African American reference library)
  Includes index.
  Contents: v. 1. A-D -- v. 2. E-J -- v. 3 K-R -- v. 4 S-Z
  ISBN 0-8103-9234-8 (Set : alk. paper); 0-8103-9235-6 (v. 1); 0-8103-9236-4 (v. 2); 0-8103-9237-2
    (v. 3); 0-8103-9238-0 (v. 4)
  1. Afro-Americans--Biography. I. U•X•L. II. Series.
E185.96.A44 1993
920'.009296073--dc20

[B]
                                           93-45651
                                              CIP

AFRICAN AMERICAN REFERENCE LIBRARY

AFRICAN AMERICAN REFERENCE LIBRARY

The **African American Reference Library** fills the need for a comprehensive, curriculum-related reference covering all aspects of African American life and culture. Aimed primarily at middle school and junior high school students, this nine-volume set combines appropriate reading level and fascinating subject matter with quality biographies, statistics, essays, chronologies, document and speech excerpts, and more.

The **African American Reference Library** consists of three separate components:

African American Biography (four volumes) profiles three hundred African Americans, both living and deceased, prominent in their fields, from civil rights to athletics, politics to literature, entertainment to science, religion to the military. A black-and-white portrait accompanies each entry, and a cumulative subject index lists all individuals by field of endeavor.

African American Almanac (three volumes) provides a comprehensive range of historical and current information on African American life and culture. Organized by subject, the volumes contain 270 black-and-white illustrations, a selected bibliography, and a cumulative subject index.

African American Chronology (two volumes) explores significant social, political, economic, cultural, and educational milestones in black history. Arranged by year and then by month and day, the volumes span from 1492 until June 30, 1993, and contain 106 illustrations and maps, extensive cross references, and a cumulative subject index.

Comments and suggestions
We welcome your comments on *African American Biography* as well as your suggestions for topics to be featured in future **African American Reference Library** series. Please write:

Editors, **African American Reference Library,** U•X•L, 835 Penobscot Bldg., Detroit, Michigan 48226-4094; call toll-free: 1-800-877-4253; or fax: 313-961-6348.

CONTENTS

AFRICAN AMERICAN BIOGRAPHY

Elizabeth Cotten

Ellen Craft

Countee Cullen

Angela Davis

Benjamin O. Davis, Sr.

Miles Davis

Ossie Davis

Sammy Davis, Jr.

Juliette Derricotte

Irene Diggs

David Dinkins

Sharon Pratt Dixon
  See Sharon Pratt Kelly

Thomas A. Dorsey

Frederick Douglass

Charles Richard Drew

William Edward Burghardt (W.E.B.) DuBois

Paul Laurence Dunbar

Katherine Dunham

Volume 2: E-J

Marian Wright Edelman

Elleanor Eldridge

Duke Ellington

Effie O'Neal Ellis

Ralph Ellison

Medgar Evers

James Farmer

Louis Farrakhan

Ella Fitzgerald

Aretha Franklin

John Hope Franklin

Mary Hatwood Futrell

Ernest J. Gaines

Marcus Garvey

Arthur Gaston

Henry Louis Gates, Jr.

Zelma Watson George

Althea Gibson

Dizzy Gillespie

Nikki Giovanni

Robin Givens

Danny Glover

Whoopi Goldberg

W. Wilson Goode

Charles Gordone

Berry Gordy, Jr.

Dick Gregory

Angelina Weld Grimké

Bryant Gumbel

Lucille C. Gunning

Clara Hale

Alex Haley

Arsenio Hall

Fannie Lou Hamer

Virginia Hamilton

Hammer

Lionel Hampton

Lorraine Hansberry

The Harlem Globetrotters

Barbara Harris

Marcelite Harris

Patricia Harris

Robert Hayden, Jr.

Dorothy Height

Jimi Hendrix

Matthew Henson

Aileen Hernandez

Anita Hill

Chester Himes

Gregory Hines

Billie Holiday

Benjamin L. Hooks

Lena Horne

Whitney Houston

Langston Hughes

Clementine Hunter
Zora Neale Hurston
Ice-T
Roy Innis
Janet Jackson
Jesse Jackson
Mahalia Jackson
Michael Jackson
Shirley Ann Jackson
John Jacob
Daniel James, Jr.
Mae C. Jemison
Beverly Johnson
Earvin "Magic" Johnson
James Weldon Johnson
John H. Johnson
Robert Johnson
Bill T. Jones
James Earl Jones
Jones, LeRoi
  See Amiri Baraka
Quincy Jones
Sissieretta Jones
Scott Joplin
Barbara Jordan
Michael Jordan
Vernon E. Jordan, Jr.
Jackie Joyner-Kersee

Volume 3: K-R

Elizabeth Keckley
Patrick Kelly
Sharon Pratt Kelly
Flo Kennedy
Kersee, Jackie Joyner
  See Jackie Joyner-Kersee
B.B. King
Coretta Scott King

Martin Luther King, Jr.
Yolanda King
Jewel Stradford Lafontant
Jacob Lawrence
Spike Lee
Carl Lewis
Elma Lewis
Little Richard
Louverture, Toussaint
  See Toussaint-Louverture
Joe Louis
Joseph E. Lowery
Naomi Long Madgett
Malcolm X
Annie Turnbo Malone
Eugene A. Marino
Branford Marsalis
Wynton Marsalis
Paule Marshall
Thurgood Marshall
Biddy Mason
Willie Mays
George Marion McClellan
Hattie McDaniel
Claude McKay
Floyd B. McKissick
Terry McMillan
Thelma "Butterfly" McQueen
James Meredith
Ron Milner
Thelonious Monk
Audley Moore
Garrett Morgan
Toni Morrison
Constance Baker Motley
Willard Motley
Elijah Muhammad
Eddie Murphy

Pauli Murray
Gloria Naylor
Huey Newton
Jessye Norman
Hazel O'Leary
Shaquille O'Neal
Jesse Owens
Satchel Paige
Gordon Parks
Rosa Parks
Sidney Poitier
Adam Clayton Powell, Jr.
Colin Powell
Leontyne Price
Charley Pride
Barbara Gardner Proctor
Richard Pryor
Public Enemy
Lloyd Albert Quarterman
Queen Latifah
Dudley Randall
A. Philip Randolph
William Raspberry
Ishmael Reed
Eslanda Goode Robeson
Paul Robeson
Jackie Robinson
Charlemae Hill Rollins
Diana Ross
Carl T. Rowan
Wilma Rudolph
Bill Russell
Bayard Rustin

Volume 4: S-Z

Edith Sampson
Sonia Sanchez
Dred Scott

Gloria Scott
Bobby Seale
Attalah Shabazz
Ntozake Shange
Al Sharpton
Althea T.L. Simmons
Carole Simpson
Naomi Sims
John Singleton
Bessie Smith
Wesley Snipes
George Stallings, Jr.
Shelby Steele
William Grant Still
Juanita Kidd Stout
Niara Sudarkasa
Henry Ossawa Tanner
Mildred Taylor
Susan Taylor
Susie Baker King Taylor
Mary Church Terrell
Clarence Thomas
Jean Toomer
Jackie Torrence
Toussaint-Louverture
Robert Townsend
William Monroe Trotter
Sojourner Truth
Harriet Tubman
Nat Turner
Mario Van Peebles
Sarah Vaughan
Denmark Vesey
Charleszetta Waddles
Alice Walker
Madame C.J. Walker
Maggie L. Walker
Sippie Wallace

PHOTO CREDITS

The photographs and illustrations appearing in *African American Biography* were received from the following sources:

On the covers: **Schomburg Center for Research in Black Culture, The New York Public Library, Astor, Lenox and Tilden Foundations:** Althea Gibson; **AP/Wide World Photos:** Josephine Baker; **Archive Photos:** Elijah Muhammad.

AP/Wide World Photos: pages 1, 4, 6, 9, 12, 18, 22, 26, 33, 36, 44, 47, 49, 51, 54, 62, 76, 80, 84, 94, 98, 113, 115, 117, 122, 124, 127, 141, 185, 231, 236, 238, 241, 257, 259, 270, 275, 277, 282, 287, 290, 295, 303, 305, 313, 336, 340, 343, 344, 350, 352, 356, 377, 380, 386, 388, 390, 393, 399, 415, 418, 431, 444, 447, 450, 463, 471, 475, 477, 483, 497, 499, 506, 521, 528, 534, 539, 553, 561, 566, 569, 574, 577, 584, 588, 590, 593, 612, 622, 625, 631, 633, 642, 658, 666, 668, 671, 681, 683, 692, 703, 712, 724, 737, 740, 745, 762, 765, 770, 774, 790, 794, 797, 799, 805; **Courtesy of Molefi Kete Asante:** page 24; **Schomburg Center for Research in Black Culture, The New York Public Library, Astor, Lenox and Tilden Foundations:** pages 29, 30, 41, 103, 174, 179, 208, 216, 244, 246, 267, 308, 359, 383, 420, 492, 515, 635, 679, 706, 732, 772; **Courtesy of Belafonte Enterprises:** page 56; **UPI/Bettmann Newsphotos:** pages 59, 199, 360, 434, 459, 468, 578, 637, 756, 777; **U.S. Office of War Information, Prints and Photographs Division, Library of Congress:** page 63; **Ed Haun/Detroit Free Press:** page 66; **UPI/Bettmann:** pages 68, 144, 147, 494, 526, 689, 767; **Reuters/Bettmann:** pages 72, 82, 157, 676; **Harper Brothers:** page 87; **Photograph by Larry McLucas:** page 90; **Courtesy of the United Nations (31216):** page 105; **Raymond W. Smock, Historian:** page 108; **National Education Television:** page 120; **Jazz Institute of Rutgers University:** pages 131, 229; **Photograph by Willard Moore:** page 136; **Courtesy of Shirley Chisholm:** page 139; **Courtesy of Jewel Plummer Cobb:** page 149; **Rick Diamond Photography:** page 151; **The Bettmann Archive:** pages 159, 422; **Courtesy of Marva Collins:** page 162; **Downbeat:** page 164; **Moorland-Spingarn Research Center, Howard University:** pages 167, 328, 543, 647, 708; **Photograph by Marco Sacchi:** page 169; **Photograph by Howard Bingham, Copyright © 1990 Universal City Studios Inc.:** page 172; **American Broadcasting Company:** pages 181, 316, 453; **Photograph by Anthony Barbaoza, © 1988 CBS Records Inc.:** page 187; **Universal**

Pictures: page 192; **Courtesy of Fisk University Library:** pages 194, 273, 627, 754; **Paul Oliver Collection, Woodstock, Oxford:** page 202; © **Rick Reinhold/Impact Visuals:** page 225; © **Photo by Bern Schwartz:** page 233; **Courtesy of Mary Hatwood Futrell:** page 252; **Photograph by Edward Spring:** page 254; **Courtesy of Oxford University Press:** page 262; **Photograph by Judith D. Sedwick, reproduced by permission of Ben Wallace:** pages 265, 334, 537; **Archive Photos/Tom Gates:** page 280; **Courtesy of the Collection of Mary O. H. Williamson, Moorland-Spingarn Research Center, Howard University:** page 293; **Photograph by James Estrin:** page 297; **Archive Photos/Serge Atall/Imapress:** page 300; **Cox Studios:** page 311; **Robert Nemiroff Estate, Jewell Handy, Executor:** page 318; **Episcopal Diocese of Massachusetts:** page 324; **Courtesy of Marcelite J. Harris:** page 327; **Photograph by J. Mud:** page 347; **Northwestern State University of Louisiana, Eugene Page Watson Library, Cammie G. Henry Research Center, The Mildred Baily Collection:** page 367; **Estate of Carl Van Vechten, Joseph Solomon, Executor:** page 369; © **Fotos International/Archive Photos:** page 373; **Lyndon B. Johnson Space Center:** page 395; **Archive Photos/Darlene Hammond:** page 401; **Photograph by George Frye:** page 406; **Robert Johnson Studio Portrait, circa 1935,** © **Stephen C. LeVere 1989:** page 410; **Photograph by James Salzano:** page 412; **Courtesy of Barbara Jordan:** page 425; **Photograph by Bill Smith, courtesy of the Chicago Bulls:** page 429; © **Nicola Dill/Outline:** pages 460, 660; **Martin Luther King, Jr., Center for Social Change:** page 455; **Eden Arts/Chris Eden:** page 466; **Photograph by Cecil Layne:** page 480; **Courtesy of Naomi Long Madgett:** page 485; **Photograph by Ed Druck:** page 489; © **Thomas Victor:** pages 501, 617; **Courtesy of San Francisco Giants:** page 510; **Photograph by Marion Ettlinger:** page 524; **Photograph by Bert Andrews:** page 531; **Courtesy of Constance Baker Motley:** page 545; **Charles L. Blockson, Afro-American Collection, Temple University:** pages 548, 619; **Archive Photos:** pages 550, 598; **Photograph by Janet Charles:** page 556; **Photograph by Christian Steiner, courtesy of Shaw Concerts, Inc.:** page 564; **Prints and Photographs Division, Library of Congress:** page 571; **National Broadcasting Company:** page 581; **Photograph by Thura Mack:** page 596; **Photograph by Ernie Panicioli,** © **1991 Sony Music, courtesy of Columbia Records:** page 601; **Courtesy of Tommy Boy Records:** page 606; **Courtesy of** *The Washington Post:* page 615; © **1984 by Layle Silbert:** page 608; **Courtesy of Lordly & Dame:** pages 651, 663; **Bennett College Library:** page 655; **Ed Kashi/***Time* **Magazine:** page 687; **Courtesy of Niara Sudarkasa:** page 695; **NYT Pictures:** page 698; **Courtesy of the Prints and Photographs Collection, Moorland-Spingarn Research Center, Howard University:** page 714; **Photograph by Irene Young:** page 717; © **Kelly Wise:** page 747; **Walker Collection of A'Lelia Perry Bundles:** page 751; **Photograph by Layle Silbert:** page 783; **Photograph by Margaret Ysuada:** page 788; **Courtesy of Ellen Wright:** page 802.

African American Biography

Hank Aaron

Baseball player
Born February 5, 1934, Mobile, Alabama

"The only thing I ever thought about was to be as good as I could. I never thought about being the greatest baseball player or anything, just to be as good as I could."

Hank Aaron

For years no one believed the record could be broken. Babe Ruth's major league record of 714 home runs would stand forever—until a young man from Mobile, Alabama, who'd become known as "Hammerin'" Hank Aaron, took a crack at it.

Aaron spent 23 years as a professional ball player and finished his playing days with an astounding 755 home runs and holding some of the most significant records in the sport.

Humble beginnings

Although he would go on to fame and glory, Aaron had humble beginnings. He was born in 1934 in Mobile, Alabama. the son of a boilermaker's assistant. He had two brothers and two sisters. The family lived only a block away from Carver Recreation Park, where the boys played many sports, including sand-lot baseball. While attending Central High School, Aaron excelled at football and basketball. One day Aaron's father took him to watch Jackie Robinson and the Brooklyn Dodgers play an exhibition game. Aaron was so impressed with Robinson's play, he told his father he'd be playing in the major leagues be-fore Robinson was through. His prediction came true.

When Aaron was 18, a scout from the Indianapolis Clowns Negro League baseball team signed him to a contract with a generous salary of $200 per month. While playing for the Clowns, he was scouted by several major league teams before signing in 1952 with the National League's Milwaukee Braves. They assigned him to their minor league team in Eau Claire, Wisconsin.

It didn't take Aaron long to excel with his new team. Playing shortstop, he batted a highly respectable .336 and was named the league's Rookie of the Year. The Braves quickly moved him to their affiliate in Jacksonville, Florida, where he won honors as the league's Most Valuable Player. Nonetheless, Aaron suffered from old prejudices. He was verbally abused at the ballpark, and when the team was traveling, he could not stay with the white players at hotels. Instead, he was billeted to black families in their homes. Although he was hurt by this prejudice, he never wavered from his determination to make the big leagues.

To the majors

In 1954 he finally got his chance. Although he played shortstop in the minors, the Braves wanted him to play outfield. Aaron stepped in when right fielder Bobby Thomson broke his ankle during the exhibition season. Though Aaron would break his own ankle later that season, he ended the year with a strong .280 batting average, 13 home runs, and 69 runs batted in (RBIs).

It was all uphill from then on. Aaron rose to prominence the next year by hitting .314 and driving in 106 runs. In 1956 he won the National League batting title with an average of .328. In 1957 he led the league in home runs and RBIs and the Braves to the National League pennant. Advancing to the World Series, the Braves met the New York Yankees, a team stocked with future hall of famers including Mickey Mantle, Yogi Berra, and Tony Kubek. Despite the Yankees' talent, Aaron led the Braves to victory and gave the city of Milwaukee its only World Series pennant.

In 1958, the Braves once again won the pennant, but lost to the Yankees in the World Series. Despite the team's setback, Aaron's career flourished. In 1959 he again led the National League in batting, prompting his manager, Fred Haney, to say, "a manager would be crazy to tell [Aaron] anything about hitting."

In 1963, 1966, and 1967 he led the team in home runs. In 1960, 1963, and 1966 he led in RBIs. In 1972, when he hit home run 650, fans realized he was closing in on Babe Ruth's record. Fan and media attention began to rise. And because the Braves had no prospects for winning a pennant since the club moved from Milwaukee to Atlanta, Georgia, in the mid-1960s, the focus was exclusively on Aaron. This shy man was suddenly a celebrity.

In 1973, racism reared its head and Aaron was subjected to verbal abuse at many ballparks and received death threats from people afraid he'd break Ruth's record. He also received thousands of letters of encouragement and support. Aaron ended the season with 713 home runs, one shy of Ruth's record.

On opening day in 1974 against the Cincinnati Reds, Aaron faced off against pitcher Jack Billingham in the first inning. With two men on base and one out and a three balls and one strike count, Aaron sent the next pitch into the left field seats. He tied the record before 52,000 screaming fans.

Breaking the record

Several days later, the Braves returned to Atlanta for their nationally televised home opener against the Los Angeles Dodgers. Opposing pitcher Al Downing decided not to take any chances in the first inning and walked Aaron. He later scored on an error, breaking Willie Mays's all-time record for runs scored with 2,063.

In the fourth inning Aaron came to the plate and sent the second pitch over the left field fence. Babe Ruth's record was broken! The game was stopped and Aaron was honored by the Braves, the National League, and representatives from the baseball commissioner's office. Western Union estimated that Aaron received 20,000 congratulatory telegrams. When the season was over—his twenty-first—Aaron was traded to the American League Milwaukee Brewers. He was pleased to return to the place of his baseball roots. "I always thought you people were responsible for my career," he told the audience at a civic luncheon. "When I made mistakes on the field, you stuck with me. Young players are blessed to be in a city like this."

In 1976 Aaron retired, holding records for home runs—755—for RBIs, and tied with Ruth for second place behind baseball great Ty Cobb for runs scored. He was elected to the Baseball Hall of Fame in his first year of eligibility—a feat achieved by few players.

Aaron eventually rejoined the Braves ball club as an executive. As a member of the front office staff he has promoted the hiring of blacks and other minorities in managerial and executive positions in professional sports.

Kareem Abdul-Jabbar

Basketball player
Born April 16, 1947, New York, New York

With only seconds left on the court and the hometown Los Angeles Lakers down by two, there was only one thought on the minds of their fans. Get the ball to Kareem Abdul-Jabbar. With his cat-like reflexes, intimidating height, and amazing "sky hook" shot, the game might still be saved.

And in many cases it was. As the towering 7 ft. 2 in. center for the Lakers, Abdul-Jabbar helped the team win five National Basketball Association (NBA) championships. An intimidating force as a rebounder and shot blocker, Abdul-Jabbar possessed grace, speed, and agility, as well as an amazing scoring touch.

His personal accomplishments are incredible: League Most Valuable Player six times; all star team member fourteen years; and Sports Illustrated Sportsman of the Year in 1985. When his twenty-year career ended in 1989, Abdul-Jabbar was the NBA's all-time leading scorer.

Showed superstar potential in high school

Born Ferdinand Lew Alcindor on April 16, 1947, he grew up in Harlem. At school he excelled at baseball, ice skating, and swimming, but by the eighth grade he was concentrating on basketball. While still a student at Power Memorial High School, Abdul-Jabbar was garnering headlines. As a seven footer, he dominated the New York City leagues during the 1960s.

He established a league record of 2,607 points and 2,002 rebounds while leading his school to three straight championships. His high school basketball team won 95 games and lost only 6 during Abdul-Jabbar's years with the team. At one time they had 71 consecutive victories. In the mind of most sports analysts, it was not a matter of if Abdul-Jabber would become a superstar, it was a question of when.

Over 100 universities offered Abdul-Jabbar scholarships, and he chose the University of California at Los Angeles (UCLA) in 1965. In his first game he set a UCLA record with 56 points. He set about improving his stamina and developed a dunk shot (jumping and thrusting the ball through the rim). His height, grace, and deft shooting touch led UCLA to three consecutive NCAA championships.

As a sophomore and a senior, he was chosen the top collegiate player in the country. He wound up his NCAA career as the ninth all-time collegiate scorer, accumulating 2,325 points in 88 games for an average of 26.4 points per game. In his best game he scored a whopping 61 points. During his time at UCLA they only lost 2 games. After UCLA's third championship, Abdul-Jabbar signed a $1.4 million contract with the Milwaukee Bucks of the NBA. It was also during this time that Abdul-Jabbar converted to Islam and legally changed his name in 1971.

Won numerous NBA awards

During his rookie NBA season with the Bucks in 1969–70, he wasted little time proving he was worth the money. Although the team was a newly established expansion club, Abdul-Jabbar led it to second place in the Eastern Division. They were only a few games behind the New York Knickerbockers, the division winners.

During his initial season, Abdul-Jabbar elevated his star status with his outstanding play in the all-star game. He combined with the Knicks' Willis Reed to lead the East to victory in an exciting exhibition of skills. At the end of the season he was selected the NBA's Rookie of the Year and finished second in league scoring with 2,361 points, second only to superstar Jerry West. He also

pulled down the third highest number of rebounds—1,190.

In 1971 he began dominating the league. Playing center, Abdul-Jabbar combined with newly acquired guard Oscar Robertson in making the team virtually unbeatable (they had an .805 winning percentage). He won the scoring championship (2,596 points) and game-point average (31.7), and he upped his rebound total to 1,311. He also bested his own personal scoring high of 53 points a game—when he hit 55 against the Boston Celtics. Miraculously, he seemed to be getting better and better. The Bucks easily won their division championship and went on to sweep the Baltimore Bullets for the NBA title.

The following year, he won the scoring title again with 2,596 points and game-point average with 34.8, but the Bucks were unsuccessful in duplicating their championship. They clinched their division championship

Kareem Abdul-Jabbar

with a sizzling 63–19 record but were eventually knocked out of the playoffs by the Los Angeles Lakers. Abdul-Jabbar won his second consecutive Most Valuable Player Award, nosing out Lakers Jerry West and Wilt Chamberlain.

In 1973 he finished second in league scoring with a 30.2 point average, but he grew dissatisfied with life in Milwaukee and was eventually traded to the L.A. Lakers, where he regained his motivation. He again garnered the Most Valuable Player award in his first two seasons with his new team. When point guard Earvin "Magic" Johnson arrived in 1979, it seemed to once again spark Abdul-Jabbar. The Lakers won the 1980 NBA championship with Abdul-Jabbar receiving his record sixth Most Valuable Player award.

Retired his jersey

In 1984 Abdul-Jabbar broke Wilt Chamberlain's career scoring record of 31,419 points. The Lakers won five championships during the 1980s, including back-to-back titles in 1987 and 1988. After this final championship, Abdul-Jabbar retired at the age of 41. He ended his career with records for most points (38,387), most field goals made (15,837), and most minutes played (57,446). His jersey was retired shortly afterwards, and he is now a member of the Lakers' front office staff.

During the off-seasons Abdul-Jabbar acted in several movies, including *Game of Death, The Fish that Saved Pittsburg,* and *Fletch,* and in several television shows, including "Mannix" and "Different Strokes."

In 1984 he wrote his autobiography with Peter Krobler, *Giant Steps,* revealing his deep devotion to the Hanafi Muslims. He believes the Islamic religion (which differs from the nationalistic Black Muslims) and determined personal effort have much to offer for a great life. Abdul-Jabbar is also greatly influenced by the life and struggles of late civil rights activist Malcolm X.

Besides his involvement with the Lakers, Abdul-Jabbar is also president of Canberry Records, affilated with MCA.

Ralph David Abernathy

Civil rights leader
Born March 11, 1926, Linden, Alabama
Died April 17, 1990, Atlanta, Georgia

"Mr. Abernathy was known as the 'other side' of Martin Luther King, and there is much evidence that King could not have succeeded without him."

Inspired by the success of the Montgomery, Alabama bus boycott protesting segregated public transit, Ralph David Abernathy and Martin Luther King, Jr. founded the Southern Christian Leadership Conference (SCLC) in 1957 to promote civil rights for black Americans. Following King's assassination in 1968, Abernathy took over the leadership of the SCLC and doggedly carried on the campaign. Though Abernathy retired from the SCLC in 1977 for an unsuccessful run for Congress, he continued the work he and King began until his death in 1990.

Abernathy has sometimes been called the "other side" of his longtime friend and associate King, for Abernathy found it easy to relate to the poor and working-class, while King, at least in the early years, appealed more to educated middle-class people in the cities. Together, the two men were a powerful team, attracting thousands of followers. King would have had far less impact in American society and government without Abernathy at his side.

Early life

Abernathy was the tenth of twelve children born to a farmer, William Abernathy, and Louivery (Bell) Abernathy. Originally named David, he was nicknamed Ralph by one of his sisters. Ralph aspired early to be a preacher, but once he graduated from Linden Academy, the local black high school, he was drafted into the U.S. Army to serve in the last months of World War II.

Ralph David Abernathy

After the war, Abernathy enrolled at Alabama State College in Montgomery, where he was elected president of the student council and led a successful protest to gain better living conditions for the students. He was ordained a Baptist minister in 1948, and graduated with a B.S. in mathematics in 1950. He earned an M.A. in sociology from Atlanta University the following year.

While Abernathy was in Atlanta he first heard King preach. Abernathy was impressed, and after the service he introduced himself to King. "Even then, I could tell he was a man with a special gift from God," Abernathy later wrote of King in his autobiography *And the Walls Came Tumbling Down*. Within a few years, the two young ministers were to meet again—with fateful results.

With King in Montgomery

In 1951 Abernathy became pastor of First Baptist Church in Montgomery. Three years later King became pastor of another black church in Montgomery, Dexter Avenue Baptist. The two men became fast friends, as did their families. Abernathy married Juanita Jones in 1952, and they had four children during the following years.

Sharing a mutual interest in the fledgling civil rights movement, Abernathy and King discussed how to go about bringing an end to segregation in an orderly, nonviolent manner. "While [King] was talking about strategy ... I was thinking about tactics," Abernathy would later write.

Abernathy and King first worked together to end segregation in 1955 when Rosa Parks, a black seamstress tired after a long day's work, refused to give up her seat to a white passenger on a Montgomery bus. She was arrested and fined, as were many other blacks who had previously refused to do the same, but Parks's arrest touched a nerve in the community, for she was quiet, well-respected in the community, and active in the local NAACP.

The local Women's Political Council called for the black people of Montgomery to protest by refusing to ride the buses. King and Abernathy took up this idea and made it work. They formed the Montgomery Improvement Association, and held meetings to spread the word about the boycott and had ministers explain from the pulpits how the boycott was to be conducted. They arranged for taxis to take people to work at reduced fares and, later, when the city objected to the practice, they organized carpools. The boycott began on December 5, 1955, and despite threats and other intimidation, it lasted for more than one year, until the U.S. Supreme Court ruled that segregation on Montgomery buses was illegal.

Working for the SCLC

Encouraged by the success of the boycott, King and Abernathy were now determined to push for civil rights for blacks in all areas of life. In 1957 they arranged a meeting in Atlanta, Georgia, with other Southern ministers and formed the Southern Christian Leadership Conference, an organization of churches and civic groups that would lead nonviolent desegregation protests across the South.

King was elected president of the SCLC and Abernathy secretary-treasurer. All those present at the meeting were aware of the dan-

gers they faced, knowing that their nonviolent protests were likely to be met with violence. Indeed, while Abernathy was at the SCLC meeting, his home and the First Baptist Church were bombed, as well as other homes and churches in Montgomery. Although his wife and children escaped unharmed, it was a chill warning.

In 1960 King moved to Atlanta to devote more time to the SCLC, and the following year Abernathy joined him there, becoming pastor of West Hunter Street Baptist Church. During the next few years, the two ministers devoted themselves to the SCLC, leading nonviolent marches, sit-ins, and rallies in the major cities of the South. They were arrested a number of times and threatened often, but they attracted support across the nation. Little by little the laws were changed.

By the mid-1960s the civil rights movement had achieved most of its aims, but African Americans were still disadvantaged and many were very poor. To draw attention to the poverty, King organized a Poor People's Campaign in 1968, intending to march on Washington, D.C., but he was assassinated in Memphis, Tennessee, before he could carry out his plan. It was left to Abernathy to complete the task.

Abernathy had been vice-president of the SCLC since 1965, and on King's death he was elected president. In May 1968 he led the march to Washington to protest for economic and civil rights. He and his followers set up a campsite called Resurrection City near the Lincoln Memorial, to which poor and homeless people came from across the country. The results of their efforts were disappointing, largely because Congress was preoccupied with the problems of the Vietnam War. After little more than a month, Abernathy disbanded Resurrection City.

Last years

As president of the SCLC, Abernathy led several other desegregation protests in the South, including a major one in Charleston, South Carolina. He resigned in 1977 to run for Congress, but he failed to gain the seat. Undaunted, he formed an organization called Foundation for Economic Enterprises Development (FEED) to teach blacks job skills, continued his ministerial duties at his church, and lectured across the United States. He published his autobiography, *And the Walls Came Tumbling Down,* in 1989, the year before he died.

Alvin Ailey

Choreographer, director, dancer, and actor
Born January 5, 1931, Rogers, Texas
Died December 1, 1989, New York, New
  York

"I'm interested in putting something on stage that would have a very wide appeal without being condescending; that will reach an audience and make it part of the dance."

A lvin Ailey has been credited with permanently embedding African American modern dance in American culture. As the founder of the Alvin Ailey American Dance Theater in 1958, Ailey went on to international acclaim for his innovative, vibrant,

and celebratory choreography. His troupe began with a mere eight dancers dedicated to black folk arts, and has grown to a main company with 30 dancers, a repertory of over 150 works, a junior troupe spotlighting young dancers, and a school training more than 1,000 students.

Learned tap dancing from a neighbor

Ailey was born on January 5, 1931, in Rogers, Texas, to Alvin, a laborer, and Lula Ailey. When Ailey was twelve, he and his mother moved to Los Angeles, where she worked for Lockheed. She also cleaned homes, but did not tell Ailey. In high school he played football, joined the gymnastics team, and learned tap dancing from his neighbor, Loretta Butler, on her shellacked living room floor dance studio. He was probably attracted to tap dancing because he was exposed to Gene Kelly and Fred Astaire in 1940s Hollywood.

Ailey was introduced to the city's black dance world by a high school friend studying classical music. It was the most vibrant such community in the country after Harlem, and it was led by Lester Horton. Finding inspiration from Japanese, American Indian, and other dance forms, Horton operated a school in Hollywood, where black artists, intellectuals, and entertainers met. Ailey became one of his students.

After about a month Ailey's enthusiasm waned, and he dropped out. He headed to UCLA to study romantic languages. In the book, *The Private World of Ballet,* Ailey said, "I didn't really see myself as a dancer. I mean, what would I dance? It was 1949. A man

Alvin Ailey

north to attend college in San Francisco. To make ends meet, he loaded baggage for Greyhound and eventually started dancing in a nightclub. The show toured Los Angeles and Ailey ran into Horton once again. Horton told him he was staying away from the mainstream and began choreographing dances that were inspired by the painter Paul Kee, the novelist Garcia Lorca, and composers such as Duke Ellington and Igor Stravinsky.

Ailey begins choreographing in Horton's style

Ailey dropped his college studies and became a dance student again in 1953. When he was not dancing, he was teaching children. That winter Horton suffered a heart attack and Ailey tried to follow in his footsteps. Facing a season at the prestigious Jacob's Pillow festival the next summer, Ailey choreographed two pieces in Horton's style. One was a tribute to Horton entitled *According to St. Francis,* and the other was based on themes by Tennessee Williams, *Mourning Morning.* The works were a flop. The festival manager wrote a scathing letter, calling the works "kitchen sink ballets" without form.

The troupe dissolved a few months later, but Ailey was not out of work long. Broadway producer Herbert Ross invited him to New York City to join the cast of *House of Flower,* a musical adaptation of Truman Capote's book. The musical was in disarray when Ailey arrived. Legendary choreographer George Balanchine had just been dismissed, the director and the performers were not speaking, and attendance was poor. The show managed to last five months, providing Ailey with a foot-

didn't just become a dancer. Especially a black man. I mean, you could be a (Katherine) Dunham dancer, or you could be a tap dancer — you know, show business, big swing." But Horton thought Ailey had potential. He offered him a scholarship and Ailey returned to the school.

Horton believed dancers should know every part of the production, so Ailey found himself doing things he had not reckoned. He mopped the stage, worked in the costume shop, and painted scenery. In his spare time he earned extra money as a waiter. "I was happy," he recollected in *The Private World of Ballet.* "Lester let us know that we were all beautiful. There were Japanese and Mexicans and blacks, whites, greens and pinks. And it was great. I was very happy being in the milieu of the dancers. I was 18."

That happiness lasted for about a year, when Ailey dropped out again and moved hold in New York. He spent his spare time studying dance with Martha Graham, ballet with Karel Shook, composition with Doris Humphrey, and acting with Stella Adler.

Ailey worked with the musical *Jamaica* in 1957 and continued to dance with small companies. In March, 1958, he and a friend, Ernest Parham, pulled together thirty-five dancers and gave eight performances at the 92nd Street YMHA. The performances contained the premier of *Blues Suite,* some Latin dances, and a solo by Ailey as a tribute to Horton.

The favorable press reviews convinced Ailey to form his own company. In 1958 he assembled a troupe of eight black dancers dedicated to black music and culture called the Alvin Ailey American Dance Theater. The troupe was based out of the Clark Center for the Performing Arts at Eighth Avenue and 51st Street. The company stayed there until 1969, when they moved to a new venue in Brooklyn. That borough lacked Manhattan's sophistication and the company moved back after three years. Among the kudos the troupe received during this time was that of P.W. Manchester, who wrote in *Dance News,* "the stage world created by Alvin Ailey [is] an altogether stimulating, exciting, beautiful, funny and original entertainment, meticulously presented."

With a chronic weight problem, Ailey's dance career had come to an end by the time the company moved. But the company did well, furthering its reputation as the country's most renowned modern dance troupe. The company starred Judith Jamison, and Ailey

decided to integrate white and black dancers. He felt whites should be allowed to dance black dance. "It's like saying only French people should do Racine or Moliere," he told the *New York Times Magazine.*

In 1971 the troupe established itself as a major company and Ailey founded the Alvin Ailey American Dance Center, his official dance school and home of the Alvin Ailey Repertory Ensemble, an apprentice group. The U.S. State Department sponsored a series of world tours during the 1970s in which the troupe performed in forty-four countries on six continents. Despite the company's popularity, Ailey still faced financial problems. Sometimes he would take a commission to choreograph a dance and use the money to pay an old phone bill.

Ailey suffers a mental breakdown

Ailey suffered a mental breakdown in 1980 which hospitalized him for several weeks. He blamed a midlife crisis, the death of close friend Joyce Trisler, and financial pressures for his condition. When he returned to the company, he had a new philosophy. He told *Newsday:* "Give up something. Do less. Concentrate on what's really important."

Ailey's principal dance works included *Revelations,* which the original program called a study of the "motivations and emotions of American Negro religious music; *Mountain Way Chant,* which is based on Navajo Indian ceremonies; and *Labyrinth,* a reworking of the Greek myth about the minotaur. His troupe served as a showcase for the modern dance creations of such popular choreographers as

Talley Beatty, Bill T. Jones, and Ulysses Dove.

"The black pieces that come from blues, spirituals and gospels are part of what I am," Ailey told the *New York Times Magazine*. "They are as honest and truthful as we can make them. I'm interested in putting something on stage that would have a very wide appeal without being condescending; that will get everyone into the theater. What do they mean when they say it's Broadway? If it's art and entertainment — thank God, that's what we want it to be."

During his lifetime, Ailey received numerous awards including first prize at the Paris International Dance Festival in 1970; *Dance* magazine award, 1975; Spingarn Medal from the National Association for the Advancement of Colored People (NAACP), 1976; Mayor's Award (New York City) of Arts and Culture, 1977; proclamation in New York City of Alvin Ailey American Dance Theater Twentieth Anniversary Day, 1979; and Samuel H. Scripps American Dance Festival Award for lifetime contributions to American modern dance, 1987. Ailey was among five outstanding artists to receive the annual Kennedy Center Honors award for lifetime achievement in 1988. He received honorary degrees in fine arts from many universities and colleges including Princeton University, Bard College, Adelphi University, and Cedar Crest College.

Ailey died of dyscrasia, a blood disorder, on December 1, 1989, in New York City. Gerald Arpino, a colleague, told the *Washington Post* upon his death that Ailey would be remembered for "works [that] have elated amd moved audiences throughout the world."

Muhammad Ali

Boxer
Born January 17, 1942, Louisville, Kentucky

"Float like a butterfly, sting like a bee!"

K nown as "The Greatest," boxer Muhammad Ali began his career as a light heavyweight gold medalist at the 1960 Olympic Games and went on to become the world heavyweight champion in 1964–67, 1974–78, and 1978–79. Light on his feet and deadly with his fists, it was Ali's boast that he could "float like a butterfly, sting like a bee."

The mix of boastfulness and charm is a well-known feature of Ali's character, as is his bold stand on issues he cares about. He dared to refuse war service in Vietnam in the late 1960s, and both before and afterwards he championed the disadvantaged, speaking out against racism and injustice. In his later years, he has concerned himself with world affairs, trying to bring peace in troubled areas. He is also fighting a private battle with a Parkinson-like disease.

Muhammad Ali took his present name in 1963 after becoming a Muslim. He was born Cassius Marcellus Clay, Jr., the son of Cassius and Odessa Clay. It was as Cassius Clay that he first gained fame in the ring.

Won Olympic gold medal in Italy

Although Cassius Clay was an outspoken young man, he is said to have been rather shy as a child. He was raised in his parents' clap-

Muhammad Ali

board house in Louisville, Kentucky, and took up boxing because he thought it was "the quickest way for black people to make it." At the age of twelve, he started working out in the Columbia Gym in Louisville. His original trainer was Joe Martin, a white Louisville patrolman, but it was his black trainer, Fred Stoner, who taught young Cassius to move lightly and gracefully.

The combination of Stoner's training and Cassius' strength, skill, and will to succeed resulted in his winning a gold medal at the 1960 Olympics in Italy. This was a great triumph for eighteen-year-old Cassius, and he was immensely proud of his success, wearing his medal day and night. But he received a shocking setback one day when he went into a five-and-dime store to order a burger and soda pop. The waitress looked at him and said, "Sorry. We don't serve coloreds."

The young boxer was furious. He had gone all the way to Italy and won a gold medal for his country, and here he was back home unable to get served in a five-and-dime store. This incident had great impact on Cassius. "That gold medal didn't mean a thing to me," he said, "if my black brothers and sisters were treated wrong in a country I was supposed to represent."

Cassius became interested in the civil rights movement, especially to activist Malcolm X, who inspired him to join the Nation of Islam and become a Muslim. This was when Cassius took the name Muhammad Ali. He was twenty-one at the time and was already beginning to attract media attention—for his personality as much as his boxing.

Knocked out Sonny Liston for world heavyweight title

After winning the Olympic gold in 1960, Ali turned professional and signed the most lucrative contract ever negotiated by a beginner. It gave him a 50–50 split with a twelve-member group of millionaires called the Louisville Sponsoring Group. Just four years later, in February 1964, Ali fought world heavyweight champion Sonny Liston. This was a dramatic fight, for although Liston could punch with deadly power, Ali used intelligence and skill as well as strength and knocked out his opponent. At the age of twenty-two he became heavyweight champion of the world.

During the next three years Ali successfully defended his title nine times, adding to his legend with each match. His clever, controlled boxing, his dancing footwork, and the speed of his powerful punch placed him head and shoulders above other boxers. Fans thronged to see him—he was a popular idol—

until he began to speak out against the Vietnam War.

In 1966, when Ali was due to be drafted into the Armed Forces, he announced that he was a pacifist that his Muslim beliefs prevented him from going to war. "I ain't got nothing against them Viet Congs," he said. This attitude raised a storm. Sports writers, radio and television commentators, and many other Americans young and old, denounced him as unpatriotic and a disgrace to his country.

The public outcry had its effect. In May 1967 the New York State Athletic Commission and the World Boxing Association stripped Ali of his title and banned him from boxing in the United States. Ali faced a prison sentence too, yet he refused to back down. He was sentenced to five years in prison and was released on appeal, but he was at length cleared in 1970 when the Supreme Court overturned his conviction.

U.S. Supreme Court put Ali back in the ring

Returning to the ring after a three-and-a-half-year layoff, Ali prepared for another shot at the title. He won against Jerry Quarry in November 1970, and this restored his confidence, but the following year he lost against the current world champion, Joe Frazier. This was Ali's first loss, and it shattered him. "It was like death," he said.

Not until 1974 did Ali regain the world title, first by defeating Frazier and then by defeating reigning champion George Foreman (who had knocked out Frazier the previous year). Foreman was younger and stronger than Ali, and most fans expected Ali to lose, but his speed and intelligence gave him the necessary superiority, and he knocked out Foreman in the eighth round.

World heavyweight champion once again, Ali defended his title successfully for the next four years. In 1978 he lost to Leon Spinks, but he regained the title later in the year. By this time Ali was old for a boxer—in his late thirties—and in 1979 he was persuaded to retire. He found it hard to stay out of the ring, though, for he loved the limelight and the cheers of the crowds. Twice more he returned, but he each time he lost, no longer having the speed and control of his earlier years.

Tells school children, "Find your purpose."

In 1975 Ali published a book, *The Greatest: My Own Story,* and in 1976 starred in a film about his life, *The Greatest*. His boxing slower and less precise over the years, Ali was diagnosed in the early 1980s as having a form of Parkinson's disease—possibly the result of taking so many blows to the head, but the fighter has continued an active public life.

He has been involved in politics, working for the Democratic party, and in 1985, went to Lebanon in a fruitless attempt to free four kidnapped Americans. He tried successfully in Iran in 1990, returning home with fourteen Americans who had been held hostage.

Ali's commitment to helping others has focused increasingly on the young, and especially on young African Americans. At the Our Children's Foundation in Manhattan in 1990 he told the youngsters: "The sun has a purpose. The moon has a purpose. The snow has a purpose. Cows have a purpose. You were born for a purpose. Go to school. Learn to read and write.... Find your purpose."

Marian Anderson

Singer
Born February 27, 1902, Philadelphia, Pennsylvania
Died April 8, 1993, Portland, Oregon

"If there is a tragic aspect to Marian Anderson's career, it is simply that later generations, black and white, would view her as something of a tattered social symbol rather than as the greatest contralto of the twentieth century."—Donald Bagle

As the first African American artist to entertain at the White House and the first to sing a major role with the Metropolitan Opera in New York, Marian Anderson's career symbolized the move toward racial equality. With quiet dignity and great perseverance, she made her way into forbidden territory, performing in places no African American had been allowed before.

Anderson's achievements were due to the superb quality of her singing. Her rich contralto voice stretched three octaves and was as roundly trilling in its high notes as it was mellow and warm in the deep lower notes. She possessed a superb musicality, using her voice like a skillfully played instrument. Despite her talents, this great contralto was not easily accepted by American audiences. Only after she was hailed as a superstar in Europe was she

able to break through the barriers at home. Yet break through she did. As Jesse Jackson said, "Beyond her extraordinary singing talents, she was a source of light and hope in one of the dark periods of American history."

Singing for her supper

Even as a small child, Anderson had an exceptional voice. She joined her church's junior choir at the age of six, and when she was eight she earned her first money, fifty cents, by singing "The Lord Is My Shepherd" at a recital. Even such a small sum was a welcome addition to the Anderson household. Anderson's father, John, made only a small income from the ice and coal he sold at a downtown Philadelphia market. When he died in 1912, Anderson's mother, Anna, could not support her three daughters on her own, so she took them to live with her in-laws and went to work as a cleaning woman.

As the eldest in the family, Anderson saw it as her duty to help support her mother and two sisters. At William Penn High School, she learned shorthand and typing, thinking she might have to get a job as a stenographer, though what she most wanted to be was a singer. Fortunately, the school authorities decided she was wasting her talents taking a commercial course, and she was transferred to South Philadelphia High School for Girls, which had better music teaching than William Penn.

When Anderson was in her mid-teens, her mother fell sick and could not work; Anderson became the family's sole wage earner. She was already bringing in a little money from singing in local churches and at social events,

Marian Anderson

and she now increased her schedule as much as her schoolwork would allow. Her accompanist, Billy King, helped arranged some tours for her. Meanwhile, she was given free singing lessons by a local soprano, Mary Patterson, who realized that the teenager had an exceptional voice. She was also taught by the contralto Agnes Reifsnyder.

Like many others in the community, Anderson's music teachers encouraged her to seek further training, yet when she applied at a local music school, she was told coldly, "We don't take colored." This was a tremendous shock, for Anderson had simply assumed that she would be admitted. Her high school principal then arranged for her to audition before the Italian-born teacher Giuseppe Boghetti, who had trained some of the most prominent concert performers. When Boghetti agreed to take Anderson as a student, the Union Baptist Church formed a fund to pay for her first year's studies. Boghetti taught her free of charge during the second, knowing she could not possibly afford his fee.

Celebrated concert singer

After graduating from high school, Anderson was able to spend more time on her music and soon had a busy schedule of performances in the churches, clubs, and colleges of the black community. She had learned French at school, and under Boghetti's instruction she began to sing French songs. He also taught her some Italian and coached her in German songs and various operatic pieces. This greatly increased Anderson's repertoire, which until then had consisted mainly of hymns and spirituals.

In 1924, she gave her first concert to a predominantly white audience at the Town Hall in New York. It was a dismal failure. The reviews were so scathing about Anderson's pronunciation of foreign words that she gave up singing in public for almost a year. She was almost ready to go back to the idea of being a typist, but Boghetti persuaded her to enter a contest sponsored by the National Music League in the summer of 1925. Three hundred singers entered this contest, eager to gain the coveted prize, which was a performance with the New York Philharmonic Orchestra. Anderson won first prize, and on August 26 she appeared at the Lewisohn Stadium where, she sang "O Mio Fernando" from Donizetti's opera *La Favorita*. This time, there was no problem with her pronunciation, for she had practiced diligently with Boghetti. The reviewers went wild. They could not praise her enough.

Despite this success, Anderson's career did not immediately take off. She was still singing mainly to black audiences and putting up with the discomfort and humiliation of segregated railway carriages when on tour. To advance her career, she studied in England in 1929 and 1930, and the following year she returned to Europe, having gained a Julius Rosenwald Fellowship to study in Germany.

Two years later, Anderson was back in Europe again, this time on a concert tour of Scandinavia. This highly successful tour was a turning point in her career. Singing a mix of classical songs and spirituals, she gave 108 concerts in twelve months, performing before such eminent people as King Christian of Denmark and King Gustav of Sweden. The Scandinavian tour was followed by a sensational series of concerts in London, Paris, Rome, and many other European capitals, where again she was a phenomenal success. The conductor Arturo Toscanini voiced the general feeling of awe when he said, after an Anderson concert, "What I heard today, one is privileged to hear only in a hundred years."

In Paris, American impresario Sol Hurok was so impressed that he insisted on becoming Anderson's manager and arranged a concert series for her in the United States. She made her debut at the Town Hall in New York—where she had been such a failure a decade earlier. As usual, she included some spirituals along with the songs of Schubert and other classical composers. The audience loved it, as did the reviewers. The *New York Times* hailed Anderson as "one of the great singers of our time." Thus, in 1935, Anderson at last won recognition in her own country.

Anderson was soon so busy that theaters were booking her two years in advance. She was invited to perform before President Franklin Roosevelt at the White House, and she sang for King George VI and Queen Elizabeth of England on their visit to America. Yet the racial issue had not gone away. Touring in the United States could still be unpleasant, though now that Anderson was such a celebrity, she did have a little more control. When performing in the South, she always insisted that the separate seating portioned off for blacks must be equal to that provided for whites.

Civil rights heroine

The racial issue came to a head in 1939, when the Daughters of the American Revolution (DAR), who owned Constitution Hall in Washington, D.C., refused to let Anderson sing there. This blatant act of racism so enraged First Lady Eleanor Roosevelt that she resigned from the DAR and arranged for Anderson to give a free outdoor concert at the Lincoln Memorial on Easter Sunday. Overnight, Anderson became front-page news, attracting the attention of millions who had never even been to a concert.

Those who were present on that cold Easter Sunday will never forget it. Standing before the massive figure of Abraham Lincoln, Anderson opened the concert by singing "My Country 'Tis of Thee." More than seventy-five thousand people had gathered to hear her, and millions more listened on the radio. Unintentionally, Marian Anderson had become a powerful symbol in the struggle for racial equality.

In 1943, partly because of increasing pressure, the DAR at last permitted Anderson to sing at Constitution Hall. That same year,

Anderson married a friend from her youth, New York architect Orpheus Fisher. By this time, she was universally recognized as a superstar. Having long ago seen that her family was well provided for, she gave away much of her earnings to charity.

Anderson continued to tour throughout the 1950s, and in 1955 she achieved a longstanding ambition when she was invited to sing at New York's Metropolitan Opera. She sang the role of Ulrica in Verdi's *Un Ballo in Maschera.* In 1958, after a goodwill concert tour in the Far East, she received an unexpected accolade when President Eisenhower appointed her a delegate to the United Nations.

Anderson was now approaching the end of her singing career, which she wound up in 1964–65 with a triumphant four-continent tour that began in Constitution Hall and ended in Carnegie Hall. After her retirement, she gave a few concerts on special occasions. She also made some recordings of her songs, and in 1991 she was given a lifetime Grammy award. She died at the age of ninety-one at the home of her nephew, symphony conductor James De Preist.

Maya Angelou

Writer, poet
Born April 4, 1928, St. Louis, Missouri

"The pervasive theme, naturally developed in all [Angelou's] autobiographies, is the strength of the Black woman, her ability to prevail despite the awful hurting put upon her by the world."

W ell-known poet Maya Angelou has been an actress, a journalist, a singer, a professor, a songwriter, a nightclub waitress, an aide to Martin Luther King, Jr., a scriptwriter, a dancer, an editor, a Creole cook, and even a streetcar conductor. Above all she is a writer, creating a warm and perceptive picture of what it is like to be a black woman in the United States.

Provided a stable life with her grandmother

Maya Angelou was born Marguerite Johnson, the daughter of Bailey and Vivian (Baxter) Johnson. The name Maya was given to her by her brother, Bailey, Jr., who called her "my-a-sister." When Maya was three, her parents divorced, and she and little Bailey were sent by bus to their grandmother, Annie Henderson, who lived in Stamps, Arkansas. With no one to accompany the two small children, they were simply put on the bus with tags tied to their wrists, saying who they were and where they were going.

Their grandmother ran a general store, which enabled her to support the children despite the hardships of the Depression years. But this stable phase of Maya's life came to an abrupt end when she was eight. While visiting her mother in St. Louis, she was raped by her mother's boyfriend, Mr. Freeman. She then had to appear at Freeman's trial. The harrowing experience confused and frightened Maya, and when Freeman was later kicked to death, she felt responsible for his murder. The whole ordeal was too much for her, and she simply stopped speaking. Maya remained silent for the next five years.

Knew small town and big city life

Back with her grandmother in Stamps, Arkansas, Maya gradually emerged from her nightmare. She was helped in her recovery by Bertha Flowers, who talked to her about books, gave her poetry to read, and encouraged her to write poetry. Even more supportive was her grandmother, who encouraged the silent child by telling her that she could become anything she wanted, even a preacher. If she worked hard and believed in herself, she would be able to achieve wonders, despite the difficulties. They were well aware of the difficulties blacks faced in that era of segregation. Like many communities throughout the South, Stamps was totally segregated and offered few opportunities for African Americans.

Nevertheless, by the time Maya graduated from eighth grade in 1940, she believed she could have control of her life and make something of it. "I am the captain of my fate,

Maya Angelou

I am the master of my soul," quoted a classmate at the graduation ceremony, and Maya agreed wholeheartedly. She graduated at the top of her class and had high hopes, but soon afterwards she and Bailey left the security of their grandmother's home and went to live with their mother in San Francisco. Their mother had become a professional gambler and ran a rooming house.

Maya attended George Washington High School in San Francisco and took drama and dance lessons at the California Labor School. While in high school she became the first female streetcar conductor in San Francisco, but her lifestyle in her mother's rooming house was very different from her grandmother's home. Maya became pregnant, and at the age of sixteen she gave birth to a son, Guy.

Achieved some success as dancer and actress

After her son was born, Maya moved out of her mother's home to be independent and support herself, but this was not easy. She applied for several jobs before being taken on as a cook in a Creole restaurant. Over the next few years Maya worked as a nightclub waitress and for a time became a prostitute. At the age of twenty-two she married a white man, Tosh Angelos, a former sailor. Maya hoped to bring some order into her life, but the marriage failed after two-and-a-half years. Although Maya had gained security, she missed the freedom of being single.

Once more on her own with a child to support, Maya worked as a dancer in a bar, which led to a job dancing at the Purple Onion, a well-known nightclub. For the first time

Maya worked with whites who treated her as an equal. The Purple Onion proved to be a turning point in Maya's life, for it led to performances in other nightclubs, including the Blue Angel in New York, and within a few years she became a successful nightclub singer and actress. During 1954–55 she toured Europe and Africa in *Porgy and Bess.* She also changed her name to Maya Angelou, "Angelou" being a variation of her former husband's surname.

Wrote multivolume autobiography

Angelou's visit to Africa made a great impression on her, and when she returned to the United States, she continued her career as a performer, but she became active in the civil rights movement. In 1960–61 she served as Northern coordinator for Martin Luther King, Jr.'s Southern Christian Leadership Conference. Late in 1961 Angelou and her son went to Cairo, Egypt, with Vusumzi Make, a South African freedom fighter. Angelou lived with Make for several years, but gradually their relationship became strained. This was partly because Angelou took a job as editor of the *Arab Observer* to bring in much-needed money, and Make resented the independence this gave her.

After leaving Make, Angelou traveled with her son to Ghana, which had recently gained independence from Britain. She taught music and dance at the University of Ghana and served as an editor of the *African Review* and as a writer for the *Ghanaian Times* and for radio. However, Ghana was a disappointment for Angelou. She was treated as a foreigner—an American—rather than a fellow African. In 1966 she returned to the United States. Acting, composing poems and songs, and producing a television series, "Africanisms in American Life," occupied Angelou, and in 1972 she was the first black woman to have a screenplay, *Georgia Georgia,* produced. In 1973 she married Paul de Feu, the ex-husband of Australian feminist Germaine Greer (the marriage ended in 1981). In 1977 she earned an Emmy nomination for her performance in the TV production of Alex Haley's *Roots.*

Spurred on by James Baldwin and other friends, Angelou began to write her autobiography. The first volume, *I Know Why the Caged Bird Sings* (1970), was widely recognized as an outstanding work and in 1979 was made into a television movie. To date, there have been four more volumes of the autobiography: *Gather Together in My Name* (1974), *Singing' and Swingin' and Gettin' Merry Like Christmas* (1976), *The Heart of a Woman* (1981), and *All God's Children Need Traveling Shoes* (1986). Angelou has also written several books of poetry, including *I Shall Not Be Moved* (1990). Her poetry, like her prose, deals with issues affecting African Americans as well as those of society as a whole. Most critics view her work as an important contribution to the personal literature of America, and especially to African American literature.

Wrote and delivered poem for Clinton inauguration

Angelou has been writer-in-residence and visiting professor at several universities, and since 1981 has held a lifetime appointment as Reynolds Professor of American Studies at

Wake Forest University in Winston-Salem, North Carolina. She teaches one course each semester and lectures across the country.

In 1993, Angelou received great attention when she was invited to write a poem for the inauguration of President Bill Clinton. Following President Clinton's swearing-in, she delivered a magnificent and moving poem before the massed crowds thronging as far as the eye could see, boldly and clearly reading her tribute, "A Rock, A River, A Tree." She was the first poet to appear at a presidential inauguration since Robert Frost spoke at President Kennedy's inauguration in 1960.

Louis Armstrong

Jazz trumpeter and singer
Born July 4, 1900, New Orleans, Louisiana
Died July 6, 1971, Long Island, New York

"Music's my language. On all those trips all over the world, maybe the musicians can't speak with you, but play 'Struttin' with Some Barbecue' and they'll know their parts and chime right in."

For the last twenty-five years of his life, Louis Armstrong was one of the most famous people in the entire world and by far the most famous jazzman. As popular in Ghana as in Georgia, as well known in Lithuania as in Louisiana, he was said to be the greatest jazz performer ever.

During a career that spanned more than fifty years, Armstrong played a central role in the development of jazz as it changed from Dixieland to more modern styles. His versatile trumpet playing and rich, gravelly voice inspired many younger musicians while thrilling his adoring fans. His records sold in the millions and still continue to sell in vast numbers more than twenty years after his death. Among the many songs he made famous are "West End Blues," "When It's Sleepy Time Down South," "What a Wonderful World," and "Hello, Dolly."

Little Louie

Louis Armstrong has said that he was "brought up around music," yet it was by pure chance that he even learned to play an instrument. He grew up in one of the poorest and toughest areas of New Orleans, spending his early years mainly with his grandmother, since his parents were separated. Occasionally he stayed with his father Willie Armstrong and with Willie's second wife and children, but he was happiest when living with his mother Mayann and his younger sister Beatrice. All of them were desperately poor, and there was never any money to spare. To help his mother make ends meet, Louis ran errands and sold papers in the street, and when he was about nine he found work with a local coal merchant, selling buckets of coal from door to door.

Louis's mother lived in the seedy but lively Storyville district of New Orleans, where the streets were filled with the music overflowing from the many dance halls and bars. Often honky-tonk ragtime bands marched through Storyville, and Louis and his friends merrily tagged along behind them. When Louis was about ten, he and some friends formed a street quartet. They would sing a few songs, pass round the hat, and then run home to give their earnings to their parents.

Although Louis was obviously very musical, he might never have become a famous trumpet player if he hadn't been overexcited one night when he was thirteen. While celebrating New Year's Eve, he fired a pistol loaded with blanks. This led to his arrest, and he was sent to the Colored Waifs' Home, a reform school for boys, where he was taught to read music. Before long he was playing the drums … and then the bugle … and by the time he left the school, he was an accomplished cornet player.

Louis had no cornet of his own, but after leaving the school he borrowed one until he was able to buy one second-hand. In his late teens, while working at odd jobs by day, he haunted the nightspots in the evenings, absorbing the styles of the different bands. Occasionally he had a chance to perform, filling in for a missing player. "Run and get little Louie," the bandleader would say, and Louis would come running. He impressed people from the beginning, for he learned at an astonishing speed and could play anything he could whistle.

The jazz world of the 1920s

From 1917 to 1922, Armstrong improved his style while playing with various Dixieland jazz bands in New Orleans, incuding the band of the legendary King Oliver. Oliver gave Armstrong lessons and took a fatherly interest in the talented young player. When Oliver left New Orleans in 1919 he found Armstrong a job with Kid Ory's Band, and three years later he invited Armstrong to join him in Chicago.

As second cornetist in King Oliver's Creole Jazz Band, Armstrong played in the clubs and dance halls of the Midwest and made his first recordings. His playing attracted considerable notice, especially the duets he played with Oliver, which became the talk of Chicago. Moving to New York City two years later, Armstrong emerged from under Oliver's shadow to joined the Fletcher Henderson Band, and he made some memorable recordings with blues singer Bessie Smith.

The year 1925 saw two important developments: Armstrong changed from the cornet to the trumpet, and he returned to Chicago, where he started playing with his own groups and with the band of jazz pianist Lillian Hardin, whom he had married the previous year. Hardin was Armstrong's second wife— his brief first marriage had ended in divorce a few years earlier—and she had convinced him that he was good enough to work independently.

The next few years were enormously significant in the history of jazz because of Armstrong's inspired improvisations. As he experimented in his playing, giving his musical imagination full rein, he broke free from the rigid Dixieland style and set jazz on a new path. His trumpet playing was so jubilant and brilliantly versatile that he automatically took center stage, and he began to add some dancing and singing to his performances. Around this time, he is said to have invented scat singing—the type of improvised singing that uses syllables instead of words. During this period, too, Armstrong joined with fellow New Orleans musicians to make the immensely popular "Hot Five" and "Hot Seven" recordings, which had such a profound influence on the course of jazz.

In 1927, Armstrong formed his own big band called Louis Armstrong and His Stompers, and two years later he scored his first triumph with a popular song when performing Fats Waller's "Ain't Misbehavin'" in the revue *Hot Chocolates*. By the end of the 1920s, his fame had spread throughout the country, and he was regarded as the leading jazz musician of the day.

Satchmo the Great

Armstrong gained the nickname Satchmo on his first tour of Britain in 1932, the first of many overseas trips. He followed up by touring Europe in 1933–35, before returning home to film *Pennies from Heaven* with Bing Crosbie. Yet the early 1930s were not a good time for Armstrong. He had fallen deeply in debt, partly because of his divorce from

Louis Armstrong

Hardin, but mainly because of the incompetent men who had been acting as his managers. Not until he hired a new manager, Joe Glaser, did his fortunes pick up. With Glaser, Armstrong began to focus on popular music more than on jazz; he appeared frequently in movies and became the first African American to have his own sponsored radio show. This change of direction lost Satchmo many of his old fans, though their departure was only temporary. By the late 1940s, he was once again playing vintage jazz.

Throughout the 1950s and 1960s, Satchmo was at the peak of his popularity, one of the most beloved entertainers in the world. Wherever he went, he was greeted by adoring crowds. Accompanied by his third wife Lucille, he was a particular success on his first visit to Ghana. He was almost constantly on tour during the 1950s, but had to slow down during the 1960s as his health began to fail.

One of Armstrong's greatest successes in the 1960s was his recording of the song "Hello Dolly," which ousted a Beatles record from the top of the charts. He also scored hits with "Mack the Knife" and "Blueberry Hill." These were but a few of the many hits Armstrong had during his life. In his more than fifty-year career, he made almost two thousand recordings, many of which are now considered classics. He appeared in numerous Broadway shows and some thirty-five movies. Most of all, he loved making music, and his music gave pleasure to all the world. When asked what he thought about when he was playing, he once said, "I just think about all my happy days and memories, and the notes come out. Always has been that way. To me, jazz has always got to be a happy music. You've got to love it to play it."

Molefi Kete Asante

Educator and writer
Born August 14, 1942, Valdosta, Georgia

"There is nothing more correct for African Americans than to search for and follow our own historical traditions."

T he author of more than one hundred scholarly articles and some thirty-five books, Molefi Kete Asante is the founder of the Afrocentric movement, which calls for a more global and comprehensive view of human behavior. Afrocentricity places Africa rather than Europe at the heart of the social universe, giving a new perspective to anthropological study. As Asante explained to *Newsweek,* "African people for 500 years have lived on the intellectual terms of Europeans. The African perspective has finally come to dinner."

Asante holds that Africa, not Europe, is at the heart of all African American behavior. During his thirty-year career in education, communication, and anthropology, he has made an in-depth study of the African American experience, and he is credited with establishing the first doctoral program in African American studies. Since 1969, Asante has been editor of the *Journal of Black Studies* and, since 1984, he has been professor and chairman of the Department of African American Studies at Temple University in Philadelphia.

The childhood of Arthur Lee Smith, Jr.

Until 1973, Asante was called Arthur Lee Smith, Jr. He changed his name after talking to a librarian in Ghana who had one of his books in the library but thought it was written by an Englishman. This made the author realize the importance of having a name that clearly affirmed his African heritage. He chose Asante because it reflected his family's ethnic origins.

Although neither of his parents, Arthur Lee Smith, Sr., and Lillie (Wilkson) Smith, finished elementary school, they were inquiring, intelligent people who possessed deep wisdom and were a great inspiration to their son. "My father was perhaps the most brilliant person I've ever met," Asante has said. "I get my curiosity and quest for knowledge from him. From my mother, I get a sense of the joy of life and the value of communication and interaction with human beings."

Determined that their son would get a good education, Asante's parents sent him to Nashville Christian Institute, one of the few black church boarding schools in the South. Returning home during summer holidays, Asante helped out in the cotton and tobacco fields, and when he was twelve he had his first paying job—as a shoe-shine boy. It lasted only a day. He left in fury after a white customer spat on his head.

At school, Asante learned about the magnitude of racial discrimination from an older student, Fred Gray. Gray later became a civil rights lawyer and represented Martin Luther King, Jr. Meanwhile, he had a strong influence on Asante, who became so concerned about racial issues that he joined in the Fisk University civil rights march in Nashville, even though he was only a high school student.

Like other students at Nashville Christian Institute, Asante learned to value hard work and discipline, for the school had a strong respect for the work ethic. Because of this and with the encouragement of his teachers, Asante made it into college, which he had never expected to do. He did extremely well academically, gaining a string of degrees: an A.A. from Southwestern Christian College in 1962, a B.A. with honors from Oklahoma Christian College in 1964, an M.A. from Pepperdine College in 1965, and a Ph.D. from the University of California, Los Angeles (UCLA), in 1968.

Chronicling the African American experience

While Asante was a student at Southwestern Christian College, he met a Nigerian named Essien, who fascinated him with tales of Africa. Asante had already done some research into the history and culture of Africa, but now he was inspired to go further. After completing his undergraduate courses, he embarked on an intensive study of the ancient Egyptian language and of African literature. The more Asante read, the more he came to realize how closely his own past and culture were linked with that of Africa.

Africa and the African American culture became a central interest as Asante launched his academic career at Purdue University and then at UCLA, where from 1970 to 1973 he was director of the Center for Afro-American

Molefi Kete Asante

Studies. He then moved to the State University of New York, as professor of communication, before becoming head of the Department of African American Studies at Temple University in 1984.

During these years, Asante produced some important writings on African American culture. His first major work, *The Rhetoric of Black Revolution* (1969), related the black experience to the civil rights movement, whereas *Toward Transracial Communication* (1970) and *Transracial Communication* (1973) were about communication between blacks and whites.

Asante's studies led him to travel to Africa—he has visited the continent more than eighteen times—and in 1981–82 he spent a year in Zimbabwe as Fulbright professor at the Zimbabwe Institute of Mass Communication. Since Zimbabwe has such an ancient culture, it was an appropriate place for Asante to be as he formed the Afrocentric movement.

The Afrocentric movement

Asante launched the Afrocentric movement with his first book on the subject, *Afrocentricity: The Theory of Social Change* (1980). He has said that he founded the movement in order "to examine why it was that we as a people were so disoriented." Having been brought to the United States as slaves, he explains, African Americans have been cut off from their heritage and denied their uniqueness, their basic humanness. The Afrocentric movement aims to repair this damage by turning the attention back to Africa. "There is nothing more correct for African Americans," says Asante, "than to search for and follow our own historical traditions."

His 1987 book, *The Afrocentric Idea,* enlarged on the original themes, emphasizing the role of Africa to such an extent that the book drew criticism from some quarters. In *Newsweek,* historian Arthur Schlesinger, Jr., complained: "What … Asante has been saying, essentially, is that Africa is the source of all good and Europe is the source of all evil." To this, Asante has responded: "We are not seeking a position of superiority. We're simply looking to have all human cultures alongside each other so that *everyone* is respected."

Asante feels that Afrocentricity is gaining ground and that many people throughout the world are now looking at things from an Afrocentric viewpoint. In the United States, his particular concern is to imbue young people with this viewpoint. As a consultant to several school districts, he has been working to make the curriculum more Afrocentric by incorporating African history and culture into the general study courses—not only into lessons on history and culture, but into those on science, religion, politics, and the arts.

To aid the growth of Afrocentricity, Asante has helped produce a number of books that serve as rich resource material on African American culture and the African heritage. These include *A Guide to African and African American Art and Antiquities* (1979), *African Myths: New Frames of Reference* (1982), *Historical and Cultural Atlas of African Americans* (1991), *The Book of African Names* (1991), and *Thunder and Silence: The Mass Media in Africa* (1992).

Arthur Ashe

Tennis player
Born July 10, 1943, Richmond, Virginia
Died February 6, 1993, New York, New York

"He was out doing things, making his point and taking care of business right up until the end, and I guess that sums up everything that he stood for."

One of the world's greatest tennis players, Arthur Ashe was in 1968 the first African American to be the nation's top-ranking player, and in 1975 he not only won the World Championship Tennis Singles but became the first black player to win the singles championship at Wimbledon in England.

The wiry Ashe was famous for his 115-mile-per-hour serve and also for his gracious and dignified behavior on the tennis court. A true gentleman-athlete, he turned his attention to social issues when forced to retire from active tennis because of heart surgery. He helped younger players, championed the cause of black athletes, and, towards the end of his life, promoted AIDS awareness. Ashe was elected to the Tennis Hall of Fame in 1985 and was chosen Sports Illustrated Sportsman of the Year in 1992.

Entered a world of white country clubs

Ashe's father, Arthur Ashe, Sr., was superintendent of the largest park for blacks in Richmond, Virginia, during the era of segregation when there were separate parks for blacks and whites. The Ashe family lived in the caretaker's cottage in the park, and young Arthur began tennis playing at the age of seven, the year after his mother died. "Books and sports were my way of bandaging the wound," he later said. "I was too light for football and not quite fast enough for track, which left tennis."

Arthur Ashe

Tennis was not an easy choice, as Arthur was to discover over and over again. With African American, Mexican, and native American ancestry, he was simply an intruder who had no right to be there at the white country clubs. Sometimes he was refused entry to competitions by being told that he had applied too late; and when he was admitted, he was usually made to feel unwelcome. As the only black person among a crowd of whites, Ashe was very careful how he behaved. Though this made him a very courteous player, it also had a lasting effect on his self-esteem. Later in life, he said that "growing up in the South, you get the impression that the world doesn't like you."

Nevertheless, Ashe rose quickly in the tennis world. Ronald Charity, a part-time instructor at the playground, noticed his talent and referred him to Dr. Walter Johnson, a tennis coach and promoter. Johnson acted as Ashe's sponsor, overseeing the young player's training, and by the time Ashe was fourteen he was already playing at the national level. In both 1960 and 1961 he won the Junior Indoor Singles title. These victories brought him to the attention of Richard Hudlin, a coach in the St. Louis area, and Ashe finished high school in St. Louis while being coached by Hudlin. By 1962 he was the fifth-ranking junior player in the United States.

Achieved international fame

After high school Ashe enrolled at the University of California, Los Angeles (UCLA), on a tennis scholarship, and in 1963 he was chosen for the Davis Cup team—the first black player ever picked for the team. His tennis triumphs continued throughout college, and by his 1966 graduation he was ranked second-top amateur player in the United States. Ashe performed his military service as a first lieutenant in the Reserve Officers' Training Corps (1967–69) and continued to play tennis, during which time he became top-ranking player in the United States, winning the U.S. Open Championship in 1968. The following year he turned professional.

The next ten years saw Ashe at the peak of his form, winning one championship after another and beating some of the best players in the world. His greatest triumph was in 1975 when he defeated Jimmy Connors at Wimbledon and Bjorn Borg at the World Championships. This twofold victory made Ashe undeniably the world's top player. But he was more than just a brilliant tennis player. His good manners on the court were a notable contrast to the tantrums thrown by some of the white players, and his personal style set an example to blacks and whites alike.

Contracted AIDS from a blood transfusion

By the 1970s black players were finding it easier to get into sports such as tennis, but Ashe's tennis career was nearing its end. In 1979 he suffered a massive heart attack, and the following year, after heart bypass surgery, he realized he would no longer be able to play.

Ashe faced this bitter blow the way he had faced other challenges—with quiet determination and courage. He changed direction, focusing on helping younger black athletes. For this reason he researched and wrote a three-volume history of America's black athletes, *A Hard Road to Glory,* published in 1988. Ashe also tried to better conditions for black people in other countries. In 1970 he helped get South Africa banned from the Davis Cup because of its racist policies and afterwards continued to press for reforms in that country. In 1985 he was among those arrested for protesting outside the South African embassy in Washington.

Working as a commentator and columnist, writing regularly on tennis for newspapers and magazines, as well as writing books, Ashe was very busy, even though his health was failing. He underwent another heart operation in 1983 and in 1988 a brain operation, then during tests following his brain surgery, the doctors discovered that Ashe had AIDS. Apparently, he had caught the disease through a blood transfusion given him during his 1983 surgery.

Ashe told only his wife Jeanne and other close family members at first. Tests revealed that neither his wife, Jeanne, nor their daughter, Camera, had contracted the HIV virus responsible for AIDS. Ashe faced his illness by taking on additional responsibilities.

Not until 1992 did Ashe make public the fact that he had AIDS, and then only because of rumors about him in the newspapers. Having been unwilling to tell people earlier for fear that he would be shunned as a leper, he now turned the publicity to good purpose, educating people about AIDS. In the few months remaining, he lectured widely, organized exhibitions, and set up the Arthur Ashe Foundation for the Defeat of AIDS. "He was out doing things, making his point, and taking care of business right up until the end," said former tennis champion Jimmy Connors. "I guess that sums up everything he stood for."

Pearl Bailey

Singer
Born March 29, 1918, Newport News,
   Virginia
Died August 17, 1990, Philadelphia,
   Pennsylvania

"The biggest mistake most people make is to want to become something before they are something. You first have to be something and be it wholeheartedly, and then you can become what you want."

T he renowned performer Pearlie Mae captured the hearts of her audiences with her sultry voice and easy charm in a career that spanned fifty-seven years. Pearl Bailey performed as actress and singer, and was known for her great sense of showmanship, appearing on stage glittering with rhinestones and wearing a feather boa, which she flipped nonchalantly as she sang.

Not so well known is her service as a U.S. representative to the United Nations, appointed to the position by President Ford. She was deeply committed to racial equality and to friendly relations between blacks and whites.

Sang with the big bands

Pearl Bailey grew up in the hard years of the late 1920s and early 1930s. She had two sisters, Virgie and Eura, and a brother, Bill, who became a tap dancer and later a minister. Their father, Joseph Bailey, was a minister, and Bailey learned her singing style in his church. She had no formal training in music, but by the time she was three, she was copying the techniques of those around her.

The family moved to Washington, D.C., when Bailey was four, and her parents divorced a little while later. Bailey's mother, Ella Mae Bailey, married again, and took the children to Philadelphia, where Bailey went to school. Her early ambition was to be a teacher, but she dropped out of William Penn High School when she was fifteen to launch her career in show business. This was in 1933, when she won first prize in a talent contest at the Pearl Theater in Philadelphia, where her brother was appearing.

The prize was five dollars and a paid two-week engagement at the theater—enough to excite Bailey's ambitions about the business. She performed for the two weeks but she was not paid, because the theater closed down. Later that year she won a prize at a contest in Washington, D.C., and over the next few years, the young singer scraped by, singing and dancing with vaudeville groups that toured coal-mining towns in Pennsylvania. Occasionally she performed at small clubs, but it was not until the 1940s, after she had started singing with the big bands, that she had her first important solo engagements at exclusive nightclubs, such as the Blue Angel in Manhattan.

From 1941 on, Bailey performed on United Service Organization tours, entertaining the troops during World War II, and in 1943–44 she toured with Cootie Williams, Count Basie, and other jazz "greats." Audiences loved the way she tossed in chatty asides in the middle of a song or paused to crack a joke. They warmed to her personality as much as her singing.

Enjoyed success on stage, film, and television

Singing led to acting, and in 1946 Bailey appeared on Broadway in "St. Louis Woman," an all-black drama. Her acting won her a Donaldson Award as the year's most promising new performer. Other roles followed. She enjoyed success in her first starring role in the stage musical "House of Flowers" (1954), and in the same year she played in the film version of *Carmen Jones.* Other film parts followed, including the role of Maria in *Porgy and Bess* (1959). Her most famous performance was in the black production of "Hello Dolly!" (1967), for which she won a special Tony Award.

Now a major star who performed frequently at the White House, Bailey continued her tours to entertain the armed forces into the last years of her life. She also appeared frequently on television and made numerous record albums. The songs for which she is best remembered are "Won't you come home, Bill Bailey," "Saint Louis Blues," and "Toot, Toot, Tootsie, Goodbye."

On a personal note, Bailey had two early marriages that failed, but in 1952 she married a white man, jazz drummer Louis Bellson, and the marriage endured until her death thirty-seven years later. The couple adopted two children, Tony and Dee Dee, who were raised in a very different world than the one Bailey had been born into. In 1968 Bailey published her autobiography, *Raw Pearl,* followed by a second autobiographical book, *Talking to Myself,* in 1971. Other books were *Pearl's Kitchen* (1973), the collection of prose, poetry, and letters titled *Hurry Up, America, and Spit* (1976), and *Between You and Me* (1990).

Appointed ambassador of love

In 1981 Bailey was the voice of the owl in the Disney movie *The Fox and the Hound,* a story was about two friends who didn't know they were supposed to be enemies. The role was symbolic of Bailey's outlook, for she worked hard to bring people together. In 1970 President Nixon appointed her "Ambassador of Love," and in 1975 President Ford appointed her special representataive in the U.S. delegation at the United Nations, a position she retained for the rest of her life.

Late in life, Bailey went back to school. After she received an honorary degree from Georgetown University, she enrolled there and

Pearl Bailey

at the age of sixty-seven graduated in theology. She said she wanted to be a teacher, but in fact she had already taught, through her involvement in charitable causes and her lifetime of outgoing behavior, the lessons of kindness, understanding, tolerance, and humanity. She had indeed been an "ambassador of love."

Augusta Baker

Librarian and storyteller
Born April 1, 1911, Baltimore, Maryland

"I began to tell stories because it was part of the job of being a children's librarian. Then as time passed I grew to love it."

African American children today have a wide choice of suitable books to read largely because of the efforts of Augusta Baker. When Baker started work as a young librarian in New York, she found few children's books portraying black people in a realistic manner. During the next thirty-seven years Baker corrected this situation, not only by adding appropriate books to the New York Public Library's collection, but also by meeting with authors and publishers to get more African American stories written. By the time she retired in 1974, libraries and bookstores throughout the nation could offer black children—as well as others from minority groups—a wide selection of suitable books.

A few of these books had been compiled by Baker herself. She published four collections of stories: *Talking Tree* (1955), *Golden Lynx* (1960), *Young Years: Best Loved Stories and Poems for Little Children* (1960), and *Once Upon a Time* (1964). Many children knew Baker more as a storyteller than a librarian. It was the part of the job she liked best, giving her the opportunity to spark the imagination of her young listeners and to inspire them with a lifelong love of books.

Earned two college degrees

Augusta Baker was the only child of Winfort and Mabel (Gough) Braxston, both teachers who made sure she had a thorough education. Baker's grandmother, who lived with the family, also stressed the importance of education. Some of Baker's fondest childhood memories are of quiet times spent with her grandmother, who told wonderful stories that had been passed from generation to generation. Baker would later pass on these stories and folktales to the next generation of children in the libraries where she worked.

Augusta Baker

Baker enjoyed her years at the all-black high school where her father taught but found it harder to adjust when she began attending college at the predominantly white University of Pittsburgh in 1927. At the end of her second year she married fellow student James Baker and moved with him to Albany, New York. There she attended New York College for Teachers, from which she earned a bachelor of arts degree in 1933 and a degree in library science the following year. Soon afterwards she and her husband moved to New York City, where their son James Henry Baker III was born.

Called for reform in black children's literature

With library positions hard to find in New York, Baker began her career as a teacher, until 1937, when she landed a job as a children's librarian at the 135th Street branch of the New York Public Library, in the heart of Harlem.

Baker was glad to find that the library had a sizable collection of books on black history and culture, but she considered the fiction shockingly inadequate: "Most of the books which included black characters represented them as shiftless, happy, grinning, dialect-speaking menials. This was what was being written for children and what they read. I was distressed and frustrated but I found I was not alone. Others were recognizing the need for a special kind of children's literature."

These "others," parents, teachers, and community leaders, supported Baker in her work assembling a collection of books that would give black children pride in their race while offering white children a realistic picture of African American life. When she started the James Weldon Johnson Memorial Collection in 1939 she wrote: "It is the purpose of this collection to bring together books for children that give an unbiased, accurate, well rounded picture of Negro life in all parts of the world.... In order to give children more democratic attitudes toward all the racial groups that make America the great nation it is, we must use literature that will strengthen the growth of democracy."

To promote the project, Baker met with a number of children's authors and gave speeches at gatherings of publishers and editors. Her ideas were eagerly taken up, and several leading publishers began to bring out the type of book she advocated. By 1957, when the bibliography of the collection was published under the title *Books about Negro Life for Children,* Baker had assembled literally hundreds of books.

As well as amassing this superb collection of children's literature, Baker organized concerts and other activities for the children who came to the library. Above all, she gained a reputation as a storyteller. "I began to tell stories as part of the job of being a librarian," she said. "Then as time passed I grew to love it.... I also enjoyed reading the literature that folktales came from and wanted to share this enjoyment with children."

First black library administrator in New York Public Library

In 1953 Baker was officially appointed "storytelling specialist" and assistant coordinator of children's services. She was the first black librarian to have an administrative position in the New York Public Library. In 1961 Baker was promoted to the highest position in her field—coordinator of children's services.

This appointment put Baker in charge of children's policies and programs in all 82 branches of the New York Public Library. Baker took full advantage of this tremendous opportunity to build the type of collection she dreamed of, adding audiovisual materials as well as books. Baker's influence spread far beyond the library itself. Working with a staff of more than 100 she involved schools and community groups, and she also consulted for the television program "Sesame Street," moderated television and radio programs, and gave courses and talks on storytelling and children's literature.

In 1974, after serving for 37 years with the New York Public Library system, Baker retired—but she did not give up her role as a storyteller. She moved with her second husband, Gordon Alexander, to Columbia, South Carolina, where she was appointed storyteller-in-residence at the University of South Carolina. Baker still takes great pleasure recounting stories, as her grandmother did so many years ago. Like her grandmother, Baker is inspiring the younger generation and building a pride and love for the African American culture.

Josephine Baker

Entertainer, dancer
Born June 3, 1906, St. Louis, Missouri
Died April 14, 1975, Paris, France

"Josephine left Paris rich, adored, famous throughout Europe. But in New York, in spite of the publicity that preceded her arrival, she was received as an uppity colored girl."

The dashing Josephine Baker was the first black woman to be an international star. She created a sensation in Paris in the 1920s performing almost naked in a revue. The crowds loved her cheerful brashness, and she willingly played up to them. As publicity for one show, she took to walking a pet leopard cub through Paris (the leopard wore only a diamond-studded choker).

Despite such flamboyance, Baker practiced seriously to perfect her dancing and singing. When committed to any cause, she pursued it relentlessly, and for her humanitarian efforts during World War II, Baker was decorated with the French Legion of Honor and the Medal of the Resistance.

Helped support her family

Josephine Baker came from a very poor home. Her mother, Carrie McDonald, worked as a domestic and was not married to Josephine's father, Eddie Carson. Carson left before Baker was a year old, and the only father she knew was her stepfather—a violent man who often hit her. Baker's mother gave birth to three more children and was so short of money that Baker was sent out to work when she was eight years old. The laws of the time permitted eight-year-olds to work, provided they also went to school. Baker worked as a kitchen helper to a white family who treated her very harshly. She left the family when the woman of the house plunged her arm into a pot of

Josephine Baker

boiling water. Baker's next employer treated her more kindly, but life was still very tough.

At thirteen, Baker ran away from home and found a job as a waitress. That same year she also married and then separated from her first husband, Willie Wells. All her life Baker never managed to have a stable relationship. She married five times, and not one of the marriages lasted.

First appeared on Broadway as a chorus girl

At fourteen Baker joined a street band, which led to work with a traveling show called the Dixie Fliers. She was taken on as a dresser, but her aim was to be a dancer. Baker practiced the dances so well that she was able to fill in when any of the chorus girls were sick. From the first, she was brighter and more vivacious than the other girls in the chorus line.

On tour in Philadelphia in 1921, the teenager met and married a Pullman porter, William Baker, whose surname she used from then on, even though she left her husband almost immediately to dance in a Broadway show, "Shuffle Along." Again too young to be taken on, she was given work as a dresser, and as before, she learned all the songs and dances to fill in when one of the chorus girls fell sick. Baker made the most of her first appearance on Broadway, but instead of kicking along with the other chorus girls, she clowned outrageously, crossing her eyes, tripping over her feet. The audience loved it. So Baker was hired by the company, touring with the show for the next three years as well as playing in their next production, "Chocolate Dandies."

Took Paris by storm

When dancing at Harlem's Plantation Club in 1925, Baker was approached by Caroline Dudley, a wealthy white woman who had a passion for black shows. Dudley invited Baker to join the troupe of black performers she was taking to France to appear in "La Revue Negre."

The revue was an instant success—mainly because of the "Dance Sauvage," in which Baker performed seminude with a male partner. Baker's nudity was considered both shocking and stunning, and she became a star overnight. When the tour ended, she was invited to join the Folies Bergère, France's famous music hall, and she played there for the next three years.

The French could not get enough of the exotic and lively "dark star," and this sparked a fashion for Josephine perfume, Josephine dolls, Josephine hair-dos. The star herself took advantage of the publicity to make records of her songs, and in 1927 Baker made the first of several movies, *La Sirene des tropiques* (The Siren of the Tropics).

In 1928 Baker toured Europe and South America, and during this period her style of performance changed. When she returned to France in 1930, she was less the comic actress and more the polished dancer and singer performing at the higher class Casino de Paris.

One of Baker's songs at Casino was "J'ai deux amours" (I have two loves, my country and Paris). This became her theme song. Her love for her country was sorely tested when she returned home in 1936, expecting to be hailed as a star. When she performed in New York with the Ziegfeld Follies, instead of being praised for her style, she was regarded as "a rather uppity colored girl." So Baker went back to Paris.

Decorated for her work in the French Resistance

Baker's 1937 marriage to a Frenchman made her a French citizen, even though the marriage soon dissolved. When World War II broke out the French recruited her as a spy, because she had useful contacts with the Italian embassy. She fled Paris when the Germans invaded in 1940, escaping to Portugal, then returned to the south of France, where she set up her operations in Marseilles.

As a performer Baker was allowed to travel, providing her a convenient cover for her intelligence work. She went to both Morocco and Portugal, but while in Morocco in 1941 she became seriously ill. Baker spent much of the next year in the hospital, where she carried on her undercover work, passing messages by means of her visitors. At the end of the war France awarded her the Medal of the Resistance and the Legion of Honor in recognition of her dangerous work as a spy.

Adopted twelve children

During the 1950s Baker added her clout to the cause of civil rights, working with others to end segregation in the United States. On a visit home in 1951 she refused to perform anywhere that was segregated, and during the following years she gave several concerts in the United States to benefit civil rights organizations.

Meanwhile, Baker set up an "ideal community" in her villa in France. She adopted twelve children of different ethnic backgrounds, calling them her "Rainbow Tribe." This "experiment in brotherhood" proved costly, and Baker returned to the stage to earn money to pay her many debts. Money problems plagued her last years, when she also gained a reputation for being very difficult. But when she died, thousands flocked to her funeral, which was shown on French television, and the French Government gave her a twenty-one gun salute. She is the only American woman who has been so honored by France.

James Baldwin

Writer
Born August 2, 1924, New York, New York
Died December 1, 1987, St. Paul de Vence,
    France

"Once I found myself on the other side of the ocean, I could see where I came from very clearly, and I could see that I carried myself, which is my home, with me.... I am the grandson of a slave, and I am a writer. I must deal with both."

A passionate writer on racial matters, James Baldwin was one of the most respected modern American authors. He emerged as a writer in the 1950s, when segregation was still legal, and his fame grew as the civil rights movement developed. In his novels, essays, and poems, Baldwin portrayed the problems faced by African Americans, describing their hopes and disappointments and how they coped in a hostile white society. He saw himself as a "disturber of the peace," revealing truths that many Americans would rather not have known.

In one of his early works, Baldwin pointed out that the much-discussed "negro problem" was in fact a white problem. "I am only black," he wrote, "if you think you're white." This theme ran through his writings, as did his belief that racism was harmful to whites as well as blacks, that it hurt the oppressors as well as the oppressed. Baldwin's works were immensely popular, and he was recognized as a major writer on both sides of the Atlantic Ocean.

Gained prestige as a teenage preacher

James Arthur Baldwin was the eldest of nine children, the son of David and Berdis (Jones) Baldwin. He was raised in Harlem in a family that was desperately poor. The most powerful figure during his childhood was his stepfather, a fiery preacher who held strict religious views and ruled the household with an iron rod. Baldwin did not get on with his stepfather—he felt unloved—and as a form of escape he turned to books (and also to movies and plays, when he could slip away to them without anyone knowing).

As Baldwin entered his teens he began to worry about his sexuality. Later in life he openly accepted his homosexuality, but as a teenager in a strict religious household, he felt horribly sinful and feared that he was depraved. Turning to the church for help, Baldwin was converted by a woman preacher of the Pentecostal faith and became a junior minister at the Fireside Pentecostal Assembly. Baldwin was only fourteen at the time and still in high school, but he proved to be a powerful preacher and gained a great reputation in the Harlem churches. His rousing language and vivid imagery were a foretaste of the skills he would later employ as a writer.

Possibly because Baldwin read so much, he showed a talent for writing at quite a young age. He was encouraged by his teachers, first at Frederick Douglass Junior High School and then at DeWitt Clinton High School, where he was editor of the school magazine. By the time Baldwin graduated from DeWitt in 1942, he no longer considered preaching to be his calling. His wide reading caused him to question Christianity, and he concluded that African Americans should have little to do with a religion that had been used to enslave them.

Succeeded abroad as a writer

After leaving school Baldwin worked to support his brothers and sisters. College was out of the question, because his stepfather was ill and the family was struggling to make ends meet. With World War II underway, Baldwin found work in a Defense Department factory, but he hated the whole experience: the workplace was segregated, and the white workers were unpleasant. When his stepfather died, Baldwin struck out on his own.

He moved to New York's Greenwich Village, where he started to write seriously and supported himself with whatever odd jobs he could get. In 1944 Baldwin met author Richard Wright, who helped him obtain a Eugene F. Saxton Fellowship, which provided Baldwin with enough money to write full time. In 1948 he sold his first short story, "Previous Condition," about the difficulties of a young black man trying to live in the white world of Greenwich Village.

Over the next few months Baldwin sold several more short pieces, but the professional encouragement he felt could not overcome the stifling racial situation in the United States. He felt he would never develop fully as a writer unless he were to leave the country, so when he won another fellowship, he set off for Paris, France.

Baldwin's Parisian years marked an important, prolific period. He settled easily into the intellectual life of the city, getting to know other writers and artists as well as getting to know himself. "Once I found myself on the other side of the ocean," he told the *New York Times*, " I could see where I came from very clearly, and I could see that I carried myself, which is my home, with me.... I am the grandson of a slave, and I am a writer. I must deal with both."

Baldwin dealt with both by producing some magnificent books during the next few years. The storyline in his first novel, *Go Tell It on the Mountain* (1953), mirrored his own youth—growing up in Harlem and being saved by the Pentecostal church. His first play, "The Amen Corner" (1955), was about a family torn between religion and art and love, and his second novel, *Giovanni's Room* (1956), was a homosexual love story set in Paris. All these books took a fresh and honest look at the subject matter, especially problems associated with race, as did the articles and essays Baldwin wrote during this period. Many critics view Baldwin's essays as his most insightful and brilliant work.

Lectured and wrote best-selling books

Baldwin often visited the United States, and he never gave up his American citizenship.

James Baldwin

By the mid-1950s his books had brought him considerable fame at home, and he was welcomed as a speaker on lecture tours. However, his personal success was tinged with bitterness over the continued oppression of black Americans

Realizing that his books were widely read by whites, Baldwin became a spokesman for the growing civil rights movement, calling on white Americans to stop the oppression and to change their ways before it was too late. He pointed out that African Americans had reached the limit of their patience—they were no longer prepared to suffer meekly. In two nonfiction works, *Nobody Knows My Name* (1961) and *The Fire Next Time* (1963), Baldwin warned that black anger could easily erupt into violence (as indeed it did later in the decade). Both books were best-sellers, selling more than a million copies.

Baldwin's energetic writing and lecturing throughout the United States in the early 1960s also brought him criticism. Black Panther activist Eldridge Cleaver accused Baldwin of "fawning on whites" and hating blacks, and members of the Black Arts Movement felt that as a black writer he should be writing only for and about fellow blacks. However, Baldwin refused to call himself a black writer; he said he was an American writer, concerned with the issues of his multiracial country.

In 1964 Baldwin's second play, "Blues for Mr. Charlie," opened on Broadway. Like virtually everything he wrote in this period, it dealt with civil rights issues—in this case, nonviolent protest versus violence. The following year, Baldwin's earlier play, "The Amen Corner," also opened on Broadway be-fore touring overseas. Baldwin joined the tour and then lived for a while in Turkey, where he settled down to do more writing. He returned to America in 1968, living in Hollywood and writing a screenplay for Alex Haley's *Autobiography of Malcolm X,* then moved to the south of France in the early 1970s, where, except for occasional travel, he lived for the rest of his life.

"This man saved our lives"

The author of seven novels and eight major works of nonfiction, as well as numerous shorter pieces, including his plays and his screenplay, Baldwin succeeded in touching America's conscience, stressing that all people have much in common, whatever their race or sex or color. His efforts encouraged other black writers, such as Orde Coombs, who wrote, "It is not too much to say that this man saved our lives, or at least, gave us the necessary ammunition to face what we knew would continue to be a hostile and condescending world." At the time of his death, Baldwin was working on a book about Martin Luther King, Jr.

Amiri Baraka

Writer, educator
Born October 7, 1934, Newark, New Jersey

"I'm fully conscious all the time that I'm an American Negro, because it's part of my life. But I know that if I want to say, 'I see a bus full of people,' I don't have to say, 'I am a Negro seeing a bus full of people.'"

B est known for his controversial plays, poems, novels, essays, and short stories, Amiri Baraka has helped awaken the social conscious of a nation. As he gained prominence in the 1960s, he lived his belief that blacks and whites could live together in social harmony. Later he abandoned that concept and shifted his attention towards black nationalism and political activism. In time he turned his attention to socialism and now writes about the destruction of capitalism and the establishment of a communist society.

Always controversial, Baraka helped shift the focus of black literature from a faceless and classless vision to an intimate look at the black experience.

Espoused ideals of Beat Generation

Baraka was born LeRoi Jones in 1934 in Newark, New Jersey. His family was considered middle class, and he was one of only a handful of black students attending his high school. Although his parents were proud of their status, Baraka felt alienated and isolated. His parents may have promoted assimilation, but Baraka came to fiercely oppose it.

In 1951 Baraka received a scholarship to Rutgers University, but continuing feelings of isolation prompted him to transfer to Howard University, a black college, the following year. He studied philosophy, religion, and literature, and he concluded that blacks were given the hopeless position in society. Baraka wrote that Howard University shocked him "into realizing how desperately sick the Negro could be, how he could be led into self-destruction and how he would not realize that it was the society that had forced him into a great sickness."

After graduating with a bachelor's degree, Baraka enlisted in the U.S. Air Force and served in Puerto Rico and Germany as a weatherman and gunner. After three years he returned to civilian life and aligned himself with the Beat Generation, a group well known for challenging the literary and moral establishment.

Baraka began living in Greenwich Village, the center of the budding Beat cultural revolution, where he met and married Hettie Cohen. A young Jewish woman, Cohen worked at the *Partisan Review,* which published Baraka's first writing in 1958. This article defended the Beats and declared that young writers should resort to "violence in writing" to overcome stereotypes.

Baraka and Cohen also organized *Yugen,* a literary magazine showcasing Beat poets. Baraka wrote a letter on toilet paper to Allen Ginsberg asking for submissions and was rewarded with contributions from Ginsberg and other notable writers, including Philip Whalen, Gregory Corso, and Gary Snyder. With such well-known contributors, *Yugen* quickly gained popularity, and this led to other projects, including the formation of Totem Press. Baraka also wrote extensively for many of the important smaller magazines of the day.

Disillusioned with lack of change

His writing began to change after he visited communist Cuba in 1960. He met many young Cubans who told him he should tackle society's problems in a more aggressive manner. Although the Beats criticized the system, they had no agenda for changing it. Baraka returned to Greenwich Village with a new sense of political mission and a stronger identification with Third World artists. He also became involved with the social life of Harlem.

He wrote two of his most serious works of fiction at this time—*The System of Dante's Hell* and *Tales,* both of which reflected his evolution away from the Beats in Greenwich Village. In 1961 he and poet Diane Di Prima founded *Floating Bear,* an underground magazine, and also helped organized the American Theater for Poets.

Most of Baraka's early writings espoused the belief that blacks and whites could live in racial harmony. But his writing slowly changed as he grew disillusioned with that concept. In his best-known play, the highly praised "Dutchman," he describes a subway scene between Lula, a free-thinking white woman; and Clay, a young middle-class black man. She taunts him about trying to be a white man and to let his true black self appear. When he finally does, Clay angrily denounces Lula and the white world. At the end of the play Lula calmly stabs Clay to death and awaits her next victim. The play won the 1964 Obie Award for best American play and propelled Baraka into a whirlwind of lectures, panel discussions, readings, and teaching assignments at several universities.

Moved from black nationalism to socialistic views

By 1964 Baraka had completely rejected Beat values and began verbally attacking his Green-

wich Village friends, white liberals, and the larger white community. Inspired by black activist leader Malcolm X, Baraka began believing that an integrated society was not only impossible but also undesirable. Ironically his new writings boosted his popularity in the white world even further. He received numerous invitations to society gatherings, but he turned them all down, stating there could be no ties with whites, since they would only serve to make him a traitor to black nationalism. By late 1965 he ended his marriage to Hettie Cohen, broke all ties with the white literary establishment, and moved to Harlem.

In Harlem he founded the Black Arts Repertory Theater School, a short-lived establishment that greatly revolutionized black theater in the United States. Plays performed there emphasized black nationalist philosophy, and several other theaters sprang up around the country modeled on this approach. In 1966

Amiri Baraka

the theater, which was supported by federal funds, was shut down by police because an arms cache was allegedly found there.

Baraka returned to Newark and dropped his given name in favor of the Bantu Muslim title Imamu (meaning "spiritual leader," which he later dropped), Ameer (meaning "blessed" which he later changed to Amiri), and Baraka (meaning "prince"). He urged black artists to discuss the plight of their race in the United States, believing it would shame the white community into taking action to assist them. In 1970 Baraka became a key organizer for the Congress of African Peoples, and two years later with the National Black Political Assembly.

By 1974 he underwent another transformation. He rejected black nationalism and declared himself to be a Marxist-Leninist-Maoist. He described his new beliefs in the *New York Times:* "It is a narrow nationalism that says the white man is the enemy.... Nationalism, so-called, when it says 'all non-blacks are our enemies,' is sickness or criminality, in fact, a form of fascism." Since 1974 Baraka has produced a great deal of socialist poetry and essays and states that the end of capitalism and the creation of a socialist community are his goals.

Ida B. Wells Barnett

Journalist, social activist
Born July 16, 1862, Holly Springs,
  Mississippi
Died March 25, 1931, Chicago, Illinois

"There is only one thing left that we can do; save our money and leave a town which will neither protect our lives and property, nor give us a fair trial in the courts, but take us out and murder us in cold blood when accused by a white person."

I da B. Wells Barnett was born into slavery, grew up during Reconstruction, and spent her adult life fighting racism. She was noted for her fiery columns in *Free Speech* and the *New York Age*. She also lectured on America's inhumanity to blacks, was a founder of the National Association for the Advancement of Colored People, helped lay the groundwork for the National Association of Colored Women, and played a key role in many other black rights organizations.

Sued the railroad for denying her seat in first class

Barnett was born a slave on July 16, 1862, in Holly Springs, Mississippi, to James and Elizabeth Wells. With the Emancipation Proclamation signed six months later, Barnett and her four brothers and four sisters were raised in freedom. She attended Rust College, a freedmen's high school and industrial school. After her parents died in 1878 from yellow fever, Barnett was responsible for the family. She passed the teachers' examination and taught for a short time in the rural district of Holly Springs, earning twenty-five dollars a month.

In the 1880s Barnett moved the family to Memphis, Tennessee, so she could be closer to her father's sister, Fannie Butler, and to find a higher-paying teaching job. She taught at a rural school in Woodstock, just outside the city, while preparing for the teachers' examinations for the Memphis black public schools.

In May 1884 Barnett purchased a first-class ticket on a local Memphis-to-Woodstock line operated by the Chesapeake, Ohio, and Southwestern Railroad Company. After she took her seat in the ladies' coach, she was asked by the conductor to move to the forward car, which was a smoker. She refused, got off the train, returned to Memphis, and filed suit against the railway company for refusing to provide her with first-class seating. In December 1884 the Memphis circuit court ruled in her favor and fined the company $300. Barnett was awarded $500 in personal damages. The company appealed the decision to the Tennessee Supreme Court, which, on April 5, 1987, reversed the earlier decision on the grounds that the company had satisfied the statutory requirements to provide "like accommodations."

From 1884 to 1891 Barnett taught in Memphis city schools. She spent Friday afternoons with other teachers at the Memphis Vance Street Christian Church reading essays and discussing literature. The meetings closed with the reading of the *Evening Star,* an internal publication that was prepared and read by the editor. Barnett eventually became editor, and her writing came to the attention of Reverend R.N. Countee, pastor of the Tabernacle Missionary Baptist Church. He asked her to write for the *Living Way,* a religious weekly. She soon began writing regularly for the black press throughout the country. At the 1889 meeting of the Colored Press Association in

Ida B. Wells Barnett

Washington, D.C., she was elected secretary. Later that year she was invited to become editor and partner in the *Free Speech and Headlight,* a militant journal owned by the Reverend Taylor Nightingale, pastor of the Beale Street Baptist Church, and J.L. Fleming.

Barnett became known for her scathing opinions. She wrote an editorial that criticized the Memphis Board of Education for its unequal distribution of resources between black and white schools. The board fired her in 1891, so she devoted all of her time to the paper. She shortened its name to *Free Speech* and worked hard to increase its circulation. In less than a year, circulation jumped by 38 percent.

Incited the white population with her editorials

In May 1892 Barnett went to Philadelphia to attend the African Methodist Episcopal church convention. Shortly before she left, she wrote an editorial to be printed in *Free Speech* about the lynching of eight blacks. Barnett questioned the excuses whites used for executing blacks without due process of the law. She declared: "Nobody in this section of the country believes the old thread-bare lies that Negro men rape white women. If Southern men are not careful they will overreach themselves and public sentiment will have a reaction; a conclusion will be reached which will be very damaging to the moral reputation of their women."

Other newspapers in the city protested that the editorial, which they falsely credited to J.L. Fleming, had gone too far. A group of leading white citizens met and voted to send a committee to warn the proprietors of *Free Speech* to never publish such comments again. Neither Barnett or Fleming were there to meet the delegation. On May 27, 1892, the *Free Speech* offices and presses were destroyed and Barnett was warned not to return to Memphis.

Barnett exchanged the circulation list of the *Free Speech* for a quarter interest in the *New York Age*. She became a columnist, and on June 7, 1892, the paper published a full page about lynching and debunked the myth that white men in Memphis intended to shield white women from rape. Ten thousand copies were sold across the country, including 1,000 in Memphis. This report became the basis for two booklets, *Southern Horrors,* published in 1892, and *A Red Record: Tabulated Statistics and Alleged Causes of Lynching in the United States, 1892, 1893, and 1894,* that was published in 1895.

Wanting to do more than just write about these problems, Barnett began lecturing throughout the Northeast. In 1893 she was invited to speak in England, Scotland, and Wales. While overseas she learned about the endeavors of English women through their civic groups. When she returned home she advised her friends to become more involved in the community, city, and the nation through civic groups.

Later that year she worked with Frederick Douglass, Ferdinand Lee Barnett, and I. Garland Penn to produce an eighty-one page pamphlet entitled *The Reason Why the Colored American Is Not in the World's Columbian Exposition: The Afro-American's Contribution to Columbian Literature.*

Also in 1893 Barnett moved to Chicago to work for the *Chicago Conservator,* the first black newspaper in the city. She continued her interest in women's clubs and organized Chicago's first civic club for black women, which was later named in her honor. She also lectured in England and in the northern and western United States.

On June 27, 1895, Barnett married Ferdinand L. Barnett, a black attorney and editor and founder of the *Chicago Conservator.* They had four children. The marriage did not lessen her activities. In 1898 she was a member of a delegation that called on President William McKinley to seek redress in the case of a black postmaster lynched in South Carolina. She was also active in the Afro-American Council and served as secretary until 1902.

Helped form the NAACP

In 1909 Barnett was one of two women (Mary Church Terell was the other) who signed the "Call" for a conference on blacks, which came after three days of racial violence in Springfield, Illinois, in August 1908. The conference convened on May 31, 1909, in New York City and led to the formation of the National Association for the Advancement of Colored People (NAACP). She delivered one of the major speeches and was placed on the executive committee. Barnett also encouraged black men to register for the vote. She worked in the women's suffrage movement, and on January 30, 1913, she founded the Alpha Suffrage Club of Chicago, the first black suffrage organization. When the National Association of Colored Women met in Chicago in 1924, Barnett ran for president but lost to Mary McLeod Bethune. Six years later she was an independent candidate for state senator but was handily defeated.

On March 21, 1931, Barnett became ill and was rushed to Daily Hospital on March 23. She died two days later and was buried in Chicago's Oakwood Cemetery.

Marguerite Ross Barnett

Educator
Born May 22, 1922, Charlottesville, Virginia
Died February 26, 1992, Wailuku, Hawaii

"The role of research universities is to help society 'solve its key conundrums ... in the same way land-grant institutions helped solve the problems of the 19th century.'"

Marguerite Ross Barnett became the first African American and the first woman to head the four-campus University of Houston (Texas) system. She had already won accolades at the University of Missouri-St. Louis, where she was chancellor and a tenured professor in political science. Through her hard work and superior organizational skills, Barnett greatly boosted the prestige of both institutions.

An academic career

Barnett was the daughter of Dewey Ross and Mary (Douglass) Barnett. She graduated from Bennett High School in Buffalo, New York, in 1959. Four years later she received an A.B. degree in political science from Antioch College. She had intended to become a scientist, but changed her mind after taking a course on Indian politics. Barnett attended the University of Chicago, receiving an M.A. degree in 1966 and a Ph.D. six years later. As part of her doctoral studies, she conducted research in south India for two years. Her doctorate was published as *The Politics of Cultural Nationalism in South India*. The American Political Science Association awarded her its top book prize in 1981.

Barnett began her teaching career as a lecturer at the University of Chicago in 1969. The next year she was named assistant professor of political science. From 1974 to 1976, she was the James Madison Bicentennial Preceptor at Princeton University. In 1976 she became a political science professor at Howard University, chairing the department from 1977 to 1980. While still at Howard in 1980, Barnett became co-director of the Ethnic Heritage Program within the United States Department of Education. She moved to Columbia Univer-

Marguerite Ross Barnett

sity and, from 1980 to 1983, she was professor of politics and education, political science professor, and director of the Institute for Urban and Minority Education. In 1982 to 1983 Barnett was the co-principal investigator on the Constitution and American Culture and on the Training Program for Special Projects Directors, sponsored by the National Endowment for the Humanities. She also served as a consultant for the Presbyterian Church of the United States from February to August 1983.

In 1983, Barnett was appointed political science professor and vice-chancellor at the City University of New York, a twenty-one college system serving 180,000 students. She stayed there until 1986, when she became chancellor and political science professor at the University of Missouri-St. Louis. She held the post until she was named the president of the University of Houston in 1990. Barnett was the first African American and the first woman to head the university, and one of only three women to lead universities with more than thirty thousand students.

Although she was the only black leading a major educational institution, Barnett was more concerned with her agenda at the university, and the role that it should play in addressing a wide range of issues, from homelessness to space exploration. In *Chronicle of Higher Education,* she was quoted as saying universities must help society "solve its key conundrums" and they must do so "in the same way land-grant institutions helped solve the problems of the 19th century."

Barnett had boundless enthusiasm, was an effective school booster, and was a woman with strong views who was not afraid to hear the opinions of others. With an abundance of self-confidence, Barnett was as comfortable in the corporate boardroom as she was in her staff meetings.

Many awards and honors

A committed volunteer, Barnett served on the board of directors of the Houston Grand Opera and the board of advisors of the Houston Symphony. She also was on the boards of the Monsanto Company, the Educational Testing Services, the Student Loan Marketing Association (SALLIE MAE), the American Council on Education, and the Committee on Economic Development. Barnett was a member of the Overseas Development Council, the Council on Foreign Relations, and the Cleveland Council.

Despite her workload, Barnett still found time for writing. She authored fifty articles and was the writer or editor of five books. In addition to her doctorate, she wrote or co-edited *Public Policy for the Black Community: Strategies and Perspectives; Readings on Equal Education, vol. 7; Comparing Race, Sex, and National Origin Desegregation: Public Attitudes of Desegregation;* and *Educational Policy in an Era of Conservative Reform.*

Barnett won numerous awards and honors during her life. She received the Bethune-Tubman-Truth Woman of the Year Award, 1983; Association of Black Women in Higher Education Award for Educational Excellence, 1986; American Political Science COBPS Award for Excellence in Scholarship and Service to the Profession, 1986; Golden GAZELLE Award from the Project on Equal Education of the NOW Legal Defense Fund (1987); and the Award of Achievement, Jefferson City (Missouri) NAACP, 1988. In 1989 she was named Woman of the Year by the St. Louis Variety Club, and the next year the Women's International Leadership Forum presented her with its Woman Who Has Made A Difference Award.

While at the University of Missouri, Barnett designed and implemented the Partnerships for Progress Program, and in 1991 the American Council on Education gave the program its Anderson Medal. She began developing a similar program at the University of Houston called the Texas Center for University-School Partnerships.

While she was married to Stephen A. Barnett, Barnett had one daughter, Amy, who was born on December 18, 1962.

In November 1991, Barnett announced she would have to take periodic leaves from her duties at the University of Houston be-cause of an unspecified neuro-endocrinological condition. She was on medical leave when she died of a blood disorder involving hypoglycemia with metastatic cancer on February 26, 1992, at Maui Memorial Hospital in Wailuku, Hawaii.

Marion Barry

Mayor of Washington, D.C., 1978–90
Born March 6, 1936, Itta Bena, Mississippi

"Some people are destined and some are determined, and I am determined."

Marion Barry was a country boy who fought his way out of poverty and segregation to become an educated man, grassroots political activist, and a powerful public official. In his early days, Barry worked hard for black civil rights as a leader with the Student Nonviolent Coordinating Committee. As his popularity grew, he was elected to several public positions before becoming mayor of Washington, D.C., in 1978. Although Barry received high marks for promoting downtown and economic development, his career was rocked with scandals during the late 1980s. He was convicted in 1990 in a hotel-room cocaine sting that made headlines around the world. In a city ravaged by drugs, the arrest of the mayor on cocaine charges was considered disastrous, and Barry left his office in disgrace.

A childhood of several jobs

Barry is the son of Marion and Mattie Barry, who made a subsistence living as sharecroppers in the 1930s. His father died when he was four years old, and his mother moved her three children to Memphis, Tennessee. She worked several jobs, and when Barry was old enough, he also joined the workforce. Barry had two paper routes and sold a third paper on the street corner. He also bagged groceries, inspected sodapop bottles, and waited tables.

After graduating from high school, Barry went to LeMoyne College, a mostly black school in Memphis. Barry was almost expelled in 1958 when he criticized a college trustee for making patronizing remarks about blacks. He later went to Fisk University in Nashville, where he became interested in the civil rights movement. In 1960 Barry helped organize lunch counter sit-ins in Nashville and other Southern cities. Within a few months he became the first national chairman of the Student Nonviolent Coordinating Committee (SNCC).

Five months later Barry left the South to begin doctoral studies in chemistry at the University of Kansas. His civil rights involvement was restricted to a part-time basis, but he still conducted nonviolent workshops, registered voters, and raised funds during the summers. In 1964 he quit school and a teaching job at Knoxville College to become a full-time SNCC member. He moved to Washington the next year to lead the organization's District of Columbia statehood drive in the Free D.C. Movement.

Becomes a politician

In 1967 Barry co-founded Pride Inc., a multimillion dollar, federally funded youth-training program, which later became a na-

tional model in the so-called War on Poverty. That same year Barry resigned from SNCC, believing that blacks must concentrate on economic and political power. In 1971 he was successfully elected to the D.C. board of education. He was re-elected twice and served as president from 1972 to 1974. In 1974 he ran for city council president and won. It was the first election of its kind as the district had been previously under congressional control. Barry focussed on economic issues, and he helped develop one of the strongest municipal ordinances in the country to protect homosexual rights. He became a hero in the eyes of many when he was shot and wounded by Hanafi Muslims during their attack on the District Building.

With his popularity on the upswing, Barry decided to run for mayor in 1978. Many considered him a long shot at best, but last-minute endorsements from the *Washington Post* and several city unions helped him to an upset victory over incumbent Walter Washington. Barry's first term in office was a success. He promoted a downtown development and revitalization boom, restored investor confidence, built roads, improved services, and provided new services to poor neighborhoods. The *Washington Post* summed up his first years in office: "Barry was an effective and formidable chief executive. He could prod sluggish bureaucrats into action, articulate policy initiatives that brought sweeping changes, go face-to-face with powerful politicians and business leaders, besting them on their own terms."

Barry took 60 per cent of the vote in the 1982 election. He continued to promote down-

Marion Barry

town and economic development, but new problems arose. The city's public housing and the prison system were starting to deteriorate. Scandals hurt his credibility. Ten top city officials, including Barry's top aide, were convicted of corruption. Barry's former wife, Mary Treadwell, was also convicted of defrauding the government. In 1983 a woman with whom Barry was having an affair was arrested and convicted of selling cocaine. Rumors spread across the city that Barry had a drug problem, but he denied these allegations.

Accusations mount

During the 1986 election campaign, Barry was opposed by a mother of three who tried to make an issue of Barry sending his son to a private school. Barry won the election by a landslide, capturing 61 per cent of the vote. Despite the victory, he was still the target of criticism, accused of bloating the bureaucracy for his own political purposes at the expense

of city services. He responded by saying he was the victim of a smear campaign that was run by the white power structure and the press.

In 1988 Barry was spotted visiting a friend, Charles Lewis, several times at a downtown hotel known for its drug traffic. Lewis was later arrested, and he told police that he sold Barry crack cocaine on several occasions. Barry denied the charges, but his conduct became the topic of many newspaper and magazine articles.

In 1987 Barry had an affair with a stripper, and his limousine was often seen in the seedier parts of the city late at night. Things finally came to a head on January 18, 1990, when Barry was caught in an FBI sting operation. Rasheeda Moore, a former model and ex-girlfriend of Barry, invited him to her room at the Vista International Hotel, where FBI agents videotaped Barry smoking crack. He was arrested and charged with cocaine possession.

Barry called the arrest a trap, but a few days later he admitted having a substance abuse problem and enrolled in a treatment program. Many black leaders felt that Barry was set up, but others said he was long overdue to pay for his actions. As the trial progressed, Barry announced he would not seek a fourth term as mayor. On August 10, 1990, a federal jury convicted Barry on one misdemeanor drug charge, but failed to resolve twelve other charges. A day after the verdict, Barry apologized to the city, saying, "to young and old, black and white ... rich and poor, I ask you to forgive me for any hurt I may have caused. Let us come together to heal ourselves and our city."

Count Basie

Pianist, bandleader
Born August 21, 1904, Red Bank, New
  Jersey
Died April 26, 1984, Hollywood, Florida

For over forty years Count Basie upheld his particular style of deeply-rooted Southwestern jazz. His band began in a Kansas City nightclub and eventually reached worldwide acclaim as the leading purveyor of swing. They contained an infectious pulse whose essence was a clean, unified, four-beats-to-the-bar swing. Although the band changed over the years, Basie insisted that it keep an uncluttered, swinging sound, anchored by the rhythm section and accented by his own "less is more" solos. He won numerous awards, including nine Grammys, and his name will always be associated with the big band era.

Visited Harlem music parlors

Basie was born on August 21, 1904, in Red Bank, New Jersey, to Harvey, a gardener, and Lillian, a domestic, Basie. At age eight he began taking music lessons for 25 cents. Despite his protests, Basie's mother was once quoted as saying he was "going to learn how to play the piano if it kills you." He attended public schools until grade nine. During the early 1920s, he visited Harlem music parlors, where he met legendary pianists James Johnson and Fats Waller. Basie took informal instruction on the piano and organ from Waller. He became a piano soloist and accompanist to

several acts including Walter Page's Blue Devils. He eventually worked his way to St. Louis, where he spent some time as a silent film organ accompanist, before playing with several local bands including Bennie Moten's.

When Moten died in 1935, Basie took over most of the band, and moved to Kansas City with a nine-piece group that embarked on a long run at the Reno Club. The band became one of the hottest in the city. One night a radio announcer discussing the "royal family" of jazz, which included "Duke of Ellington" and "King of Oliver," dubbed him "Count of Basie." He never really liked the title, and in 1982 said, "I wanted to be called Buck or Hoot or even Arkansas Fats"—all silent-film heroes.

John Hammond, a jazz impresario, heard one of the band's regular broadcasts on an experimental radio station and helped them to get bookings in Chicago and later New York. Basie wanted to increase the band to thirteen pieces, but initial reaction was disappointing.

In 1937 the band finally seemed to come into its own. Freddie Green solidified the rhythm section and booking agent Willard Alexander managed to get them an engagement at the Famous Door in the heart of New York's 52nd Street. NBC radio broadcast the performance. Basie's recordings with Decca—"One O'Clock Jump," "Jumpin' at the Woodside," "Swingin' the Blues," "Lester Leaps In"—and several others began to sell. As word spread, the band attracted huge audiences, often in excess of the venue's seating capacity.

The band's music evolved over a period of time as the leader and the players experimented with short phrases (riffs) and accents that bounced from the trumpets to the reeds to the trombones. In the early 1940s the band benefited from the writing and arranging of Buster Harding, Buck Clayton, and Tab Smith. Their work helped pave the way for the band's later reliance upon outstanding writing and arranging by Neal Hefti, Frank Foster, Ernie Wilkins, and Sam Nestico. In time the band grew to sixteen pieces.

Royal command performance in England

Basie and his orchestra toured in Europe and Asia, performed regularly at Broadway's Birdland, as well as at countless dances, festivals, and concerts. They gave royal command performances in England and won recognition by Presidents John Kennedy and Ronald Reagan. They delighted audiences with their new hits—"Li'l Darlin'," "Cute," "Every Day I Have the Blues," "All Right, OK, You Win," and "April in Paris." Although his band and music changed over the years, he always displayed a devotion to blues-based swinging, an uncluttered pulse, and the effective use of dynamics.

Basie's bandstand demeanor seemed laid back; some called it laissez faire, others called it lazy. His bandmen and arrangers defended his demeanor. Basie's greatest skill was probably as an editor and personnel manager. He told the *New York Times,* "I wanted my 13-piece band to work together just like those nine pieces ... to think and play the same way.... I said the minute the brass got out of hand and blared and screeched instead of making every note mean something, there'd be

Count Basie

some changes made." He stated in his autobiography, *Good Morning Blues,* that, "I'm experienced at auditions. I can tell in a few bars whether or not somebody can voice my stuff."

The writers and arrangers became used to Basie's editing out of all material that he considered contrary to the band's ultimate goal—to swing. Such was the case with Neal Hefti's "Li'l Darlin'." Basie insisted on a much slower tempo than Hefti had envisioned, and the end result was one of the band's greatest and most enduring hits. Basie's conducting included such simple movements as a pointed finger, a smile, a raised eyebrow, and a nod. Any of these movements would kick the band into high gear.

Basie played the piano with smaller groups, including duets with Oscar Peterson. His solos, usually brief, cut to the essence of swing. With the full band, he was increasingly content to support and cajole soloists with carefully distilled single notes and chords of introduction and background. A modesty about his piano skills combined with Basie's understanding of the role of the big band piano to form his style.

In his book *Night Creature,* jazz critic Whitney Balliett stated Basie "pilots his ship from the keyboard with an occasional raised finger, an almost imperceptible nod, a sudden widely opened eye, a left-hand chord, a lifted chin, a smile, and plays background and solo piano that is the quintessence of swinging and taste and good cheer, even when almost nothing happens around it."

Inspired other artists

Several critics have observed that Basie's spare playing inspired such important artists as John Lewis, music director of the Modern Jazz Quartet; and Thelonious Monk, one of the architects of the Bop Era. Mary Lou Williams and Oscar Peterson also say that they were influenced by Basie. Mature jazz artists say great playing consists not only of the notes one chooses to play, but those that one leaves out. In this arena, Basie was considered the master.

Basie received a host of awards during his career. He received *Esquire*'s All American Band Award in 1945; *down beat*'s International Critics' Poll winner, 1952–56; Metronome Poll 1956 winner; received an honorary doctorate from Philadelphia Music Academy, 1974; named to *Ebony*'s Black Music Hall of Fame, 1975; named to *Playboy*'s Hall of Fame, 1976; named to Newport Jazz Hall of Fame, 1976; received Kennedy Center Performing Arts Honor Medal, 1981; received Black Music Association Award in 1982; and

won nine Grammy Awards. The Governor of New York declared Count Basie Day on September 22, 1974.

In his later years Basie was crippled with arthritis and suffered a heart attack in 1976. His last performance was on March 19, 1984, at the Hollywood Palladium in California. He died later that year from pancreatic cancer. In commenting on Basie's death, blues singer Joe Williams said, "we have just lost a national treasure, but the happiness that his music gave us will live."

Daisy Bates

Journalist, civil rights activist
Born 1920, Huttig, Arkansas

"Instinctively I threw myself to the floor. I was covered with shattered glass. L.C. rushed into the room. He bent over me as I lay on the floor. 'Are you hurt? Are you hurt?' he cried. 'I don't think so.'"

Daisy Bates assured herself a place in the history books with her courageous efforts to integrate Central High School in Little Rock, Arkansas, during the late 1950s. Despite threats, criminal charges, and mob violence, Bates lead nine black children through a gauntlet of white supremacists so they could attend school. As the leader of the Arkansas conference of the National Association for the Advancement of Colored People (NAACP), Bates was in the forefront of the civil rights movement. "She was a good infighter, persistent, intelligent, unintimidated—

a woman who made a choice of this career fully aware of its dangers to her person and also its rewards in the prestige and service of her people," Elizabeth Huckaby, vice-principal of Central, once said of Bates.

Journalism and activism

Bates was born in 1920 in Huttig, a small town in southeast Arkansas. She was raised by adoptive parents, Orlee and Susie Smith, and never knew her birth parents. She attended a segregated public school in Huttig, where the students used textbooks that were discarded from the white school. When she was fifteen, she met Lucius Christopher Bates, an insurance salesman and close friend of her father. In 1941 the two married and settled in Little Rock. They used their savings to lease the *Arkansas State Press,* and within the first few months, they increased circulation to ten thousand.

The *State Press* was a successful paper that strived for better social and economic conditions for blacks throughout the state. It exposed police brutality in Little Rock, which eventually brought about charges. Black policemen were eventually hired to patrol black neighborhoods, and race relations improved.

When the U.S. Supreme Court declared segregation in public schools unconstitutional in May 1954, the superintendent of Little Rock public schools, Virgil Blossom, announced that the board would seek gradual integration. The state and the local NAACP branches decided to challenge the school board's policy of gradualism. This placed Bates (who had been president of the state conference of NAACP branches since 1952) and a group of

children at the center of national and international attention for months.

Several hundred African American children were polled by school officials to see if they were eligible for admission to Central High School. Eighty were chosen, and then when additional factors were considered—scholastic achievement and emotional stability—officials stated only seventeen could apply. Of those seventeen, only nine agreed to attend an integrated school. Bates promised to protect these children, despite threats of violence and economic retaliation.

Bates took the children to the white public school with photographers from the *State Press* and other newspapers present to see if they could enroll in the school. On May 31, 1955, the Supreme Court announced that public school integration must proceed "with all deliberate speed." During the 1955–56 and 1956–57 school years, the NAACP leader-

Daisy Bates

ship kept the pressure on the Little Rock school board to move on its announced integration program. In February 1956, NAACP lawyers Wiley Branton and U. Simpson Tate filed suit in federal court to gain the admittance of Bates's children to white public schools at mid-semester. Federal Judge John Miller decided to go along with Little Rock School Board's timetable for integration, but stated integration would have to begin on September 4, 1957.

Violence erupts

On August 22, 1957, a rock was thrown through the front window of Bates's home. In her autobiography, *The Long Shadow of Little Rock,* Bates said, "Instinctively I threw myself to the floor. I was covered with shattered glass. L.C. rushed into the room. He bent over me as I lay on the floor. 'Are you hurt? Are you hurt?' he cried. 'I don't think so.'" The rock had a note attached: "Stone this time, dynamite next."

The nine students chosen to attend Central High School had some misgivings about putting themselves in a potentially dangerous situation, but they and their parents had faith in Bates. She had put herself on the line before and had successfully challenged white school authorities with the legal backing of the NAACP.

On August 29, 1957, Judge Murray O. Reed issued an injunction halting the integration of Central High School based on a rumor that white and black children were forming gangs, with some of them carrying knives and guns. NAACP lawyers successfully appealed the decision. On September 2, 1957, the Arkansas National Guard were summoned to Central High School to prevent an outbreak of violence. The school board asked the black students not to try to enroll at any white school.

With rumors circulating that a mob of whites was forming around the high school and other areas of the city, Bates contacted members of the Interracial Ministerial Alliance and asked that a group of ministers accompany the students to the school. Some ministers agreed, and they planned to walk with the children the next morning. Bates called the parents of all the children, except Elizabeth Eckford since the Eckfords did not have a phone. That morning Eckford went to Central High School by herself and was taunted, jeered, and accosted by hundreds of white students and citizens in front of reporters and photographers from around the world. She displayed dignity under pressure and became a source of inspiration to other blacks.

Federal involvement

The attack on Eckford set off a round of mob violence in the city that lasted seventeen days. On September 23, Bates had the children gather outside her home, and she quietly escorted them into the school. Her actions sparked mob action throughout the downtown. The children had to be sneaked out of the school through a delivery door. The next day the students stayed at home, while President Dwight Eisenhower federalized all units of the Arkansas National Guard and ordered Secretary of Defense Charles Wilson to enforce the integration laws. Wilson ordered a thousand paratroopers to the area, and President Eisenhower went on television to announce that the troops would enforce federal law in Little Rock.

On September 25, the children again met at Bates's home, and she escorted them to school under federal troop supervision. The paratroopers remained at Central High School until September 30, when they were withdrawn to a base twelve miles away from the city. The federalized Arkansas National Guard remained on patrol at the school.

On October 31, the Little Rock City Council ordered the chief of police to arrest Bates, Reverend J.C. Crenshaw, and all other NAACP officials he could find on the charge of violating a recently enacted statute requiring an organization to supply the city clerk's office with information regarding its membership, contributors, and expenditures. The arrest of Bates was generally denounced in editorials across the country, and she was eventually fined one hundred dollars.

Despite the best efforts of white racists, Bates was able to get the nine students through the school year. For the rest of the 1950s and early 1960s, Bates turned her attention toward voter education and registration programs. Although recent illness has slowed her actions, she is still active on numerous boards in community organizations and is sought out by the press and politicians to comment on problems facing the black community.

Kathleen Battle

Opera singer
Born August 13, 1948, Portsmouth, Ohio

"I learned to sing listening to my father. He was a singer in a gospel quartet. My sister taught me how to read music.... The piano I kind of picked up, getting a fingering here, a chord there, looking over people's shoulders."

Kathleen Battle is one of the premier opera singers in the world. An attractive woman dubbed "the undisputed best-dressed concert performer in the business" by *Time,* Battle is noted for her roles in the coloratura and soubrette repertoires. After debuting with the Michigan Opera Theater in 1976, Battle has appeared in major festivals, toured and recorded extensively, and appeared on Grammy Awards shows. She has also performed with major orchestras including the New York Philharmonic, Cleveland Orchestra, and Los Angeles Philharmonic.

Learned to sing from her father

Battle was born on August 13, 1948, in Portsmouth, Ohio, to a steelworker. She was the youngest of seven children, and learned to sing from her father. He was a singer in a gospel quartet and her sister taught her to read music. By looking over other people's shoulders she learned how to play the piano.

Battle's first audience was at the African Methodist Episcopal Church, where she sang at civic functions, banquets, and church affairs. Charles Varney, a Portsmouth High School teacher, told *Time* he was very impressed when he heard the eight-year-old sing. "I went to her later and told her God had blessed her, and she must always sing."

As an excellent student in school, Battle considered a career in music or math. Varney convinced her to pursue music after she graduated from Portsmouth High School in 1966. She won a National Achievement Scholarship and enrolled at the College-Conservatory of Music at the University of Cincinnati. Since she felt she would never become a major performer, she took classes in art, dance, piano, and languages to increase her job opportunities. Battle received a B.A. in music education in 1970, and her M.A. the next year.

After leaving university, Battle taught music at inner-city elementary schools while taking private voice studies at the College Conservatory. In 1972 she auditioned for Thomas Schippers, the conductor of the Cincinnati Symphony. He chose her to perform Brahm's *Ein Deutsches Requiem* at the Festival of Two Worlds in Spoleto, Italy.

Leaves teaching for full-time music career

Deciding to concentrate on music full time, Battle resigned her teaching position. She was introduced to James Levine, the music director and principal conductor of New York's Metropolitan Opera. Levine was a Cincinnati native, who had come home to be the visiting director at the orchestra's renowned May Festival. He auditioned Battle and was so impressed that he chose her to sing a short soprano role in Mahler's *Eighth Symphony* at the festival the next year. "Some singers have little instinct but do have the intellect to balance the technical and musical issues. Some have instinct and a beautiful voice but less intellect. I had never come across a more com-

plete talent than hers," Levine told the *New York Times Magazine*.

Levine encouraged Battle to develop her repertoire to include sacred music and emphasized Mozart. Her reputation grew as she began making appearances across the country. Battle went to New York, where she was offered an understudy part in Scott Joplin's opera *Treemonisha*. In 1976 she made her operatic debut at the Michigan Opera Theater, and debuted as Susanna in *The Marriage of Figaro* with the New York City Opera. She then auditioned at the Metropolitan Opera, and two years later on September 18, 1978, she made her debut under Levine's direction as the shepherd in Wagner's *Tannhauser*.

In 1985 *Time* declared her as the "best lyric coloratura Soprano in the world." She not only has the lyric fare of typical coloratura opera singers—Adinas, Despinas, Norinas, Zerlinas, Paminas, and Rosinas—but has also

Kathleen Battle

added spirituals and suitable works by Schubert, Duparc, Brahams, Haydn, Mahler, and Bach. In 1986 her recital at Alice Tully Hall in New York was sold out months in advance. Battle averages sixty performances a year, with her most memorable roles being the young servants (soubrettes) and heroines of Mozart.

"She won't do Tosca or Mimi, but concentrates on the coquettish '-ettas' and 'inas' of the opera repertoire. Next to those like Jessye Norman's, her voice sounds small. But that sound is so ravishing, the intonations so true, the voice is so flexible, and the timbre so pure, that Kathleen Battle is one of our most adored divas, reigning as the finest coloratura soprano of her generation," a 1986 *Vogue* article described her.

Knowing the limits of her voice

Although some critics have charged that she is limited in her roles, the majority of them feel her confined set of roles may actually concentrate her talents. Her roles are usually limited to the soubrette and coloratura repertoires that accommodate her range. "I won't stretch or pull my voice beyond its capacity and capability," Battle told *Opera News*. "And I know what the limit is." Terry Teachout in *High Fidelity* was baffled by the criticism of Battle's voice as "a vocal fragment" in 1987. In his review of her album *Salzburg Recital,* he stated, "Artists like Battle should be cherished, and not dismissed with a vulgar sneer."

Despite her successes, some critics have claimed Battle is difficult to get along with.

This criticism first surfaced during rehearsals with opera diva Kiri Te Kawana. They were appearing together in Strauss's *Arabella* in 1983 when Battle objected to cuts to her role as Zdenka. After consulting with members of the production staff, Battle requested that her role be restored to its entirety. Te Kawana refused her request, and the relationship between the two quickly deteriorated. Matthew A. Epstein, the producer of Handel's *Semele* at Carnegie Hall in which Battle starred, defended Battle's image in an article in the *New York Times Magazine*. "She is not a pushover; she's a professional liberated woman," he said.

During her career, Battle has received numerous awards and Grammy nominations (including one for *Salzburg Recital*) and an honorary doctorate from the University of Cincinnati College-Conservatory in 1983.

Battle maintains a home in Quogue, Long Island. Eventually she would like to teach at the conservatory level, or commission music composed for soprano and small orchestra. Having conquered the United States, she intends to make performances in the great opera houses of the world.

Harry Belafonte

Singer, actor, activist
Born March 1, 1927, New York, New York

"The environment [in Jamaica] was terribly musical. People sang while working in the fields, while selling their wares in the streets, in church, during festivals. That background had a great impact on me."

In the 1950s Harry Belafonte burst on the scene as a handsome young calypso singer, scoring record-breaking hits with "Banana Boat Song" and "Matilda," and other bouncy Caribbean melodies. As the star of such films as *Carmen Jones* and *Island in the Sun,* he became a teenage heartthrob.

In the 1990s, Belafonte is famed at a deeper level as a champion of civil rights and a worldwide humanitarian. In 1985 he helped organize the recording of *We Are the World,* the album that raised millions of dollars for victims of famine in Africa. In 1987 he was appointed a goodwill ambassador of UNICEF, the United Nations Children's Fund, and his dedicated work on behalf of UNICEF has caused him to be dubbed "the children's patron saint." In 1989 the U.S. Committee for UNICEF honored him with the Danny Kaye Award.

As Belafonte has made his way through life, he has achieved many firsts. His recording of Caribbean songs, *Calypso,* was the first album to sell more than a million copies, and its success led to the establishment of the Grammy awards. As well, Belafonte was the first male African American to win an Emmy award and the first African American to be a television producer. He was also the first entertainer—black or white—to be made cultural advisor to the Peace Corps, an honor bestowed on him by President John F. Kennedy. Whether Belafonte will be remembered most for his humanitarian work or his music, there is no doubt that he has left his personal mark on the world.

The young performer

The strong Caribbean flavor of much of Belafonte's music dates back to his childhood, when he spent five years in Jamaica. Although Harold George Belafonte, Jr. was born in New York, both his parents came from the West Indies—his father, Harold George, from Martinique, and his mother, Melvine (Love), from Jamaica—and he was taken to Jamaica by his mother when he was eight. There, as well as absorbing the music, he learned what it was like to live under colonial rule, for Jamaica was at the time a British colony. Belafonte's activism on behalf of civil rights both at home and abroad can be traced back to his time in Jamaica in the 1930s.

On returning to the United States as a teenager, Belafonte attended St. Thomas the Apostle School in New York and then spent two years at George Washington High School. In 1944 he left school in order to enlist with the U.S. Navy, though his military service was very brief because World War II ended

Harry Belefonte

the following year. By the end of 1945 Belafonte was back in New York, where he took a job as a maintenance worker in an apartment house—and it was there that the small incident happened that change the course of his life. As a tip, one of the tenants gave the young man two tickets for a show put on by the American Negro Theater. This was the first real theater Belafonte had ever seen, and he was tremendously excited by it. From that moment on, he was determined to become an actor.

Through the GI Bill, which funded college courses for former soldiers, Belafonte trained at the Dramatic Workshop run by the famous German director Erwin Piscator. But there were very few jobs available for young black actors, and to earn a living, Belafonte found a job working for the garment industry, pushing a dress cart. Not for long, though. The owner of a Broadway jazz spot, the Royal Roost Nightclub, had heard Belafonte sing at the Dramatic Workshop, and he offered the young singer a two-week engagement. Belafonte proved such a success, with his husky, lilting voice and charming smile, that the two weeks were extended to twenty.

Belafonte spent the next two years singing popular songs in nightclubs throughout the United States. Although he delighted his audiences and was making good money, he was not entirely satisfied, for he had a longing to be a folksinger. At the end of 1950 he cancelled all his bookings so that he could take time off to study folk music, and during the next few months he spent long hours at the Library of Congress playing literally hundreds of records. Together with his friend Millard

Thomas, who became his accompanist, Belafonte selected the folk ballads that formed the basis of his new repertoire. Once again, he was an instant success, with two-week engagements lengthening into year-long runs.

The superstar

In 1948 Belafonte had married Marguerite Byrd, a child psychology teacher whom he had met when he was in the Navy. With his growing family of children and his well-filled schedule, he seemed all set for a steady career as a singer. But he had not yet fulfilled his dream of being an actor, and he jumped at the chance when he was offered a leading role in the film *Bright Road* (1952). Belafonte followed up with a delightful performance in the revue *John Murray Anderson's Almanac,* which opened on Broadway in December 1953 and which won him a Tony Award the following year. Next came his starring role in the movie *Carmen Jones* (1954), the all-black musical that made Belafonte a familiar figure to filmgoers throughout the country.

In 1956 Belafonte brought out his first hit record, *Calypso.* It made him a superstar overnight with its lilting West Indian numbers—especially "Banana Boat Song" with its catchy refrain, "Day-o, day-ay-ay-o." Since then, Belafonte has made a vast number of recordings and has extended his repertoire to take in the music of many cultures. One of his most acclaimed albums is *Paradise in Gazankulu* (1988), a recording of black South African music with vocals by Belafonte. He has also been a hit singing African American spirituals. Nevertheless, the bouncy calypso remains his trademark.

Alongside his recordings, Belafonte has given live concert performances in many parts of the world and has starred in several other films, including *Island in the Sun* (1957) and *Uptown Saturday Night* (1974). His television specials include "Tonight with Belafonte" (1960), which won him an Emmy Award. He received a Grammy in 1985 for his album *We Are the World*, which he organized to help the thousands of people who were suffering from famine and drought in the Horn of Africa.

The *We Are the World* album is just one of the many ways in which Belafonte has used his position as a celebrity to help others. In the 1960s, he played an active role in the civil rights movement. He was a friend of Martin Luther King, Jr., and after King's assassination he was one of the three executors appointed to handle the King estate. As well, Belafonte served as chairman of the Martin Luther King, Jr., Memorial Fund and was on the board of directors of the Southern Christian Leadership Conference (SCLC), a leading civil rights organization.

Belafonte has also campaigned for civil rights overseas, especially in South Africa. He was one of the prominent Americans who repeatedly urged the South African government to release from prison the African National Congress leader, Nelson Mandela—which it eventually did. Belafonte has shown a similar determination in his work for UNICEF. He was only the second American ever appointed UNICEF Goodwill Ambassador, and he has thrown himself into the work wholeheartedly. In his efforts to improve the lives of children in developing countries, Belafonte has supported a widespread immunization program to protect them from disease. As each year passes, he continues to help others both at home and abroad. Few superstars have put their celebrity to such good use.

Chuck Berry

Singer
Born October 18, 1926, St. Louis, Missouri

"It struck me that my material was becoming marketable, a recognizable product, and if these guys could do such a good job to get a hit, well, fantastic. I'm glad it was my song."

With his famous hip-swinging duckwalk, a mean guitar, and a smooth voice, Chuck Berry was propelled into rock and rock stardom. During the 1950s and 1960s, Berry cut one hit song after another during a troubled career that saw him tangle with the law on more than one occasion. He has made numerous albums, appeared in movies and television shows, and was inducted into the Rock and Roll Hall of Fame in 1986. His music was considered on the leading edge of its time, and he influenced many British bands that would become popular in the United States. Many American singers have tried to emulate Berry's heavy beat and melodic pattern.

Troubled youth

Berry is the son of Henry and Martha Berry. His early years were filled with trouble, and it was difficult to believe that he would one day go on to music stardom. He learned to play

Chuck Berry

the guitar when he was in his teens, but he was mainly interested in country music. In 1939 he and a friend played a steamy version of "Confessin' The Blues," which delighted a high school audience. The reaction convinced Barry to learn some guitar chords with his partner during his spare time. When he was sixteen, Berry was arrested and convicted of armed robbery and served three years in prison in Algoa, Missouri.

When he was released in 1947, music was still not his career choice. Instead, he went to work on the assembly line at the General Motors Fisher Body plant in Detroit. He studied hairdressing and cosmetology in night school with the hope of one day improving his career choices. In 1948 he married Themetta (Toddy) Suggs, and they eventually had four children.

Since he was always interested in music, Berry decided to put his talents to good use. Near the end of 1952, Johnnie Johnson, a piano player, asked him to play a New Year's Eve gig at the Cosmopolitan Club. Berry accepted and for the next three years, the band, Sir John's Trio, was the biggest act in the club. Besides Johnson and Berry, it featured Ebby Harding on drums. The trio played mainly blues, hillbilly, country, and honky tonk music in Detroit's black nightclubs. Berry wanted to be a big band guitarist, but by that time the style was not as popular. Berry borrowed sounds from T-Bone Walker, Carl Hogan, and Charlie Christian to make his own sound.

First hit single

In 1955 Berry bundled up a number of songs he had written and headed to Chicago. The Windy City was already famous for the number of outstanding black musicians that had made the South Side the blues capital of the world. It was here that Berry met one of his idols, blues legend Muddy Waters. "It was the feeling I suppose one would get from having a word with the president or pope," Berry wrote in his autobiography. "I quickly told him of my admiration for his compositions and asked him who I could see about making a record."

Waters told Berry to see Leonard and Phil Chess of Chess Records. The Chess brothers listened to Berry's rendition of "Ida Red" and were immediately impressed. They renamed it "Maybellene," and the record company struck a deal with Russ Fralto and New York disc jockey Alan Freed that gave them writing credits with Berry. The deal, which was made without Berry's knowledge, made the song the number one hit on rhythm and blues charts. However, the arrangement left Berry short of two-thirds of his royalties and convinced him to take charge of his own deals.

Berry's career snowballed from there. He cranked out a string of popular songs including: "Roll Over Beethoven," 1956; "Rock and Roll Music," 1957; "Sweet Little Sixteen," 1958; and "Back in the USA," 1959. Berry managed to combine the blues with wry, country-based topics such as young love and fast cars. He combined a standard heavy beat with his own special brand of ironic lyrics. He was singing rock and roll before it even had a name!

With his arms flapping and legs waddling, Berry became popular on the concert circuit with his dance known as the duckwalk. His stage presence also helped him to land several acting roles in movies such as *Mister Rock and Roll; Roll, Roll, Roll;* and *Go, Johnny, Go.*

The money from touring and record royalties began to add up. Around 1957 Berry opened Berry Park, just outside of Wentzville, Missouri. It featured a guitar-shaped swimming pool, golf course, hotel suites, and a nightclub. Berry also owned a fleet of Cadillacs.

Berry ran afoul of the law again in 1961 when he was found guilty of transporting a teenage girl across a state line for immoral purposes. He spent from February 19, 1962, until October 18, 1963, at the Federal Medical Center in Springfield, Missouri. He used this time to complete his high school diploma and write some of his most notable songs.

He returned with two hits in 1964 entitled "Nadine" and "No Particular Place to Go." But his star was beginning to fade. As the British rock invasion swept through the United States, Berry's singing style was no longer considered unique. Many of these overseas bands as well as some American bands had successfully adapted his songs to their collection. The Rolling Stones, for example, have done ten of his tunes.

Berry seemed to fade from public view in the sixties. He switched from Chess to Mercury Records from 1966 to 1969, but it had little effect. He continued to tour throughout the 1960s, but did not have a regular backup band. Berry's method has always been to use pickup bands comprised of musicians from the city he was playing in. This led to many complaints that his performances are sometimes shoddy and careless. He reportedly accepts no less than $10,000 per gig and plays for no more than forty-five minutes with no encores.

"My Ding-a-Ling" tops charts

Berry rose to prominence again in 1972 with the smash hit, "My Ding-a-Ling," that sold over two million albums for Chess Records. It was his first gold record and a number one hit in the U.S. and Europe. In the ensuing years he performed only occasionally, while problems with the law continued to crop up. In 1979 he pled guilty to a charge of income tax evasion and was sentenced to four months imprisonment and a thousand hours of community service doing benefit concerts.

Despite his personal problems, Berry has been recognized by the industry for his accomplishments. He received a National Music Award from the American Music Conference in 1976; a Grammy Award for Lifetime

Achievement in 1984; and a Lifetime Achievement Award by *Guitar Player* magazine in 1987. That same year he received his own star on the Hollywood Walk of Fame.

Halle Berry

Actress, model
Born around 1967

"Berry's radiant looks belie the strengths that have made her a young actress worth watching."—Lawrence Chua, Elle *magazine*

A former model and first runner-up in the Miss USA pageant, Halle Berry is making a name for herself as a television and movie actress. She made her debut in movies in 1991, when she appeared in three separate films, and has since continued to gain praise in a wide selection of roles.

The stunningly beautiful Berry has said that she does not "want to be just a sex goddess." In fact, she has already proved herself far more than this and has repeatedly shattered the Hollywood myth that models can't act. As Lawrence Chua commented in the magazine *Elle,* "Berry's radiant looks belie the strengths that have made her a young actress worth watching."

Growing up in Cleveland

Halle Berry and her sister Heidi are the children of a white mother and a black father. Their parents separated in the early 1970s, and the girls were brought up by their mother, Judith, who was a registered nurse. They spent their childhood in Cleveland, Ohio, living first in an inner-city neighborhood and later in a suburb.

Halle was a very shy child, partly because she was so conscious of being biracial. After moving to suburban Cleveland, she was often teased for having a white mother. Some of the neighboring kids called her "zebra," and placed Oreo cookies in the mailbox. But her mother built up her confidence. "What do you see when you look in the mirror?" she asked Halle. "You see what everyone else sees. They don't know that you're biracial. They don't know who your mother is, and they aren't going to care."

With such encouragement, Berry settled in well at school and during her high school years she was a cheerleader, prom queen, and class president. When she was seventeen, one of her boyfriends entered her name in the Miss Teen Ohio beauty contest, and she won the title. Thrilled by this success, she went on to compete in other pageants, including Miss World, in which she won the dress competition. However, her best year was 1985, when she was selected as Miss Ohio and then was named first runner-up in the Miss USA pageant.

In 1986 Berry enrolled at Cleveland's Cuyahoga Community College to study journalism, but she soon discovered that she disliked reporting and left the college without completing the course. Since grade school, Berry had dreamed of being an actress, and now she decided to give it a try. Her mother was encouraging, so in 1987 she left home for Chicago to work as model while studying acting.

An actress who is going places

While in Chicago, Berry heard that producer Aaron Spelling was doing a pilot for a new television show to be called "Charlie's Angels '88." She auditioned for a part, and although the show did not come off, her screen tests impressed Spelling, and he encouraged her to keep on with her acting.

It was not long before she had her first big breaks—a three-week United Service Organizations (USO) tour with Bob Hope and a starring role as a teenage fashion model in the television series "Living Dolls." Although "Living Dolls" was soon cancelled, Berry's acting attracted considerable notice, and filmmaker Spike Lee picked her for his controversial film, *Jungle Fever,* which was released in 1991. In this film, Berry played a crack addict named Vivien. In preparation for the role, she went ten days without a bath and interviewed a number of addicts.

Halle Berry

In 1991 Berry also appeared in the films *Strictly Business* and *The Last Boy Scout.* In the former, she had the leading role as the seductively attractive Natalie—though she almost failed to get the part because her skin was considered too light. "I found out that they hired me, thought I was too light-skinned, hired someone darker, realized that was a mistake, and then hired me again," Berry told *Elle* magazine. In *The Last Boy Scout* she again had a lead role, this time starring as an exotic dancer. She researched the role by paying the owner of a Hollywood strip joint to let her dance, and she gave such a strong performance in the film that Vincent Canby of the *New York Times* enthused, "The best thing in the film is Halle Berry. She is an actress who is going places."

Berry took on a totally different role in her next film, *Boomerang* (1992), an Eddie Murphy comedy in which she played the doe-eyed Angela. The year 1992 was a good one for Berry. She became engaged to Atlanta Braves outfielder David Justice and also starred in the television mini-series "Queen." As Berry makes her way in films, she has continued to take television parts. These include her recurring role as Debbie Porter in the series "Knots Landing."

In recent years Berry has developed diabetes, but she has refused to let the condition stand in the way of her career. She is a volunteer for the Juvenile Diabetes Association and enjoys a quiet life when not acting. As an actress, she specifically looks for roles that are not concerned with the conventional "black issues." She feels it is time to get away from racial themes.

As Berry moves from success to success, she has said that she does not want to rise to superstardom overnight. "There's no place to go but down," she explains. Most moviegoers would feel that she need not worry, for she is very clearly an actress on her way up.

Mary McLeod Bethune

Educator and civil rights activist
Born July 10, 1875, Mayesville, South
  Carolina
Died May 18, 1955, Daytona Beach, Florida

"The scattered work and independent programs of national organizations of Negro women needed the strength that unity could bring."

Ironically barred from doing missionary work in Africa because of her race, Mary McLeod Bethune taught in missionary schools in the South. The school she opened in Daytona Beach, Florida, became renowned for her methods and her students' success. Bethune campaigned nationwide on behalf of education and civil rights, and President Franklin D. Roosevelt appointed her director of the Division of Negro Affairs of the National Youth Administration. She earned a reputation as one of the most influential black women in American history.

Life on the farm

Bethune was born on July 10, 1875, in Mayesville, South Carolina, the fifteenth of seventeen children of former slaves Samuel

and Patsy McLeod. The family owned and farmed on a small plot of land purchased from Patsy McLeod's former owners. With no schools in existence that African Americans could attend, the children all worked the cotton fields. When Bethune was nine, she attended the new Presbyterian Church mission school five miles from home. The one-room school, with a blackboard of painted cardboard, was a great experience for the young girl. She learned how to read and taught the rest of her family in the evening.

At twelve Bethune received a scholarship to Scotia Seminary, a Presbyterian facility in Concord, North Carolina, and for seven years she studied high school and junior college courses, which included academics, religion, and the "culture and refinement" and "industrial education" subjects: sewing, cooking, laundering, and cleaning. Bethune's dream, however, was to serve as a missionary in

Mary McLeod Bethune

Africa, so she attended the Bible Institute for Home and Foreign Missions (later Moody Bible Institute) in Chicago as a scholarship student, but when she completed her training in 1895, Bethune was devastated to learn that the church did not permit African Americans to go abroad.

Builds own school

Bethune taught at several small schools for black children in the South. She married Albertus Bethune, also a teacher, and gave birth to a son. The couple moved several times and taught at various mission schools before Bethune opened her own school in 1904. Albertus Bethune died in 1918.

The school for which Bethune is best known is the facility she started in 1904. A major railroad construction project along the east coast of Florida attracted hundreds of black families hoping to find work. Hearing of the poor conditions near Daytona Beach, Bethune offered to establish a school. Though people were critical of the idea, Bethune pressed ahead. She rented a frame building in need of great repair and earned rent money by selling sweet potato pies, ice cream, and fried fish. She scrubbed every corner until the building was presentable. She made ink from wild elderberry juice and pencils from charred firewood. She rescued discards from the city's hotels and raised money door-to-door.

Daytona Normal and Industrial School for Negro Girls opened for business October 3, 1904. With an initial student body of 5 girls and Bethune's son, the school offered reading, writing, arithmetic, cooking, sewing, and other vocational skills. In just two years, a faculty of 5 served 250 students. The success was gratifying, but money remained a constant struggle. Bethune continued to sell food and salvage junk, and the school choir gave concerts in the area. Eventually she purchased thirty-two acres of property surrounding the school, and using secondhand material and labor supplied mainly by her students' fathers in exchange for tuition they built a new school called Faith Hall in 1907. Impressed with Bethune's determination, several businessmen and philanthropists provided operating funds. Several other buildings were added over the years, and the school offered adult education and community outreach programs and even contests to encourage civic pride.

In 1928, to secure the school's financial future, Bethune merged her school with Cookman Institute in Jacksonville, Florida, a boys' school affiliated with the Methodist Episcopal church. It was renamed Bethune-Cookman College, and Bethune was its president until 1942.

Mrs. Bethune goes to Washington

During the 1930s Bethune lectured widely and contributed to many magazines and newspapers. An authority on education and civil rights issues, she spoke dynamically on such topics as granting African Americans the right to vote, which she regarded as the true mark of freedom and citizenship. Bethune also served as vice-president of the National Association for the Advancement of Colored People and the National Urban League's commission on interracial cooperation.

In 1935 she established the National Council of Negro Women (NCNW) in Washington D.C. When Bethune stepped down from the presidency in 1949, the NCNW included twenty-two professional and occupational groups and sororities at the national level and eighty-two metropolitan councils. Bethune gained national prominence for advising President Franklin Delano Roosevelt on minority issues, and in 1936, he appointed her director of Negro affairs for the National Youth Administration, where she supervised the development of recreational facilities and vocational training programs for young black people. In the early 1940s she was influential in President Roosevelt's creation of the Federal Committee on Fair Employment Practices intended to end employment discrimination. Bethune was special assistant to the secretary of war during World War II, charged with selecting candidates for the first officers' training school for the Women's Army Corps, and in 1945 she attended the organizing conference of the United Nations as a special representative of the Department of State.

Bethune continued working throughout her seventies until she suffered a fatal heart attack just two months short of her eightieth birthday. She is buried on the grounds of her college, which at the time of her death in 1955 had an enrollment of more than 1,000 students and 100 faculty members. Bethune-Cookman College now has over 2,000 students and nearly 200 faculty members.

Dave Bing

Businessman, former basketball player
Born November 29, 1943, Washington, D.C.

"You need to work to be productive. Not so much for income. I'm not working for income, if you will. It's to be productive, it's to keep myself busy, to keep me doing something that's positive."

B asketball stars today sign multimillion dollar contracts to perform on the courts. But when Dave Bing was one of the game's most dominant guards, the biggest contract he ever signed was for $225,000. Shortly after his basketball career ended, Bing formed his own steel company, and through hard work and determination, he was finally able to ink his million dollar contract. Besides being an astute businessman, Bing devotes much of his time to charity and is seen as a role model for young African Americans.

Hard work, long-term thinking, teamwork

Bing was raised in a poor neighborhood of Washington, D.C. His parents taught him the value of hard work and long-term thinking. William Roundtree, his basketball coach at Spingarn High in Washington, impressed on him the value of teamwork. "If I'd had a different philosophy, David could have scored forty points a game," Roundtree told *Sports Illustrated*. Foregoing personal statistics for team play, Bing was still named to the *Senior Scholastic* High School All-American team, and in 1962 he was recruited by Syracuse University.

At Syracuse Bing majored in economics and marketing, and he was an All-American on the court. He averaged 24.8 points per game over four years and set a school scoring record that lasted more than twenty years. Bing was never a great shooter, but he made up for it by taking a lot of shots. At six feet three inches, many considered him too short for the National Basketball Association. But the Detroit Pistons were impressed with his speed, agility, and extraordinary jumping ability, and they made him the number two pick in 1966.

Bing sizzled in his first year, averaging 20 points a game and finishing tenth in league scoring. He was named Rookie of the Year. The next year Bing scored 2,142 points to lead the NBA, averaging 27.1 points per game. He was named to the All-Star game, a feat he would accomplish six more times. For the first time in years, the Pistons left the East Division cellar.

In 1975 Bing was traded to the Washington Bullets, his original hometown, and though he was past his prime, he played in all eighty-two games and was named Most Valuable Player of the 1976 All-Star game. After two years with the Bullets, Bing spent a year with the Boston Celtics before retiring. After twelve years, Bing had scored 18,327 points, including 54 shots in one game, and 5,397 assists, placing him twenty-fourth and twelfth, respectively, in the all-time rankings in these categories.

Despite his impressive statistics, basketball did not make Bing a millionaire. His salary during the 1966–67 season was only $15,000, and the most he made was $225,000 with the Washington Bullets in 1977. Fortunately, Bing had made arrangements for a smooth off-court transition. In 1967 he went to the National Bank of Detroit to apply for a

Dave Bing

mortgage and a job as a management trainee. For the next eight years he worked for the bank during the off-season. "I ... learned everything there was to know about money, financing, and the banking industry," Bing said in a *Black Enterprise* interview.

Works his way up

Bing gave up his bank position when he moved to Washington. After retiring from basketball, Paragon Steel in Detroit offered him a position in the warehouse, involving inventory control. Bing worked his way through the ranks, spending time in accounting, credit, purchasing, sales, and marketing.

After two years Bing decided to establish his own steel processing business, Bing Steel. To boost sales, Bing worked as a radio and television commentator, covering Michigan State University's basketball games throughout the Midwest for two years. Since Bing Steel's marketing area coincided with the states where the basketball team played, Bing's appearances were free advertising for his company.

The first few months were difficult for Bing. He used $80,000 of his own money and a $250,000 loan to start his company. He started the company during the worst recession in the American steel industry since the 1930s. He lost $90,000 in his first six months, but the company turned the corner when he won a contract to supply steel to General Motors. Several other automakers followed suit. With a growing reputation, sales soared, and Bing Steel grossed $4.2 million in 1982. By 1990 sales were $61 million, making it the tenth largest black-owned company in the United States, according to *Black Enterprise*.

Bing Steel expands

Despite his success, Bing remains apprehensive. "The reality, in my opinion, is that we make peanuts," he told the *Washington Post*. "Yeah, we're doing okay. But I think gross sales is an aberration of how one looks at success. To me as a business person, success ... is what you can bring down to your bottom line." Bing has diversified his company to overcome the booms and busts of the steel industry by starting a metal stamping company, a construction company, and—with Pistons star Isiah Thomas—a fiberglass company.

Besides his professional life, Bing is also active with community organizations. He devotes fifteen hours per week to charity work, in addition to the sixty hours he puts into his business. In 1989 he set out to raise money to maintain athletic programs in Detroit schools, which were experiencing a financial crisis.

Some said that sports should not be priority in a cash-strapped school system, but Bing defended his actions in the *New York Times:* "You look at 4,500 kids who are involved at school with sports and that is a significant number. Many of them would not go to school if these things are taken away."

In 1990 Bing was elected to basketball's hall of fame. The selection process created a bit of controversy when none of the candidates received enough votes on the first round of voting. With the prospect of no inductees, a second ballet was held with fewer names, enabling Bing, Earl Monroe, and Elvin Hayes to be inducted. Hall of fame president Bob Cousy resigned during the controversy, but the *Washington Post* stated that "even Cousy would be hard-pressed to argue that this year's class does not belong."

Bing is often regarded as a role model for young African Americans. Although he recognizes this image, he tries to downplay it. In a *New York Times* interview he said, "I'm probably one of the few black males in (Detroit) in business who has a positive image." He later remarked to *Sports Illustrated,* "If I'm a role model, well, it's largely because I have a big payroll, I spend time in the community and I'm successful. I've never yet seen a role model who was broke, bankrupt, and out of work."

Julian Bond

Civil rights activist, politician
Born January 14, 1940, Nashville,
    Tennessee

"The people who say I showed no racial consciousness are probably right. The occasion to be a race champion just didn't arise. And if it had, I don't know that I would have risen with it."

W hile many blacks have viewed politicians as the opponent in their struggle for civil rights, Julian Bond decided to become one. Shying away from the militancy of many in his generation, Bond was one of the first blacks elected to a state legislature. He gained national headlines when the Georgia House of Representatives tried to bar him from taking his seat because of his statements against the Vietnam War. Bond was the first African American nominated for the vice-presidency of the United States. In his later career he has been dogged by scandals, but has still maintained his dignity and is considered an influential voice in politics, education, and the media.

Parents were civil rights activists

Bond is the son of Horace and Julia Bond. He grew up in a sheltered academic environment since his father was the president of Lincoln University, but he was still not immune to racism. Many whites resented having a black president, and tensions increased when Horace Bond began to challenge restaurant and theater segregation in nearby Oxford, Pennsylvania, and in the county school system. Using their children as plaintiffs, Horace and several other faculty members successfully integrated the schools. Horace's efforts brought him many enemies, and his children often felt much of this hostility.

Julian Bond attended an integrated school for three years, and when he reached high school age, he was sent to George School, a Quaker boarding school in Bucks County, Pennsylvania. Bond was the only black at the school. Race relations were not a problem, and Bond rarely concerned himself with the matter. His first major run-in with racism took place when he wore his school jacket to Philadelphia on a date with his white girlfriend. The next day the dean told him he should not have worn the jacket. Although the school claimed that their policy did not permit any student to wear their school jackets to places like Philadelphia, Bond felt the real reason was because he was dating a white girl.

Despite this incident, it appeared that Bond was not going to follow in his father's footsteps and become a civil rights activist. His parents hoped he would become a scholar, but Bond had different ideas. Although he

Julian Bond

was extremely intelligent, he was very selective in the projects he took on. His grades at George School were average and he graduated in the bottom quarter of his class.

Attends Morehouse College

Bond decided to follow the family tradition by attending Morehouse College in Atlanta. He was leary of moving south because he felt that race problems did not exist in the North, and that violence against blacks was commonplace in the South. Bond lived in the predominately black West End of Atlanta, where several black colleges were located. While at Morehouse, Bond's gift for expression, his charisma, and his eloquence started to shine. He became known for his expressive poetry, and he was published in six anthologies.

Bond's interest in civil rights did not come to the fore until February 1960. Lonnie King, a fellow student, showed him a copy of the *Atlanta Daily World* containing an article about college students in Greensboro, North Carolina, who staged a sit-in at a local whites-only lunch counter. King convinced Bond that they should try to do the same thing in Atlanta. A meeting was held later that afternoon, giving birth to the Atlanta Committee on Appeal for Human Rights (COHAR).

This group decided to stage a series of sit-ins at white-only eating establishments. Bond was arrested while leading a group of students to the Atlanta City Hall cafeteria on March 15, 1960. It was the first and only time he was arrested. In *The Bonds: An American Family,* author Roger W. Williams wrote, "he had no stomach for bravado. But he was leader of the student group, and leadership at that juncture

meant physical action, so Bond went through with it. Perhaps he proved something to himself. If so, he proved it so well that he has not felt compelled to prove it again—not in so direct a fashion, at any rate."

Shortly afterwards, Martin Luther King, Jr., and the Southern Christian Leadership Conference (SCLC) asked Bond and other black student leaders to work together for civil rights. Their interests gave rise to the Student Nonviolent Coordinating Committee (SNCC).

Bond began to spend less time on his studies and more time with COHAR, which was quickly becoming one of the wealthiest and best-organized student groups in the country. He was also busy with the *Atlanta Inquirer,* a black newspaper he and several other students founded. He began as a writer but soon became the managing editor. Bond also started dating Alice Clopton, a student at Spelman College. All these demands eventually caught up to him, and he dropped out of college and married Clopton in 1961.

Becomes SNCC Director of Communications

Later that year COHAR was absorbed by SNCC, and Bond was offered a position as director of communications. He sent tapes to radio stations, wrote press releases, and attended meetings throughout the South. He occasionally found himself in dangerous situations, and once had a confrontation with the Alabama Bureau of Investigation.

In 1964 many SNCC members called for more militant action. Bond began to wonder about his career with SNCC and the effect increased militancy might have on his family.

When the Georgia legislature reapportioned the state, Bond decided to run for one of the newly created Atlanta seats. He campaigned on local issues including unemployment, minimum wage, and housing. He easily won the election, taking 82 percent of the vote. Bond ran into trouble in January 1966, when he publicly endorsed a statement from SNCC that condemned U.S. involvement in the Vietnam War. He added that he admired those who had the courage to resist the draft by burning their draft cards. The Georgia legislature refused to seat him. Pressure mounted on Bond to rescind his statements, but he refused to back down. National leaders and the press sided with him, and Bond took his case to the U.S. Supreme Court. On December 5, 1966, it was unanimously ruled that the Georgia house had "violated Bond's right of free expression under the First Amendment."

During the time the Georgia house voted not to seat him, Bond ran in two elections for vacant seats and won both times. Even when he was finally able to take his seat, he was still treated as an outcast. The *Washington Post* once reported that for the first five years he would not speak on the house floor. The conservative nature of the house made it difficult for Bond to be an effective legislator.

Bond was thrust into the national spotlight again in 1968. Georgia governor Lester Maddox named only 6 black delegates of a total of 107 to the Democratic National Convention, even though the party declared that the delegates must be representative of the state's ethnic makeup. The Georgia Democratic Party Forum, which included Bond, decided to challenge the official delegation.

Bond co-chaired a rival group, and after several days of wrangling at the convention, his delegation won almost half of Georgia's delegate votes.

First black U.S. vice-presidential candidate

In 1968 Bond became the Democratic party's first black candidate for the U.S. vice-presidency. After the voting results came in from the first few states, he withdrew the nomination. At age twenty-eight, most thought he was too young for the job. Despite the setback, he continued to remain popular and was a coveted speaker. He received $2,000 per speech in 1971, and a poll the year before stated he was the first choice of African Americans for president. In the Georgia legislature he mainly focussed on issues such as street paving and garbage collection, angering some who felt he should be discussing more important matters. He was reelected in 1974 and successfully defended his seat until 1986.

In 1976 Bond turned down a request to join the administration of President Jimmy Carter. The decision placed him on the outside of the black civil rights movement. He tried to reassert his popularity by seeking the directorship of the National Association for the Advancement of Colored People (NAACP), but was rejected for being too radical. He made a few television appearances, but his popularity continued to wane. He barely won reelection in the 1980s. In 1986 Bond gave up his state senate seat to run unsuccessfully for U.S. Congress. The next year his marriage began to break up, and his wife accused him of using cocaine. She retracted the statement a bit later, but a new scandal was soon upon him. His alleged girlfriend received a twenty-two-year sentence on drug charges. In 1989 Bond and his wife divorced, and the next day he was named in a paternity suit. Bond denied the charges at first, but in May 1990, he admitted to being the father and was ordered to pay support.

As the 1980s drew to a close, Bond continued to write and lecture. He narrated both parts of *Eyes on the Prize,* a highly acclaimed Public Broadcasting Service (PBS) documentary on the civil rights movement, hosted the television program *America's Black Forum,* wrote a nationally syndicated newspaper column titled "Viewpoint," and contributed numerous articles to magazines and newspapers. Since 1988 he has been a visiting professor at Drexel University, Harvard University, the University of Virginia, and American University. His future plans are to write an autobiography and a play.

Bobby Bonilla

Baseball player
Born February 23, 1963, Bronx, New York

"Kids today are looking for idols, but sometimes they look too far. When I was growing up, my idol was there ... my father. I didn't have to look any farther. The neighborhood was bad, but my home life wasn't bad."

he pressures of growing up in the Bronx helped prepare Barry Bonilla

for the pressures of professional baseball. The switch-hitting Bonilla has helped guide the Pittsburgh Pirates to two National League East championships and has been elected several times to the National League All-Star team. He was rewarded for his efforts with a $29-million five-year offer from the New York Mets in 1991. Bonilla has become a team leader with the Mets, both on and off the field.

Living in the toughest section of New York

Bonilla was born in the South Bronx, which is reputed to be one of New York City's toughest areas. He saw shootings, drug abuse, gang violence, and poverty. Whenever the situation became too bad, his father, Roberto, an electrician, and his mother Regina, a social worker, would move the family to a new location. Bonilla turned to sports as a way out of crime. As a child he would take his bat with him to bed, in case he wanted to take a few practice swings at night. He also spent hours playing sandlot and organized baseball.

But even getting to the playground was a challenge. "I walked out of the door at 7 A.M. and there went a guy chasing somebody down the street with a .22 (rifle)," Bonilla told *Sports Illustrated.* "We were all ducking under cars to stay out of the line of fire."

Bonilla's father, Roberto, helped him past the tough times. Even after his parents divorced when he was eight, his father continued to take an active role in his life. Roberto encouraged him to excel in sports and would take him along to work sites. "Kids today are looking for idols, but sometimes they look too far," Bonilla told the *Chicago Tribune.* "When

I was growing up, my idol was there ... my father. I didn't have to look any farther. The neighborhood was bad, but my home life wasn't bad."

With good grades and behavior, Bonilla was able to attend Lehman High, a predominately white, middle-class school in another area of the city. It was here that he had his first encounter with racism. "I didn't really know about racism and had never given it much thought until I got to high school," he told *Sports Illustrated*. "There were always a couple of guys there saying, 'You don't belong here, we're going to blow your head off.'"

Bonilla caught the attention of baseball coach Joe Levine, but since he played with an inner city school, scouts did not see him play. He also played in a league with few games; one year he only played thirty-three games. After graduating in 1981, Levine managed to find a position for Bonilla with an Eastern

Bobby Bonilla

U.S. high school stars' tour of Scandinavia. Pittsburgh Pirate scout Syd Thrift, whose son Jim was playing with the team, noticed Bonilla and recommended that the Pirates sign him. Bonilla agreed to terms and was sent to their Bradenton, Florida, farm team.

Slow start in the minor leagues

While at Bradenton, Bonilla did not set the league on fire. During his first two years, he only batted .217 and .228. However, he had far less experience than other rookies, and former Pirate great Willie Stargell began tutoring him. By 1983 his batting average was raised to .256, and he was sent to a higher caliber club in Alexandria. Realizing few minor leaguers actually make it to the major leagues, Bonilla attended a technical college in the off-season to learn repair work.

In 1985 Bonilla married his high school girlfriend, Millie Quinones. Later that year the couple experienced hard times—Bonilla broke his leg at the Pirates' spring training camp. The break was severe and took months to heal. When it finally mended, Bonilla was shipped back to the minors. During the winter of 1985-86, Bonilla was left off the Pirates' forty-man roster, making him eligible to sign with another team. The Chicago White Sox signed him, but he was only there for a few months until Syd Thrift convinced the Pirates to reacquire him in a trade for pitcher Jose DeLeon. He joined the Pirates permanently in 1986, and became a starter in mid-1987.

Pirates manager Jim Leyland was impressed with Bonilla. In a *Washington Post* interview in early 1988, Leyland said: "Bobby's big and has great power from both sides of the plate. He's got a great arm. He's quick. His foot speed is okay and he's a pretty good base runner. He's always been kind of laid-back (off the field) but he plays pretty gutsy. If I were him, I wouldn't worry. I'd go ahead and buy a house here in Pittsburgh." Bonilla did not disappoint. As a switch-hitting third baseman, he hit 24 home runs and knocked in 100 runs. Leyland told the *Chicago Tribune*, "If we hadn't had Bobby Bonilla, you might have needed a flashlight to find us. We might have been forty games out."

Bonilla picked up where he left off in subsequent years. He helped guide the Pirates to two National League East championships and was named several times to the National League All-Star team. With a batting average around .300 and fine defensive play, many felt Bonilla would stay a Pirate for many years. Bonilla wanted to stay in Pittsburgh, but the team owners offered him little incentive. He was challenged even when he asked for salary arbitration. After finishing third in the voting for the league's Most Valuable Player and helping the Pirates advance to the National League Championship Series in 1991, Bonilla became a free agent at the end of the year.

Offers poured in, but the Philadelphia Phillies and New York Mets showed the most interest. The Mets finally won the bidding war with a $29-million contract paying Bonilla $5.8 million each year for five years. "People say I ran to the money, but I would have been the highest paid player in baseball with any of the deals I could have signed." he told the *New York Times*. "After I lost at arbitration in the past, people said I was underpaid. Now they say I'm overpaid. Hey, I'm home. I'm happy to be here. I have my smile and it's going to be hard to knock it off."

Arna Bontemps

Writer
Born October 13, 1902, Alexandria, Louisiana
Died June 4, 1973, Nashville Tennessee

"After having produced more than 25 books ... Arna Bontemps became a literary critic of considerable stature."

Arna Bontemps first made his name as a writer during the Harlem Renaissance, the black cultural movement of the 1920s. He is chiefly identified with that era even though he was still writing in the 1970s.

Of Creole stock, Bontemps used the Creole dialect in some of his early works. He wrote fiction and nonfiction, poetry and plays, novels and short stories, essays and articles, children's stories and histories. Many of Bontemps's books record the achievements of African Americans, such as his *Famous Negro Athletes,* which he wrote for young people in 1964. He also compiled collections of other people's work, publishing anthologies of African American poetry and books of essays and personal reminiscences, which together greatly expanded the field of African American literature.

Knew and valued his own culture

Arnaud Wendell Bontemps gained his love of literature from his mother, Maria, who had

Arna Bontemps

been a school teacher before her marriage. However, she died when he was twelve, and Arna's father, Paul Bontemps, had no love of books and could not understand why the boy wanted to be a writer. The Bontemps men had been brick masons for three generations, and Arna was expected to learn the trade too.

Yet Arna's father valued education, so he moved the family to Los Angeles in 1905 in the hope of escaping the blatant racism of the South. In 1917 he sent Arna to San Fernando Academy, a white boarding school, where Arna soon came to the conclusion that he was being "miseducated" and was in danger of losing his identity as a black American. He felt the same about the teaching at Pacific Union College, which he attended in the early 1920s. Black history and literature were virtually ignored, and Bontemps welcomed the time he spent with his family or with fellow African Americans, just to keep in touch with his culture. As a writer he intended to portray his own culture, not the one thrust upon him through his education.

The young poet

After graduating with a B.A. in 1923, Bontemps moved to New York to teach at Harlem Academy. Harlem was the best place for a budding black writer to be at that particular time, and Bontemps soon came to know such key figures of the Harlem Renaissance as Langston Hughes, Claude McKay, and Countee Cullen.

Langston Hughes became Bontemps's close friend and colleague and collaborated with him on many projects. The two men were much the same age, and both were just beginning to have their poetry published. Bontemps' first published poem appeared in the journal *Crisis* in 1924. It was not particularly notable, but in both 1926 and 1927 two vastly superior poems won him *Opportunity* magazine's Alexander Pushkin Poetry Prize. Typical of other works of the era, they harked back to ancient times in Africa.

During this period Bontemps married Alberta Johnson, with whom he eventually had six children.

Wrote the novel that established his reputation

In 1931 Bontemps left Harlem to join the faculty of Oakwood Junior College in Huntsville, Alabama. That same year he had his first novel published, *God Sends Sunday*. The story was about a black jockey whose luck runs out, so that he becomes a penniless wanderer. With its dramatic plot and its use of the Creole dialect, the book was a considerable success, and it was later adapted by Countee Cullen as the musical "St. Louis Woman," which opened on Broadway in 1946. However, the novel did not make Bontemps rich, so he continued to teach at Huntsville, which gave him the idea to write books for children as a way of giving young people a positive image of black Americans. His first children's book, *Popo and Fifina* (1932), was written in collaboration with Langston Hughes and was a moving story about two black children in Haiti. Bontemps later teamed up with Jack Conroy as co-author of his children's books, but he also wrote many as sole author, including *You Can't Pet a Possum* (1934), *Lonesome Boy* (1955), and *Mr. Kelso's Lion* (1970).

From 1935 to 1937 Bontemps taught at Shiloh Academy in Chicago, and during this period he published his most celebrated novel, *Black Thunder* (1936). The story is based on a slave rebellion that occurred in Virginia in 1800 and was brutally put down. This book established Bontemps as a writer, and it enabled him to get a Rosewald Fellowship in 1938. At last he was able to give up teaching, spend more time writing, and complete his master's degree.

Historian and anthologist

After earning his master's degree in 1943, Bontemps was appointed head librarian at Fisk University in Nashville, Tennessee, a position he held until 1965, when he accepted a professorship at the University of Illinois. As librarian Bontemps pursued a longstanding goal of making black history and literature more readily available. The library housed the rudiments of such a collection, and over the years Bontemps added many priceless original documents to it. As a result of his efforts, Fisk University Library is now a major source of material on African American life and culture.

Bontemps also published a wide range of books on African American achievement, including volumes of black history, anthologies of black poetry, collections of folklore, stories of black life during the Depression, and biographies of such outstanding figures as George Washington Carver and Frederick Douglass. Some of these books were written specifically for young people so they could get to know their culture.

In 1970 Bontemps returned to Fisk University as writer-in-residence, a position he held until his death three years later. He produced half a dozen more books, one of which was the collection *The Harlem Renaissance Remembered* (1972), a topic Bontemps lectured extensively on, for he had been one of the era's last survivors.

Riddick Bowe

Boxer
Born 1967

"I knew somehow, someday I would get out of there. I lived there, I survived and I fought my way out, and they said I had no heart."

I n a sport that is often violent and brutal, Riddick Bowe, the heavyweight boxing champion of the world is a gentle giant. He is a committed family man, who does not drink, believes in higher education, and invests his

Riddick Bowe

money wisely. He fought his way out of a New York ghetto to earn a spot on the 1988 U.S. Olympic team. When he lost the gold medal to Canadian Lennox Lewis, many felt he did not have the heart to become a professional boxer. With the odds stacked against him, Bowe embarked on a string of victories that eventually saw him take the heavyweight crown from Evander Holyfield in 1992.

Living with crack dealers

Bowe grew up in Brownsville, a tough section of Brooklyn, New York. He lived in a cramped two-bedroom apartment in a building in which crack dealers stationed armed lookouts on every landing. Murders were commonplace. One victim was shot in the head a floor below where Bowe lived, and laid in the hall for eleven hours before anyone moved the body. In 1988, Bowe's sister, Brenda, was murdered near the apartment by a drug addict who was trying to steal her welfare check. Once a friend

named Bugsy stuck a loaded .38 in Bowe's hands and told him it was the best way to take care of a neighborhood enemy. Bowe gave the gun back to Bugsy and decided to turn his back on crime. Today, Bugsy is in jail.

It was boxing that Bowe turned to as a way out of the ghetto. His early mentor was Muhammad Ali. "He saw himself as Ali," his wife, Judy, told *Sports Illustrated*. "He put Ali on a pedestal and strived to get there also."

Bowe first met Judy in Brownsville during the summer of 1982. He was walking down Christopher Avenue with one of her cousins, when he spotted her sitting on the stoop of the two-family brownstone where she lived. He asked her cousin to introduce them. Bowe used to take the bus to the New Bed-Stuy Boxing Club on the corner where Judy lived, and he would stop by her house to visit. Three years passed before they started dating. They would sneak nights together at Bowe's house while his mother worked. When Judy could not get out, they would meet at her house. They were married in April 1986, and Bowe graduated from Thomas Jefferson High School a few months later. When Judy became pregnant, she suffered fainting spells. She told *Sports Illustrated* that once, while she was slipping in and out of consciousness, she heard Bowe ask her mother, "What's wrong with her?" and start crying. "After that, I knew he was in for the long haul."

Their first child, Riddick, Jr., was born in 1986; two years later, a daughter, Riddicia, was born. In 1990, they had another daughter, Joyce. Bowe considers parenthood a big responsibility. "Having these kids gave me a reason to live," he told *Sports Illustrated*. "In my neighborhood people are always telling you that you are no good, that you can't do this, that you can't do that. But having these children and knowing they need me, well, that helped me. They are the reason I am up and running in the morning."

Losing gold at the Olympics

Bowe's boxing career was shaped in the ghetto, and he took his skills to the 1988 Olympic Games in Seoul, South Korea. He was the odds-on favorite to win the gold medal, and he made it to the superheavyweight final against Lennox Lewis. Bowe took two standing eight counts in round two. As referee Gustav Baumgardt counted off the second time, Bowe raised his arms over his head and bounced on his toes. After he reached eight, Baumgardt put his arms around Bowe and told him the fight was over. Many people questioned Bowe's "heart" and claimed he would never have what it takes to become a professional boxer. Bowe decided to seek a career in the army, and was on his way to the recruiting station when he came across trainer Eddie Futch. This boxing guru had already guided five men to the heavyweight championship. A soft-spoken man, Futch tutored Bowe with the no-nonsense demands and love of a father.

With Futch in his corner, Bowe went on to win thirty-one consecutive victories. His string earned him a shot at Evander Holyfield's heavyweight title in 1992. Bowe added Dick Gregory, a comedian who became a self-proclaimed nutrition expert, to his staff. When Bowe began training, he weighed 281 pounds, and Gregory put him on diet of 300 vitamins and protein tablets a day. Each day Gregory would arrive at camp with two or three six-inch tall jars of pills. He would stand by waiting for Bowe to swallow them all, which usually took fifteen minutes. Gregory also devised a tonic of beets, carrots, celery, lettuce, cucumbers, garlic, onions, bananas, maple syrup, and anything else he could find in his kitchen. Gregory intended to clean out Bowe's bowels, lymph glands, and red blood cells. "The hard part was to clean out the 50 trillion cells in his body," Gregory told *Sports Illustrated*. "And each cell has three billion genetic bytes, and damn if I didn't have to clean out all of those, too."

Bowe weighed in for the match at 235 pounds. The fight went the full twelve rounds, and when the final bell rang, the scoring went as expected. Judges Jerry Roth and Dalby Shirley scored it 117–110, and Judge Chuck Giampa, 115–112, with Bowe the winner in each case.

At noon the next day, Holyfield telephoned Bowe in his suite and congratulated him for a great fight. Bowe recounted his conversation with Holyfield to *Sports Illustrated*: "Hey Champ, I was going to call you. You put up a hell of a fight and have nothing to be ashamed of. You always were a class act in my book, and my thoughts have not changed. I just hope we can get together and hang out. I want you to know we are still buddies. I want you to know you got me good, and I am going to have to sit down now."

Financial success

Bowe's success in the boxing ring has also been translated into financial success. He is financially secure for the rest of his life, even if he never fights again. His earnings have been channelled into a series of low-risk investments, and his children already have trust funds to pay for college. Education is extremely important to Bowe, and he and his wife enrolled at Howard University in 1992. Judy registered for health services, while Bowe studied business administration and drama. "I've got to practice what I preach," he told *Sports Illustrated*. "If a big dummy like me can go to school, then anyone can." Knowing he is a role model for youngsters, Bowe does not drink alcohol, has never done drugs, and has dated only one woman—Judy.

Bowe lives in a comfortable suburb of Fort Washington, in Washington D.C., in a modest two-story house he purchased after his manager, Rock Newman, insisted that he move to the capital area in 1989. The first thing you see upon entering the house is a framed evaluation from Riddick Jr.'s school that states, "J.R. had a very good day at school today. When he gets home from school give him a big hug."

Bowe is now designing a new house that will be built in Fort Washington. It will contain a big "RB" on its front iron gate, an indoor swimming pool, a boxing ring, a twenty-five seat movie theater, and a ten-car garage.

Ed Bradley

Television journalist
Born January 22, 1941, Philadelphia,
 Pennsylvania

"I've always been driven—but I'm not the kind of person who says 'This is going to take me here and that's going to take me there.' I don't have goals—I have standards of achievement."

Broadcast journalist Ed Bradley has practiced his trade in refugee camps in Thailand, talked with the IRA in Northern Ireland, and reported on the Vietnam peace talks in Paris. Since 1981, as a correspondent for the highly rated CBS television show "60 Minutes," his soft-spoken and often intensely personal reports have earned him the widespread recognition as the first black reporter to succeed in national television.

Hooked on doing live news

Bradley was born on January 22, 1941, in Philadelphia, Pennsylvania, to Edward and Gladys Bradley. His parents, who worked long hours at two jobs to provide for the family, inspired Bradley to believe that if he showed the same determination, he could achieve his goals. In 1964 he graduated from college and worked as an elementary school teacher during the day and as an unpaid disc jockey at a local jazz radio station in the evenings. Reading hourly newscasts for WDAS radio was valuable volunteer experience. His first paid reporting assignment came in connection with a riot north of the city.

"It must have been about two o'clock in the morning.... I was coming out of a club and turned on the radio," Bradley later told the *Christian Science Monitor*. "I heard Gary Shepard reporting on this rioting that was going on." With the station short-staffed, Bradley picked up a tape recorder and an engineer at the station and headed to the action. "For the next 48 hours, without sleep, I covered the riots.... I was getting these great scoops.... And that kind of hooked me on the idea of doing live stuff, going out and covering the news."

First African American to cover the White House

Impressed with Bradley's efforts, the station started paying him a small salary. In 1967 he began a three-and-half year stint at WCBS, an all-news CBS Radio affiliate in New York City, followed by a move to Paris, France, to write a novel. Though he enjoyed life in Paris, he ran out of money, so he prepared reports for CBS's Paris bureau, covering the peace talks between the United States and North Vietnam. This got Bradley back into the news business full time. He became the CBS-TV war correspondent in Indochina, spending three years in Vietnam and Cambodia. A wound he suffered in a mortar attack in 1973 resulted in a temporary assignment in Washington, D.C., but he returned to Vietnam in 1975 to cover the end of the war.

Jimmy Carter's campaign for president was Bradley's next assignment, and afterwards CBS assigned him to cover the White House, the first African American to work that beat. Considered a coveted position, Bradley hated it. The second-string reporter on staff, he spent most of his time in an office, an untenable position for the talented journalist, and he developed a reputation for being hard to get along with.

In 1976 Bradley began producing documentaries for "CBS Reports." Some of his best work focused on racial issues. He examined the subject of black gangs in Los Angeles in "Murder—Teenage Style." He won an Emmy and an Alfred I. duPont Columbia University Award for his 1979 piece "Blacks in America: With All Deliberate Speed," on American race relations. Traveling to China, Saudi Arabia, and Malaysia he documented Vietnamese refugees known as "boat people." This 1979 show earned him an Emmy and several other awards.

"60 Minutes" leads to "Street Stories"

CBC executives took several years to decide to offer Bradley a position on their award-winning news program "60 Minutes" in 1981. "60 Minutes" producer Don Hewitt wrote in his book *Minute by Minute,* Bradley was "so good and so savvy and so lights up the tube every time he's on it, that I wonder what took us so long."

Bradley worried whether the television audience would accept him, but the show's ratings remained solid. Well liked by the public, he has also garnered support from his peers. Colleague Mike Wallace called Bradley's approach "instinctive—he has no idea how he does it." Bradley's interview of actor Laurence Olivier typifies the journalist's style. There was some doubt about whether Olivier, who was ill at the time, would have enough strength to finish the interview. It turned out to be one of the most memorable interviews on "60 Minutes," however. As Hewitt described it in *Minute by Minute:* "The interview went on for an another hour and a half as Laurence Olivier and Ed Bradley jousted with each other. When Jeanne finally said 'cut' neither had fallen off his horse."

Bradley has also interviewed confrontational subjects. He spoke with activist Bernadette Devlin McAliskey of Northern Ireland for "The Other Face of the IRA." The heated discussion about politics and religion concluded with McAliskey declaring, "At the end of the day, God will be on the side of the winner, regardless of who wins, regardless of how he wins, because God always was and always will be."

Bradley's investigation of the murder of CBS correspondent George Polk in post–World War II Greece presented exceptional challenges. Many of those involved were dead, and survivors had to recall events nearly fifty years past. Bradley also discovered the possible involvement of one of his journalistic heroes, retired CBS correspondent Winston Burdett, in a cover-up to protect Polk's killers.

Ed Bradley

"I'd grown up listening to [Burdett] on the radio," reflected Bradley to the *TV Guide*. The magazine called Bradley's story "one of the most riveting interviews of one journalist by another."

In 1992 Bradley began hosting another weekly newsmagazine, "Street Stories." The prize-winning journalist explained his approach to work in a 1993 *People* magazine interview: "The bottom line in this job is fun," he said. "And when it stops being fun, then I'll stop doing it."

Carol Moseley Braun

U.S. senator, politician, lawyer
Born August 16, 1947, Chicago, Illinois

"By the time I got requests from white males in Republican counties in downstate Illinois, I knew something was up."

With few financial resources and little name recognition, Carol Moseley Braun stormed into the political arena in 1993 by entering the United States Senate. She defeated two-term Senator Alan Dixon in the March 1992 Democratic primary and later bulldozed past Republican candidate Richard Williamson. She benefited from feelings of anti-incumbency and that it was time to change the old boys' network on Capitol Hill. Although she was generally ignored by her opponents and the press before the primary, she has emerged as a leader for the growing force of women who want to influence American politics.

Fights for racial justice

Braun is the daughter of Joseph and Edna Moseley. She was interested in racial justice at an early age and once staged a one-person sit-in at a restaurant that would not serve her. Braun even withstood the stone throwing of whites when she refused to leave a whites-only beach. When she was sixteen she marched with Martin Luther King, Jr., in an open-housing demonstration in an all-white neighborhood.

After graduating from high school, Braun studied political science at the University of Illinois in Chicago. In 1972 she graduated from the University of Chicago Law School and became an assistant U.S. attorney under Jim Thompson (later governor of Illinois). Six years later she sought and won election to the Illinois House of Representatives in Springfield. Sue Purrington, her former legislative aide, told *People*, "It was immediately obvious that Carol was in her element. She liked the power play and the control."

Braun combines a strong commitment to the rights of the downtrodden and an ability to bring together rival political factions. Education, welfare, health care, and gun control have been her favorite reform subjects. She is noted for disarming her ideological opponents with calm debating techniques.

In 1983 Mayor Harold Washington named Braun his floor leader in the legislature, even though she was still a junior member. The two soon had a falling out, reportedly because Braun refused to follow Washington unquestioningly. He, in turn, blocked a 1986 recruit of hers to run as the state's lieutenant governor. That same year, Braun was burdened with personal problems. Her marriage ended in divorce, her brother died from drug and alcohol abuse, and her mother suffered a stroke.

Braun was elected Cook County Recorder of Deeds in 1988, the first black elected to an executive position in the county. She oversaw an office with three hundred employees and an $8 million budget. During her term she streamlined the agency through the use of computers and eliminated political patronage by implementing a code of ethics.

Braun considered a second term as recorder, but was urged to seek election to the U.S. Senate. Many were pleased with her stand on the Clarence Thomas judicial review in 1991. Braun publicly decried his nomination on the grounds that he did not have the judicial record to warrant his serving on the U.S. Supreme Court. When he was alleged to have sexually harassed Anita Hill, Braun took an even tougher stand against Thomas. "The whole thing was an embarrassment," she was quoted in *Ebony*. "I mean, it was an embarrassment from the very beginning and by the time (it began focussing on) the sexual harassment issue, it was beyond embarrassing, it was mortifying."

Campaigning against "The Pal"

Her stance won her many friends with conservatives as well as liberals, giving her a base to jump into the Senate race. Braun was pitted against Senator Alan Dixon, who had never lost an election in his forty-three-year political career. Known as "The Pal," Dixon was the champion vote-getter in state history. In 1991 he had sided with Republican President George Bush 58 per cent of the time, more than any other northern Democrat. Braun, known for her advocacy of mainstream democratic causes, knew she would need more than the support of just the traditional camp. And she found it. "By the time I got requests from white males in Republican counties in downstate Illinois, I knew something was up," she told the *New York Times*.

Although an out-with-the-old mentality pervaded the campaign, many analysts did not give Braun a serious shot at unseating Dixon. He had strong name recognition, strong financing, and appealed to many conservatives. The press paid little attention to Braun, choosing instead to focus on Dixon and a third primary candidate, Alfred Hofeld, a multimillionaire personal injury and products liability lawyer. The only headlines Braun seemed to get were ones regarding her grassroots campaign. She was beset with resignations, disorganization, and charges of mismanagement. She also received little support from her fellow politicians—only two members of the Illinois congressional delegation endorsed her. Even Senator Paul Simon, whose 1990 reelection campaign Braun co-chaired, supported Dixon. Her biggest support came from feminist Gloria Steinem, who provided fundraising help.

The campaign featured Dixon and Hofeld embroiled in bitter advertising strategies. Hofeld spent about $5 million on advertisements that said Dixon was out of touch with his constituents and was the tool of special interest groups. Dixon responded with a $2 million ad campaign of his own that defended himself and trashed Hofeld. Neither paid much attention to Braun. Since she was not a part of the negative advertising campaigns, Braun began to emerge as the most attractive of the candidates. She traveled the state and delivered speeches that voiced the themes she felt the people in the middle of a recession and hungry for change wanted to hear. The cornerstones of her campaign were job creation, universal health care, and increased educational funding. She also portrayed the Senate as a domain for white males, discussing the need for more minorities. She told the *Nation*, "what inspires me is that that anger is focussed much more against a system of ideological patronage and a Billionaire Boys Club whose abandonment of domestic policy has brought us to a social and economic precipice."

Although Braun only spent $350,000—she could only afford two television advertisements which ran a week before the election—she was the winner. She won 38 per cent of the vote; Dixon, 35; and Hofeld, 27.

Carol Moseley Braun

Bring on the Republicans

Her next hurdle was Richard Williamson, a one-time assistant secretary of state in the Ronald Reagan administration, initially recruited by the Republican party to run as a sacrificial lamb against Dixon. Williamson made it clear that he would use any means necessary to cast Braun as a big-spending, big-taxing liberal. Braun said she supported an increase in personal income tax on the top one percent of wage earners, wanted $100 billion slashed from defense spending, a capital gains tax cut, and a universal health care plan. "It's a historic candidacy and we're going to make history," she said in a *Boston Globe* interview. "The state is ready and willing to strike a blow for revitalizing our democracy and opening the doors to the Senate."

Braun entered the campaign with a huge lead, but it soon shrank due to several scandals. A local television station reported that she mishandled a $28,750 royalty payment made to her mother on lumber sales from family-owned land in Alabama. Williamson accused Braun of lacking integrity because the money had not been turned over to the state (as required by law) to determine if it should be used to help pay Edna Moseley's nursing home bills, which were being funded by Medicaid. Braun admitted she mishandled the money and her support in the polls dropped. She was also criticized for running an anti-incumbency campaign, rather than relying on detailed, well articulated positions.

When the final vote was taken, however, it was Braun who stood as the winner. She won a decisive ten-point victory, gathering support from a broad-based coalition that spanned racial, geographic, and gender lines. In January 1993, Braun took her place in U.S. Senate.

Edward W. Brooke III

Politician
Born October 26, 1919, Washington, D.C.

"I have been a very lucky American Negro. I believe the Negro will improve his lot and improve his plight by improvement of his mind and his body and his ambition."

E dward W. Brooke once termed himself a "very lucky American Negro." But it was more than just luck that enabled him to become the African American United States Senator since Reconstruction. Brooke racked up more than one million votes in 1966 to represent Massachusetts. He served for over a decade, concerning himself with issues such as abortion, nutrition, and children's programs. A bitter divorce and a Senate investigation into his finances combined to defeat his bid for a third term. Today Brooke is a partner in a Washington law firm and is active as a Senate lobbyist.

A descendant of Thomas Jefferson

Brooke was born on October 26, 1919, in Washington, D.C., to middle-class parents. His grandfather once told him that he was a descendant of Thomas Jefferson, and also of a British admiral, Sir Philip Bowes Broke, and that he was related to the English poet, Rupert Brooke. The family lived in an integrated area,

Edward W. Brooke III

which screened blacks who wanted to settle there. After graduating from high school, he attended Howard University, earning a science degree in 1941. Although this was intended to be the first step toward a medical career, his studies were interrupted by World War II. Brooke became an infantry intelligence officer, spending time behind enemy lines to fight with Italian partisans. While in Italy, Brooke, who attained the rank of captain, met and later married Remigia Ferrari-Scacco.

After the war, Brooke and two army friends headed to Boston to begin an engineering firm. Their plans fell flat, and Brooke entered Boston University Law School, earning an L.L.B. degree in two years, and a master's degree a year later. He settled down to a law practice in Roxbury—Boston's black section.

Brooke became known as an impeccable dresser who favored conservative suits that matched his calm mannerisms. Those who dealt with him on a daily basis said they could not remember Brooke in a wrinkled suit anymore than they could remember when he lost his temper in public. The nearest most observers saw Brooke with his guard down was when he uttered a short, bitter laugh at some particular probing question, usually about his involvement with racial issues.

In 1950, he made an unsuccessful bid for the state legislature. He returned to the courtroom and ran for secretary of state in 1960. Although he lost by 112,000 votes, he received more than one million votes.

Elected state attorney general

In 1962 Brooke ran for state attorney general. He was met with charges that he was soft on communism, but he countered by saying that in one of his earlier campaigns, he had been endorsed by the Communist party, which was endorsing any black who ran for public office. He won the election and was re-elected in 1964. His tenure was noted for his handling of a series of cases stemming from the work of a blue ribbon crime commission. He successfully convicted four members of the executive council, all Democrats, and a former Republican floor leader in the State House of Representatives, for conspiracy in connection with bribery. He also convicted three men involved in larceny, in connection with the construction of an underground garage. Brooke also had several cases thrown out for lack of evidence. Most notable was a verdict of not guilty against former Governor Foster Furcolo, a Democrat, on a charge of conspiracy to arrange a bribe. On one occasion a series of indictments had to be redrawn because of faulty staff work.

From 1962 to 1964, Brooke served as chairman of the Boston Finance Commission, a watchdog agency, and was frequently in the news for exposing civil corruption. In 1964, at a time when Brooke was being suggested as a possible candidate for governor, there were strong rumors that he was having troubles with the Internal Revenue Service. Brooke called a press conference to say that his returns for the past two or three years were being audited. He said his lawyers found a clerical error involving income of $12,000 over three years in connection with an estate. No charges were laid.

In 1966, Brooke wrote a book entitled, *Challenge of Change,* which outlined his personal methods to remake the Republican Party. The book led to an unsuccessful movement within the party to block his Senate nomination. During the campaign, political pundits claimed that Brooke faced a white backlash, but it was largely confined to middle-class groups. On November 8, 1966, Brooke received 1,213,473 votes and was elected a U.S. Senator. "I have been a very lucky American Negro," Brooke said in the *New York Times* upon his victory. "I believe the Negro will improve his lot and improve his plight by improvement of his mind and his body and his ambition."

Twelve years in the Senate

Brooke kept his Senate seat for twelve years. His main issues were abortion, nutrition, and family programs. He was defeated in the 1979 election after a Department of Housing and Urban Development audit, which indicated that he became a consultant for developers who sought help in lobbying the department so they could acquire federal subsidies for housing projects. The audit stated that Brooke had arranged, with senior department officials, for subsidies worth $14.7 million, the value of rehabilitation work on 150 housing units, to be "held" for Brooke. He was not charged with any criminal wrongdoing.

Brooke took an unpaid and temporary job as the head of the National Low Income Housing Coalition. He pressed the Senate for more funds for low-income housing, a concern that preoccupied him for years as a member of the Senate Housing and Urban Affairs Subcommittee. He was quoted in the *New York Times* as telling the subcommittee in 1979 that "low-income housing had barely recovered in 1976 from the moratorium by fiat unfortunately imposed by the Nixon administration.... Each year the Carter Administration is proposing funding for fewer units, and the Congress is acceding to these requests or worse yet, cutting them back."

Brooke lobbied in other areas as well. In Senate hearings, he supported federal grants to help the poor buy fuel oil during the winter, and with feminist Gloria Steinem, he organized a pro-abortion political group called Voters for Choice. Brooke often picked up the telephone to lobby personally for legislation, although ex-staffer Meg Power told *Newsweek,* "Even a former senator has only a certain number of times he can call his former colleagues before he uses up his currency."

Besides lobbying, Brooke became a partner in a Washington law firm. His legal duties usually require travelling, but he stays in touch with his former Senate staffers. Many believe that his presence is missed in Congress.

Gwendolyn Brooks

Poet
Born June 7, 1917, Topeka, Kansas

"I have notebooks dating from the time I was 11, when I started to keep my poems in composition books. My mother decided that I was to be the female Paul Laurence Dunbar."

Gwendolyn Elizabeth Brooks, the first black writer to win the Pulitzer Prize, received the award in 1950 for *Annie Allen,* a book of poems focusing on the black urban poor. Since then she has produced some twenty poetry books as well as numerous other works, including two writing manuals for children, *Young Poet's Primer* (1981) and *Very Young Poets* (1983).

Although Brooks has written on a wide range of subjects, she is especially known for her poems about everyday life in the cities. She draws sensitive portraits of people caught up by poverty, sharing with her readers their joys and griefs. The power apparent in the poems is due to Brooks's technical mastery. "Very early in life I became fascinated with the wonders of language," she once said, "and I began to play with words. That word-play is what I have been known for chiefly."

Began to publish poems in the *Defender*

Many of Brooks's poems are set in Chicago, where she has lived since she was a baby. She and her brother, Raymond, were given a very cultured upbringing. Their mother, Keziah (Wims) Brooks, had been a schoolteacher, and she composed songs for the children and encouraged them to read and write at a very young age. Their father, David Brooks, worked as a janitor but had hoped to be a doctor. Determined that his children would have the benefit of a thorough education, he encouraged them and often read aloud to them from the *Harvard Classics*.

By the time Brooks was eleven, she was reading everything she could lay her hands on, from the novels of L.M. Montgomery to the poems of Paul Laurence Dunbar. She was particularly attracted to Dunbar, the nineteenth-century African American poet, and when she started writing poetry, her mother prophesied that one day she would become the "*lady* Paul Laurence Dunbar." Brooks, who had written her first poem when she was seven, had her first poem published in a children's magazine when she was thirteen. By the time she was sixteen, her poems were appearing in the *Defender,* a Chicago daily newspaper.

At her mother's suggestion, Brooks sent some of her poems to Weldon Johnson and Langston Hughes, two leading poets in the Harlem Renaissance literary movement. Hughes later became a good friend, guiding her development as a poet. Both men recognized the girl's talent and encouraged her to carry on writing, and Johnson suggested that she read the works of such modern poets as T.S. Eliot and e.e. cummings. This the young poet eagerly did, both at home and in school, but her school years were not entirely happy. Brooks enjoyed learning, but the many white students at High Park Branch made her feel inferior. She later attended Wendell Phillips

Gwendolyn Brooks

High School and finally Englewood High School, where she felt slightly more at home. But since she felt that her darker color made her unpopular, she kept very much to herself.

Hailed as major new poet

Brooks graduated from Wilson Junior College with an English degree in 1936, then worked for the Youth Council of the National Association for the Advancement of Colored People (NAACP), where she met her future husband, Henry Blakely, Jr., who also wanted to be a writer. Both twenty-one when they met, they married in 1939, beginning a long if sometimes stormy partnership. They had two children, Henry and Nora.

From 1941 on Brooks regularly attended a writer's workshop led by writer and scholar Inez Cunningham Stark. In 1943 she won a poetry award from the Midwestern Writers Conference and submitted a collection of poems to the Harper & Row publishing house, which appeared in 1945 as *A Street in Bronzeville.*

This book delighted critics, and Brooks was hailed as a major new poet. Her poems took a perceptive look at the ordinary black people she saw every day in Chicago. The first section of the book depicted life in a neighborhood called Bronzeville. The second section, consisting of twelve sonnets, looked at the prejudice blacks suffered in the armed forces. Critics praised her handling of the subject matter as well as her artistry and technical skill. The accomplished way Brooks chose and used words to convey her meaning indicated that here was a poet who had practiced her craft and knew how to handle words with maximum effect.

A Street in Bronzeville brought Brooks a Guggenheim fellowship as well as the honor of being named one of *Mademoiselle* magazine's Ten Women of the Year. Her next book, *Annie Allen* (1949), received the Pulitzer Prize in 1950, the first time the prize was ever awarded to any African American for a book of poetry. *Annie Allen* centered on the life of a young black woman, also the focus of the novel *Maud Martha,* which Brooks published in 1953. Brooks's only novel, *Maud Martha* has been considered as lightweight but is beautifully written and deeper than it at first seems. Brooks published *Bronzeville Boys and Girls*, a collection of poetry for children, in 1956, and another children's collection, *The Tiger Who Wore White Gloves,* in 1974.

Developed a political outlook

Among Brooks's audience were some black writers who accused her of writing for whites only and of using language that was too complicated for ordinary people to understand. When Brooks attended the Black Writers Conference at Fisk University in 1967, she met writers who made a deep impression on her. "They seemed proud and so committed to their own people," she remarked. "The poets among them felt that black poets should write as blacks, about blacks, and address themselves *to* blacks." As a result Brooks decided to write in a way that black people could easily relate to, and she developed a more open, free-verse style of writing.

The conference also made Brooks more political, more consciously concerned with social problems. Her next two books, *In the Mecca* (1968) and *Riot* (1969), examined social issues, and later books dealt with such topics as rebellion and black nationalism. *In the Mecca* marked Brooks's defection from her longtime publisher, Harper & Row, to Broadside Press, a black publishing company, and Brooks claimed she would follow this policy with future books. Her autobiography, *Report from Part One,* was published in 1972 by Broadside Press.

Uses position to mentor others

In 1968 Brooks was created poet laureate of Illinois, and she has received numerous other poetry awards, including honorary degrees from forty-nine universities and colleges. Brooks was appointed poetry consultant to the Library of Congress in 1985; a school was named for her in Harvey, Illinois; and the Gwendolyn Brooks Center for African American Literature was established at Western Illinois University.

Brooks has used her stature as a poet to help others. She has lectured widely, not only at colleges and universities, but also in jails and in drug-treatment centers—anywhere she thinks people may relate to her poems. At schools she has encouraged students to write and to keep journals. Brooks has mentored up-and-coming poets, especially young black poets, and has organized numerous poetry competitions, often providing the prize money out of her own pocket.

Brooks still sees herself very much as a voice speaking to and for black people. "My aim," she declared, "is to write poems that will somehow successfully 'call ... all black people ... in gutters, in schools, offices, factories, prisons, the consulate; I wish to reach black people in pulpits, black people in mines, on farms, on thrones." Yet, like all poets, Brooks is writing for anyone who will listen. She has said that although her writing is *to* blacks, it is also for "anyone who will open the book."

Claude Brown

Writer
Born February 23, 1937, New York, New
  York

"I didn't have any dreams of becoming anything. All I knew for certain was that I had my fears."

Claude Brown is celebrated for two realistic books he wrote about life in Harlem—his autobiography, *Manchild in the*

Promised Land (1965), and *The Children of Ham* (1976).

Brown's autobiography has often been cited as the first book to describe the experience of urban African Americans in a truly effective manner. It gives a grim picture of life for families who had moved from the plantations of the South, dreaming of a golden future and ending up in a Harlem slum, surrounded by thieves and drug addicts. This was the world Brown knew—the world of his childhood in the 1940s and 1950s.

Shot in the stomach at age thirteen

Claude Brown was the eldest of the four children of Henry and Ossie Brown, both of whom were from South Carolina. After moving to Harlem in 1935, they retained the awe and fear of whites that had been instilled in them in the South, calling white men "sir" and seldom speaking up for their rights. This deferential attitude infuriated Brown. "They were in New York," he wrote in his autobiography, "but it seemed like their minds were still down there in the South Carolina cotton fields."

Brown's father worked on the railroad and expected his two sons to take similar jobs. When Brown's younger brother said he wanted to be an airline pilot, he was immediately put down. That type of work was for whites, he was told. A boy from Harlem should be thinking of something sensible, like being a janitor.

Brown responded to his parents' behavior by becoming a rebel. Egged on by older boys in the neighborhood, he was a practiced thief before he was even old enough to go to school. At school he got into fights so often that he decided not to bother going, and he regularly played hooky. He also joined the Buccaneers gang. "By the time I was nine years old," wrote Brown, "I had been hit by a bus, thrown into the Harlem River (intentionally), hit by a car, severely beaten with a chain. And I had set the house afire."

For Brown and his friends, there seemed nothing much to do except steal and get into fights with other gangs. "Boy, why you so bad?" his mother used to ask despairingly. By the age of eleven Brown had been expelled from three schools and had frequently been up before the children's court. After repeated arrests for theft, he was sent to Wiltwyck School for Boys, where he spent the next two years. However, soon after his release, Brown was shot in the stomach by an angry homeowner whose bedspreads he had been stealing. Just thirteen years old at the time, he thought he was going to die. But he pulled through and was sent to Warwick, another reform school. This turned out to be a home away from home, because most of Brown's friends were there too.

His autobiography received critical acclaim

Brown anticipated a bleak future with no sense of purpose but to steal, drink, smoke, make out with girls—it didn't add up to much. When let out of Warwick after nine months, he found so little to do that he voluntarily went back to the school. Many of his friends were already well on the road to ruin and heavily into drugs. Several had committed murders, and some had gone to the electric chair. Brown wondered if he would end up the same way.

Claude Brown

Two things saved him: his own strength of character—demonstrated by the fact that he resisted getting hooked on heroin—and the help he received from the staff of the reform schools. Ernest Papanek, the director of Wiltwyck, was a long-standing influence, constantly trying to get Brown to realize that he could amount to something if he made the effort. Another significant influence was the superintendent's wife at Warwick, who lent Brown books about achievers such as physicist Albert Einstein. Brown was fascinated. Here was a whole world he had never dreamed of—people with a solid sense of purpose and tremendous persistence. He decided that he, too, would make the effort. He would break free of Harlem and get himself an education.

At the age of seventeen Brown moved to Greenwich Village and for the first time in his life took a real job, rather than making money by selling drugs or stealing. It was the type of job his father would have chosen for him—working as a busboy at a hamburger joint—but it brought in enough to pay for his courses at night school. Meanwhile he joined a sports club, where he met a musician who encouraged him to learn the piano. Within a year he was playing in jazz groups.

Occasionally Brown returned to Harlem to visit his parents and look up old friends, but his friends were increasingly hard to find. Some were away serving prison sentences, many were heavily into drugs, and others were dead. One of his closest friends fell off a roof while under the influence of heroin. A few of Brown's group managed to break free of drugs, but most could not do so, despite his efforts to help them.

Through all this time Brown kept in touch with Ernest Papanek at Wiltwyck, and in the early 1960s Papanek persuaded him to write an article about Harlem for *Dissent* magazine. A powerful piece, the article attracted the attention of the publishers at Macmillan, and they offered to pay Brown's expenses while he wrote a book about his life in Harlem. The result was his autobiography, *Manchild in the Promised Land,* which Brown completed in 1963. It was published in 1965, the same year he triumphantly graduated with a B.A. from Howard University.

Manchild was highly praised by the reviewers and was taken up by the civil rights movement because it gave such a faithful and devastating picture of what life was like in the black ghettos of the big cities. Brown's second book, *The Children of Ham* (1976), returned to the same subject but with a different twist. It is the story of a group of black teenagers who gather in abandoned apartments where they can live free of heroin. Their aim is to stay clean and stay in school. This book attracted less attention than Brown's autobiography, but it too gave a chilling picture of the streets of Harlem in the 1950s and 1960s.

While Brown was making his way as a writer, he carried on with his education, studying in the law schools of Stanford and Rutgers universities. He has since worked with the Harlem Improvement Project Group and other organizations. His autobiography remains a classic of American literature, while his metamorphosis from child criminal to social activist stands as an example of what can be achieved even against overwhelming odds.

H. Rap Brown

Writer, political activist
Born October 4, 1943, Baton Rouge,
　Louisiana

"I'm not happy to be here and I think it's unnecessary that we have to be here protesting against the brutality that Black people are being subjected to."

Author of the controversial book *Die Nigger Die!* and chairman of the Student Nonviolent Coordinating Committee (SNCC) in the late 1960s, H. Rap Brown was an outspoken leader who advocated violence to achieve civil rights. In the reactionary times following assassination of the movement's nonviolent leader, Martin Luther King, Jr., Brown's appearances in several large American cities provoked riots. His pro-violence

stance, which included recommending that black people use guns to assert their rights, ran him into trouble with the law, and he was eventually sent to jail in the early 1970s.

Met with President Johnson

Brown was born Hubert Gerold Brown on October 4, 1943, to Eddie and Thelma Brown of Baton Rouge, Louisiana. His father worked for an oil company. From 1960 to 1964 Brown studied sociology at Southern University, a black college in his hometown, where he felt the administration was unwilling to stand up against racial injustice.

After graduating, he worked in Washington, D.C., as a librarian for the Department of Agriculture. Then he became a neighborhood worker for a government antipoverty program, but left feeling that blacks were being co-opted for the program. "The poverty program," he later wrote, "was designed to take those people whom the government considered threatening to the structure and buy them off. It didn't address itself to the causes of poverty but to the effects of poverty."

Although he tried to use government programs to bring about social change, Brown became increasingly frustrated with them and explored other options. In 1965 he became chairman of the Washington-based Nonviolent Action Group and joined several other black leaders meeting with President Lyndon Johnson. Brown gained attention for criticizing the strong-willed president. "I am not happy to be here," he remembered telling Johnson, "and I think it's unnecessary that we have to be here protesting against the brutality that black people are subjected to."

Elected chairman of the Student Nonviolent Coordinating Committee

As an organizer for the Student Nonviolent Coordinating Committee (SNCC), Brown went to Greene County, Alabama, the next year to encourage the local black population to vote and hold public office. He was successful despite hostility from white citizens and the police, and he became SNCC's Alabama project director a few months later. In 1967 he was elected chairman of the entire organization.

Brown's position brought him national attention, as did the controversial comments he made about the need for a violent confrontation against racism. He suggested that the riots sweeping the country at this time were part of a political rebellion. Riots broke out after his speeches in the cities of Dayton, Ohio; East St. Louis, Illinois; and Cambridge, Mary-

H. Rap Brown

land. Authorities in Maryland charged Brown with inciting the Cambridge riot and engaging in arson. For the next few years Brown had a running feud with the police, who charged him with illegally possessing a gun and violating the terms of his bail. Brown's supporters argued that he was being harassed for his political beliefs.

Die Nigger Die!

When Brown's autobiography entitled *Die Nigger Die!* appeared in 1969, it received predictably mixed reviews. *New York Times Book Review* writer Shane Stevens commented that the "cutting edge of pain is there. But so is the raucous, somtimes slightly hysterical, laughter of life." John Leonard of the *New York Times* found the work lacking both as an autobiography and as a political commentary, charging that Brown was so busy proving his manhood in the book that the point he wants to make in the book is never clear. But Brown did have his supporters. In *Black World* magazine, Kiarri Cheatwood wrote that "perhaps better than anyone before him," the author outlined "the responsibilities of black students to their people."

Lived as a fugitive

In 1970 Brown went into hiding, delaying the start of his riot trial in Maryland. The Federal Bureau of Investigation (FBI) immediately placed him on their most-wanted list. The next year, New York City police took him into custody near the scene of a bar room robbery. He remained in prison while he was tried and convicted of taking part in the robbery and was sentenced to further time in jail. Authorities in Maryland dropped their riot and arson charges after he pleaded guilty to eluding his Maryland trial.

Newsweek magazine called him a hatemonger, but despite his trouble with the law, Brown still had his supporters. Cheatwood called him a "young man with deep sensibilities."

During his time in jail, Brown converted to Islam and changed his name to Jamil Abdullah Al-Amin. He was paroled in 1976 and moved to Atlanta, Georgia, where he opened a small grocery store. Though no longer in the national spotlight, he spoke with *Washington Post* columnist George F. Will in 1985. Will observed that Brown had finally found a kind of peace. Brown reported that he no longer misses the 1960s and that the Muslim faith is the center of his life and inspiration. Instead of striving for political change, Brown was then working with neighbors on plans for a religious school.

James Brown

Singer, songwriter
Born June 17, 1928, Pulaski, Tennessee

"Sports are good. But it don't touch music. Music is the master of the soul. I can play in a place, and thirty minutes after I play, everybody is brothers. You know, I love that."

C alled the "Godfather of Soul," the "Hardest Working Man in Show Business," the "Sex Machine," and the "Minister of the New Super Heavy Funk," James Brown revolutionized the music of his generation by sidestepping the simple pop tunes of the day. He exuded a defiant independence, and his dynamic road show, innovative dance rhythms, and energized music attracted mass audiences.

Combining his own style with regular rhythm and blues and with gospel music, Brown influenced the music scene beyond his heyday, stretching to some of today's hottest stars. Mick Jagger, Michael Jackson, Otis Redding, and Prince have all stated that Brown was one of their greatest inspirations.

Succeeded with singing career

Brown was born on June 17, 1928, in Pulaski, Tennessee (some sources say he was born on May 3, 1933, in Augusta, Georgia). His parents, Joseph and Susie Brown, were poor, and Brown held a variety of jobs as a youth, including field hand, shoe-shine, boxer, and semipro basketball player, before being sentenced to an eight-to-sixteen-year term at the Alto Reform School in Taccoa, Georgia, in 1949 for armed robbery. He was paroled three-and-a-half years later and moved to Macon, Georgia, to join his friend Bobby Byrd as a member of the Gospel Starlighters. The group soon changed their name and began dabbling in rhythm and blues (R & B).

In 1956 Ralph Bass, a Federal Records executive, discovered the group, signed a contract with them, and brought them to Cincinnati, Ohio. Brown began to take control of the band and renamed them James Brown and the Famous Flames. Later that year they released "Please, Please, Please" which sold well and made the top song charts.

James Brown

Bass said in Arnold Shaw's book *Honkers and Shouters* that "Brown was way ahead of his time. He wasn't really singing R & B. He was singing gospel to an R & B combo with a real heavy feeling.... He wasn't singing or playing music—he was transmitting pure feeling." In the music business, that spelled the formula for success.

Produced an international hit

Two years later Brown and his band hit the national charts with their remodeled gospel tune "Try Me." This song attracted the attention of Ben Bart, owner of the Universal Attractions booking agency. Bart became the first and probably the most important booking manager in Brown's career. With a list of high-energy songs including "Good, Good Lovin'," "Think," "Night Train," and "Baby You're Right," Brown took his show on the road, selling out black venues across the country. His performance at the famous Apollo Theater in Harlem in 1962 was captured on the album *Live at the Apollo,* which rose to number two on the prestigious Billboard album chart.

Brown and his band changed their name to the James Brown Revue, and Brown became the center of one of the most popular R & B acts in history. He was nicknamed "Mr. Dynamite" for his showmanship, which included bright outfits, rhythmic grunts, and original dance steps. He fined the band members if they fell short of razor-sharp precision.

In the mid-1960s, with the assistance of Bart, Brown formed Fair Deal, his own production company. This gave him more control of his sound and a chance for broader distribution of the finished product. He was rewarded for his efforts with the international hit "Out of Sight" in 1964. King Records eventually convinced Brown to return to their label with the promise that he would have more control over his music. Working with band director Nat Jones, they produced several new hits including "I Got You," "Ain't That a Groove," and "Papa's Got a Brand New Bag."

Became a civil rights peacemaker

Brown became a role model for many blacks. Not only was he a successful musician, but he also owned fast-food franchises, radio stations, a booking agency, a publishing company, and his own Lear jet. He managed his own career in a white-dominated industry.

For a time Brown recorded several songs concerning black nationalism, including "Don't Be a Dropout," "I Don't Want Nobody to Give Me Nothin'," and "Say It Loud—I'm Black and I'm Proud." The songs received strong responses from both sides of the issues, convincing Brown to shy away from controversial topics. His principal role during the civil rights era was that of a peacemaker. He received a personal thank you from President Lyndon Johnson for performing a televised concert the day after Martin Luther King, Jr.'s assassination, a show credited with helping to stop riots from spreading across the country.

By the early 1970s, Brown had changed his style once again. Calling himself the Minister of the New Super Heavy Funk, he ushered in a new age of music featuring African rhythms. He recorded several songs with a group of young musicians who later became the popular group Funkadelic. Other groups began to duplicate Brown's new funk style.

Enjoying new popularity

Brown's superstardom seemed to fade in the mid-1970s. He appeared in a cameo role in the popular 1980s film *The Blues Brothers* and sang "Living in America" in the film *Rocky IV.* In 1986 this song reached the top ten and won Brown a Grammy Award for best male rhythm and blues performance.

Despite the award, Brown's career continued to fall apart. In 1988 he had repeated run-ins with the police on his 60-acre spread on South Carolina's Beech Island. Brown's fourth wife, Adrienne, complained of beatings. There were high-speed police chases involving Brown, rumors of drug abuse, and tax troubles. On September 24 he burst into an insurance seminar being conducted next-door to his offices in Augusta, carrying a shotgun and accusing the participants of using his restrooms. When the police arrived, Brown jumped into his pickup and was chased for ten miles. Eventually the police shot at Brown's truck, causing it to crash into the ditch. Brown claimed that he only deserved a speeding ticket and that the rest of the story was made up by the police.

Brown was sentenced to six years in a work-release program. He used his time in jail to rid himself of drugs and began helping children, the poor, and the elderly. He also recharged his musical batteries. His time in prison served to make him more popular than ever as musicians from all over the world began adopting his techniques. Though flattered by the attention, Brown also admitted to being angry for not being compensated for his music.

When he was paroled in 1991, Brown was prepared to capitalize on his new popularity. He appeared in a pay-per-view television concert a few months after his release, and a boxed set of four compact discs entitled *Star Time* detailed his career. He returned to the studio and produced *Love Over-Due,* which delivered more of his unique, show-stopping music. The "Godfather of Soul" was entertaining a new generation of music lovers.

Ron Brown

Secretary of Commerce
Born August 1, 1941, Washington, D.C.

"There is a tremendous vacuum in national Democratic politics when we are out of power. The national party ought to play a large part in filling that vacuum."

95

Credited with creating the campaign strategy that won the presidential election for Bill Clinton, in 1993 Ron Brown became the first African American to serve as Secretary of Commerce. In this position within Clinton's cabinet, Brown is in charge of a $3.5 billion budget and more than 36, 000 employees and has played a strong role in engineering and promoting Clinton's economic plan. Brown's mission as Secretary of Comerce, as he sees it, is to create job opportunities for all Americans, particularly African Americans and other minority groups who were overlooked during former presidential administrations. Along with fellow cabinet members, Brown seeks to change America by changing its economy.

Racism at college

Brown was born in Washington, D.C., and grew up in the Theresa Hotel in Harlem, New York, where his father was the manager. His parents were graduates of Howard University, and they bused him to exclusive preparatory schools. After high school he attended the virtually all-white Middlebury College in Vermont. Since he seldom experienced racism, he played almost no role in the civil rights movement of the 1960s.

Brown did encounter racism during his freshman year at Middlebury. As the only black in his class, he was rushed by white classmates from the Sigma Phi Epsilon fraternity (also known as the campus "jock" house). The national organization objected because of a clause in their rules that barred blacks. Brown said that he would not accept house privileges without full membership. The fraternity supported him, causing them to be expelled from the national chapters. Middlebury then barred all exclusionary chapters from campus. Today Brown is a trustee at the school.

After college, Brown became the only black officer at his U.S. Army post in West Germany. He returned home to earn a law degree, worked as an inner-city social worker, and then joined the National Urban League as its Washington lobbyist in 1968. He later became the deputy campaign manager for Senator Edward Kennedy's presidential campaign, was the chief counsel for the U.S. Senate Committee on the Judiciary, and was the general counsel and staff director for Senator Edward Kennedy. He served as the deputy chairman of the Democratic National Committee from 1981 to 1985.

In 1981 Brown joined the law firm of Patton, Boggs & Blow, where he became known for his backroom dealings. His clients included the government of former Haitian ruler Jean-Claude "Baby Doc" Duvalier and U.S. units of Japanese consumer electronics companies, which were fighting curbs on digital audio-tape records.

Jesse Jackson's campaign manager

During the 1988 Democratic National Convention, Brown was Jesse Jackson's manager. He was viewed as the peacemaker between the Jackson and Michael Dukakis supporters. When Jackson realized he couldn't win the Democratic nomination, he wanted a sign of respect from Dukakis. If the two camps remained split, it could have divided the party along color lines for many years. Brown used his skills as a negotiator to bring the two sides together. "He is not bragging when he says that his conciliation efforts played a role in turning a potential disaster into a love-in," David Broder wrote in the *Washington Post*.

His actions during the convention made him a media celebrity. *Time* wrote that Brown is "for better or worse, a symbol of his party: either an embodiment of the commitment to fairness and equality that has been at the heart of the Democrats' creed or, from another viewpoint, the final snub to those white voters who feel the party has become beholden to blacks and special interests."

Many Democrats were worried that the party was too concerned with Jackson's civil rights agenda. They felt the party should try to woo back traditional white, working-class voters. Brown seemed to be the answer. "He is such a very different guy from Jesse Jackson. He doesn't have the same inner demons. He doesn't have that bottomless thirst for respect," North Carolina Congressman David Price told the *New York Times*. *Business Week* agreed, saying, "he has a strong commitment to civil rights, but shows little interest in Jackson's theories of economic redistribution." Brown has become popular with white America since he looks like an Establishment figure. His voice is smooth, his manners are polished, and appearance is confident.

A master strategist

Brown is a master strategist who engineered his own election to become Democratic party chairman. He began the campaign as just one of five candidates for the post, but he used his carefully honed lobbying skills to the utmost. Brown contacted his former boss, Senator Kennedy, who chairs the influential labor committee, and a short time later the AFL-CIO endorsed him. To the surprise of many in the party, Brown managed to win the early support not only of liberals like Mario Cuomo, but also of moderates such as Senator Bill Bradley and former Arizona Governor Bruce Babbitt. The *New York Times* wrote, "Mr. Brown's election, the product of a meticulously organized campaign, gave him such an overwhelming advantage that his four competitors dropped out of the contest weeks before the voting."

Brown's stated goal was to overcome all of the party's ideological and sectoral divisions. He was determined to fuse the fifty state parties, the two congressional fund-raising committees, and the Democratic National Committee into a coordinated campaign organization that would help the Democrats more effectively convey their message. "What the party does over here and over there should be strategically connected," Brown told the *New York Times Magazine*. "The voter registration, the redistricting, the state party building and the campaigns—everything should be connected to winning elections."

After winning the election in 1989, Brown helped the Democrats to two major successes. The Democrats elected a black governor, Douglas Wilder, in Virginia and a black mayor, David Dinkins, in New York City. Both were firsts. The Democrats also picked up four con-

Ron Brown

gressional seats in special elections, including winning Vice-President Dan Quayle's former seat in heavily Republican Indiana. The fact that the party succeeded to such an extent is even more impressive considering President George Bush's high approval rating at the time. In these races, local party leaders praised Brown not only for bringing resources to the table—staff, money, polling, and get-out-the-vote expertise—but also for insisting that local candidates pool their own resources and run coordinated campaigns.

Brown has also been impressive with his ability to handle racial questions. Many white Southern Democrats are uneasy with the party's association with the black civil rights movement. During the Chicago mayoral election of 1989, Brown dodged the tricky issue of supporting white nominee Richard Daley, son of the late mayor, or black alderman Tim Evans, a Jackson ally running as an in-

dependent. Brown publicly stated he supported the Democratic candidate, Daley. He then promptly got out of town.

Appointed to Clinton cabinet

When Clinton named Brown as his choice for Secretary of Commerce, many Washington commentators predicted that the Senate would reject Brown in the confirmation hearings. These insiders pointed to the dealings and lobbying connected with Brown's career at Patton, Boggs & Blow. Undaunted, Brown sailed through the hearings and took his place along with three other African Americans in Clinton's cabinet.

When not at work, Brown lives in the capital with his family, drives an old Jaguar, and cheers for the Washington Bullets and Redskins. The *Atlanta Journal and Constitution* quoted his daughter, Tracey, as saying her parents were "better than Bill Cosby's Huxtables, the type that always discussed problems rather than meting out punishment." The paper also looked at his more humorous side. "[He] can get rattled on the tennis court or golf course. He has been known to heave rackets and drivers, one nearly taking out a group of nearby golfers."

With Bill Clinton in the White House, Brown has even more work. With the Democrats so long out of power, it was a painstaking transition to become the governing party. Although many have wondered how the party will deal with racial issues, Brown has promised it will not be a problem. He intends to be a strong advocate for African American business and he is in a position to accomplish this goal. "I'm the spokesman and representative of all American businesses and industries," Brown said in *Jet* magazine. "That's where all the jobs are."

Ed Bullins

Playwright
Born July 2, 1935, Philadelphia,
 Pennsylvania

"Some people said my language was too obscene, and others said the stuff I was writing was not theater in the traditional sense."

A major force in black theater, Ed Bullins has written more than fifty plays. He began writing in his mid-twenties as a political activist and soon emerged as a leading playwright about black life. Most of Bullins's dramas were written during the late 1960s and the 1970s. Since then he has been less productive, though his plays continue to be extremely popular.

Bullins's plays attract white as well as black audiences, though they are written specifically for African Americans. Bullins says he does not care what white critics think of his work: "It doesn't matter whether they appreciate it. It's not for them." Bullins has also written poems, short stories, and a novel. His plays have won him numerous awards, including the New York Drama Critics Circle Award, the Black Arts Alliance Award, and three Obie Awards.

Nearly lost his life in a street fight

Ed Bullins was raised by his mother, Bertha (Queen) Bullins, and knew little of his father, Edward Bullins. He became part of the street scene very young and joined a gang called the Jet Cobras. Because Bullins's junior high school was outside the gang's territory, he had to fight his way to school and back, and he quickly became a good boxer.

Even so, Bullins had his front teeth knocked out, and in one fight he was stabbed and nearly died. He viewed his survival as so amazing that he believed he had a special destiny: "My heart stopped. But I was brought back for a reason. I was gifted with these abilities and I was sent into the world to do what I do because that is the only thing I can do. I write."

At the time, however, Bullins did not realize that writing was his special gift. Dropping out of high school at the age of seventeen, he joined the navy and remained with the service from 1952 to 1955. During these years Bullins won his ship's lightweight boxing championship. More to the point, however, he began reading. Back in Philadelphia in 1955 he enrolled at night school, but once again he became involved in the street scene, living rough and tough and gaining some harsh experience, but not advancing his education.

Produced own plays in San Francisco

In 1958 Bullins started a new life California, where he attended Los Angeles City College and took his first steps as a writer. He started by writing short stories and poems, some of

Ed Bullins

which were printed in the campus magazine *Citadel*, which he founded and edited. Moving to San Francisco in 1964, Bullins took a writer's course at San Francisco State College and began writing plays. "I found that the people I was interested in writing about or writing to—my people—didn't read much fiction, essays, or poetry," he said. "I also found when I began writing plays I could handle the form better than most people."

At first Bullins had difficulty getting his plays staged: "Some people said my language was too obscene, and others said the stuff I was writing was not theater in the traditional sense." Nevertheless, he carried on, and he took heart after seeing two plays by LeRoi Jones—an established playwright dealing with the same aspects of black life that Bullins wrote about.

Bullins decided that if others would not stage his plays, he would do so himself. He rented a loft, gathered together a group of black actors, and put on the shows. When he and his actors were turned out of the loft, they gave performances in bars and coffee houses.

For the first time in his life Bullins was meeting a wide range of young black intellectuals—people with the same attitudes as himself—and in 1965 he joined with a group of young writers and revolutionaries to form Black House, a cultural-political organization. The Black Panthers used Black House as their San Francisco base, and for a time Bullins served as the Panthers' minister of culture. But he left the group when it became clear that the political activists regarded culture merely as a political weapon.

Celebrated as major playwright

All these activities brought Bullins quite a reputation, and in 1967 young black director Robert Macbeth invited Bullins to come to New York to join the newly established New Lafayette Theater in Harlem. Bullins stayed with Macbeth's company for the next six years, working as associate director as well as playwright-in-residence. His first work staged by the company was the 1968 trio of dramas *The Electronic Nigger,* about a pretentious black student in a creative writing class; *A Son Came Home,* a conversation between a zealously religious mother and her son; and *Clara's Ole Man,* which is generally considered to be Bullins's greatest work.

Like so many of Bullins's plays, *Clara's Ole Man* is about tenement dwellers and street people. The main characters are three women: large and hearty Big Girl, pretty eighteen-year-old Clara, and mentally handicapped Baby Girl, who is Big Girl's sister. The story revolves around a young man named Jack, who calls on Clara, believing her "ole man" to be at work. Jack doesn't know that Clara's "old man" is in fact Big Girl, with whom she is having a lesbian relationship. After he has been informed of this, Big Girl gets a gang of toughs to beat him up. The play is extremely powerful, portraying the desperation and frustrations of life in a black ghetto.

Bullins's years with the New Lafayette saw the production of some of his best plays, including *In the Wine Time* (1968), *Goin' a Buffalo* (1968), *The Duplex* (1970), and *The Fabulous Miss Marie* (1971). The New Lafayette staged many of its plays at the American Place Theater, and when in 1973 the New Lafayette closed for lack of funds, Bullins stayed on as playwright at American Place. Meanwhile, other theaters also were showing his plays. Bullins had twenty-five plays produced in New York in the twelve years between 1968 and 1980. He was also involved in teaching, and from 1975 to 1983 was coordinator of the playwriting workshops for the New York Shakespeare Festival. Bullins has since given playwrighting workshops at colleges and universities across the country.

In 1983 Bullins returned to San Francisco with his third wife, Trixie (Warner) Bullins, and their children. There he has continued to write plays. For many years he has been working on a project called "Twentieth-Century Cycle." This is a group of twenty plays that portray different aspects of African American life and feature the same characters at different times and in different places. So far, six of the plays have been staged.

Like all Bullins's work, these plays are strong and memorable. *Newsweek* magazine's Jack Kroll captured the essential character of Bullins's art when he wrote: "Although things happen in Bullins' plays, they do not really have plots: they simmer with interpersonal tensions, explode, subside, build to new tensions and explode again, ending on unresolved chords which lean out into time, forward and back, leaving an ache upon the air."

Grace Bumbry

Opera singer
Born January 4, 1937, St. Louis, Missouri

"Hers is a voice of multiple richness—radiantly lyrical at times, like that of a light soprano, opulent and resonant at other times, as if no possible range was too low for it, and no color out of its reach."—Louis Biancolli

The beautiful mezzo-soprano voice of Grace Bumbry first gained wide acclaim in 1961, when she sang the role of Venus in Wagner's opera *Tannhauser* at the Wagner Festival in Bayreuth, Germany. Bumbry was the first black performer ever to sing at the Wagner Festival. A year later, the twenty-five-year-old singer received another great honor when she was called home to sing at a formal state dinner at the White House as the guest of President and Mrs. Kennedy.

Since those days, Bumbry has performed throughout the world, delighting audiences wherever she has been heard. Although she has chosen to live in Europe, she often performs in the United States, as she did in 1982 when she appeared in Carnegie Hall for the eightieth birthday celebration of the great contralto Marian Anderson. When Bumbry was a little-known seventeen-year-old, Anderson had given her a helping hand, recognizing Bumbry's talent and knowing from personal experience how difficult it was for a black singer to be accepted in the world of classical music.

Bumbry was fortunate to be born a generation later than Anderson, therefore having a better chance of becoming an opera singer. Anderson had led the way, and by the 1960s the music-going public was beginning to accept the idea of black opera stars.

The choir girl from St. Louis

Like Marian Anderson and many African American singers, Grace Ann Bumbry had her first voice training in church as part of a junior choir. Even before she was old enough to join in, she accompanied her two older brothers to choir practice, for her parents had their own choir practice on the same day and there was no one to babysit the little girl.

Bumbry's parents were Benjamin and Meliza (Walker) Bumbry. Benjamin was a freight handler on the railroad, and Meliza was a schoolteacher from Mississippi, and both had a passion for music. When Bumbry was seven, her mother started teaching her the piano, and at family gatherings the small girl was expected to play as well as sing.

By the time Bumbry was thirteen, her voice was already attracting attention. While at Sumner High School in St. Louis, she joined the prestigious A Cappella Choir and was

given special training by the choir director. He encouraged her to enter local talent competitions, most of which she won. In 1954, the year she graduated from high school, she won a particularly welcome prize as a result of a contest on KMOX radio in St. Louis: a $1,000 war bond, a visit to New York, and a $1,000 scholarship to the St. Louis Institute of Music. The only problem was that the Institute of Music's trustees would not accept a black student. They offered Bumbry a course of private lessons instead. This her family refused.

KMOX radio then arranged for Bumbry to appear on Arthur Godfrey's "Talent Scouts," a nationwide radio contest. Singing an aria by Verdi, she won first prize. This led to scholarship offers from seven major music schools. Bumbry chose Boston, but after a year there she transferred to Northwestern University so that she could study under the world famous Lotte Lehmann. She was Lehmann's pupil for the next three and a half years.

Success in Europe

In 1958, Bumbry won $1,000 as semifinalist in the Metropolitan Opera Auditions of the Air. Despite this success, she decided to launch her career in Europe rather than in North America, because she felt that a black classical singer would have a better chance of a career overseas.

She made her European debut at Wigmore Hall in London in the summer of 1959 and then went on to Paris, where she gave several concerts. By the end of the year, she had gained a considerable reputation, which she increased enormously in 1960 when she performed with the Paris Opera as Amneris in

Grace Bumbry

Aida. The New York *Herald Tribune* gave a glowing review, describing how "the packed house showered her with applause, and at that moment one knew that Miss Bumbry had made her first step—or rather, leap—in what is certain to be a far-reaching international career."

Bumbry was immediately signed for a three-year contract with the Opera of Basel in Switzerland, though she was free to take other work and sang at several festivals in 1961, the most notable being the Wagner Festival in Germany. When Wagner's grandson chose her for the part of Venus, there was an uproar in the German music world, because Venus had always been played by a blond. Nonetheless, the composer's grandson insisted: "I don't need any ideal Nordic figures," he said. "What I was looking for was the best Venus in voice and appearance. It is an exceptionally difficult role which only a few artists are capable of singing." On opening night, Bumbry proved

herself so capable of singing this difficult role that she was given tremendous applause. Audience and critics alike could not praise her enough.

Bumbry now embarked on a very busy career, singing with the Paris Opera during 1961–62, touring Japan in the fall of 1962, and returning to the United States in between to perform in Washington for the Kennedys. This performance was arranged by the manager Sol Hurok, to whom Marian Anderson had introduced Bumbry many years earlier. Hurok brought Bumbry back that fall for a concert tour in the United States, and the following year she came back again to perform with the Lyric Opera of Chicago. Meanwhile, she also had a full schedule in Europe, performing at the Covent Garden Opera House in London in roles such as Lady Macbeth and Carmen.

In 1963, Bumbry married the Polish-German tenor Erwin Jackel, who became her manager. However, this was not a successful arrangement. Jackel objected when Bumbry began to sing soprano as well as mezzo-soprano roles, and the marriage ended in divorce.

American performances

Although Bumbry has been based in Europe for the past thirty years, she has made some memorable appearances in American opera houses. Her first performance with the Metropolitan Opera in New York was in 1965, when she played Eboli in Verdi's *Don Carlos.* In 1974, she returned to the Met to sing Santuzza in *Cavalleria Rusticana,* and that same year she also sang the part of Salome.

In the 1980s, Bumbry's American performances included the roles of Medea, Lady

Macbeth, Abigaille in *Nabucco,* and Bess in *Porgy and Bess*. She has also performed at concerts, including a gala benefit at New York's Waldorf Astoria, where she sang the pop ballad "Natalie." In the 1990s, Bumbry continues to bring pleasure to music lovers throughout the world with her superb stage presence and gloriously rich voice.

Ralph Bunche

United Nations official, diplomat
Born August 7, 1904, Detroit, Michigan
Died 1971

"I have a bias against racial and religious bigotry. I have a bias against war, a bias for peace. I have a bias which leads me to believe that no problem of human relations is ever insoluble."

Considering the depth of hostility between Jews and Arabs in the Middle East, it seems like a miracle that anyone could get them to agree to a peace treaty. But a miracle is just what Ralph Bunche performed, combining consummate diplomacy with tireless optimism to work out a peace agreement. In recognition of his efforts, he received the 1950 Nobel Peace Prize, making him the first African American ever to receive that honor. He eventually became the highest-ranking American at the United Nations and played a key role in organizing a six thousand man peace-keeping force in Egypt's volatile areas. Truly an internationalist, he worked to forge peaceful bonds between all nations. "I have come to believe," he once said, "that what is good for the world is good for my country."

Orphaned

Bunche was the son of Fred Bunche, a barber, and Olive Bunche, a musician. When he was ten years old, his mother became sick, and the family moved to New Mexico for the improved climate. Three years later both of his parents died within three months of each other. Bunche went to live with his maternal grandmother, Lucy Johnson, in Los Angeles, California. Johnson felt that Bunche had enormous potential and used her iron will to make him succeed. Bunche once called her "the strongest woman I ever knew, even though she stood less than five feet tall." In 1922, Bunche was the class valedictorian at Jefferson High School.

Since he was interested in current affairs, Bunche studied international relations at the University of California at Los Angeles. He financed his education by holding a variety of jobs including janitor, carpet layer, and petty-officer's messman. He also received many athletic and academic scholarships, starring on baseball and basketball teams, and took part in oratorical and debating contests. He was elected a member of Phi Beta Kappa and graduated summa cum laude in 1927. He then headed to Harvard University to earn a master's degree in government.

Bunche worked as a teacher at the all-black Howard University in Washington, D.C., and in 1930, married one of his students, Ruth Harris. After four years in Washington, Bunche returned to Harvard to work on his doctorate. He climbed aboard a truck and trav-

Ralph Bunche

elled across the continent, meeting people first-hand to complete his thesis on African colonialism. He also did post-graduate work at Northwestern University, the London School of Economics, and Cape Town University in South Africa. From 1938 to 1940, Bunche worked with Gunnar Myrdal, a Swedish sociologist who prepared the influential report on U.S. race relations, *An American Dilemma*. Their research took them to the deep South, where twice they were almost lynched. These experiences with prejudice and discrimination had a profound affect on Bunche. "I have a bias against hate and intolerance," he once said. "I have a bias against racial and religious bigotry. I have a bias against war, a bias against peace. I have a bias which leads me to believe that no problem of human relations is ever insoluble."

Bunche joined the Office of Strategic Services as a colonial affairs expert during World War II. In 1944 he moved to the State Department, where he helped author the United Nations Charter. Two years later he joined the U.N. and quickly became one of its most effective negotiators. He was held in high regard for his intellect, diplomatic skills, down-to-earth humor, responsibility, and kindness. Bunche often remained cool despite trying circumstances.

A peace treaty in the Middle East

As a U.N. negotiator, Bunche often found himself in dangerous circumstances. As hostilities increased between Palestinian Jews and Arabs in the Middle East, a specially appointed United Nations commission had recommended dividing the territory into separate Arab and Jewish states. Arab factions were upset over this proposal since they did not want to give up land and power to what they deemed were a relatively small number of Jews. War broke out in late 1947. On May 14 of the next year, the new Jewish state of Israel was proclaimed, but this heightened the conflict, dragging neighboring Arab states into the war against Israel. U.N. negotiators worked hard to find a solution. When chief negotiator Count Folke Bernadotte of Sweden was assassinated in September 1948, Bunche found himself in charge. He worked tirelessly and with unabashed optimism to find a compromise. Once when negotiations bogged down, Bunche pulled out a set of Rhodian pottery he had purchased as gifts for the negotiators and said, "I was going to give you these when we finished today, but now it looks as if I shall have to break them over your heads." Eventually Bunche was able to hammer out an armistice agreement, and he went on to receive a Nobel Prize for his efforts. Shortly afterwards he was elected president of the American Political Science Association and was named to the Board of Overseers at Harvard University.

Bunche considered his greatest achievement to be his work with the U.N.'s peace-keeping forces. In 1956 he helped organize a peace-keeping force in Egypt's Sinai Peninsula and Gaza Strip. This force successfully maintained peace for eleven years. "For the first time," commented Bunche, "we have found a way to use military men for peace instead of war."

Besides international affairs, Bunche was also interested in the civil rights movement closer to home. President Truman once asked Bunche to return to Washington as Assistant Secretary of State—which would have made him the highest-ranking black in the U.S. government. He refused because he objected to the oppressive discrimination practiced against blacks in the city. Bunche lived quietly with his wife and three children in New York City. Bunche was on the board of directors for the National Association for the Advancement of Colored People (NAACP) and took part in Martin Luther King's legendary 1963 demonstration at the Lincoln Memorial in Washington, D.C. He also joined King's protest marches in Selma and Montgomery, Alabama, in 1965, and attended King's funeral in 1968.

Named U.N. undersecretary

Bunche was name undersecretary at the U.N. in 1951, becoming the highest-ranking American at the U.N. One writer stated, "despite the extraordinary demands placed upon him,

Bunche was never too worried or too tired to think about the feelings—if not the inconvenience—of others.... Although he often ridiculed pretension or pomposity, I never heard him utter a malicious word. After bringing people down to earth, he was kindness itself. But he hated to see anyone humiliated or treated unjustly, and here his anger was formidable.... His personal integrity was matched by a demanding intellectual integrity. He did not let himself, or anyone else, get away with sloppy, self-serving work."

Failing health forced Bunche to resign from the U.N. in 1971 and he died six months later. United Nations Secretary General U Thant eulogized him as "an international institution in his own right." One writer commented, "Bunche had achieved a unique status. A black without color and an American who belonged to all the nations."

The Department of the Interior made Bunche's home at 115-125 Grosvenor Road, Kew Gardens, in Queens, New York, a National Historic Landmark on May 11, 1976.

Yvonne Brathwaite Burke

Politician and lawyer
Born October 5, 1932, Los Angeles, California

"I'm more interested in effectiveness than in being a firebrand."

 s a seasoned politician and lawyer with a strong commitment to public service,

Yvonne Brathwaite Burke has racked up an impressive number of "firsts." She was the first black woman elected to the California General Assembly, the first black woman to represent California in the U.S. Congress, and the first woman of any race on the Los Angeles County Board of Supervisors. She was also the first member of Congress to become a mother and the first to be granted maternity leave.

Burke regards her own achievements as merely a beginning and looks forward to seeing many more African Americans in government. She told *Ebony* magazine: "I visualize a time within the next ten years when we should have fifty black Congressmen because right now there are at least that many districts with 35 percent or more blacks. It's just a matter of time until we have a black governor, and, yes, a black President."

Set up own practice as a new lawyer

Yvonne Brathwaite Burke was born Pearl Yvonne Watson, the only child of James Watson, a janitor at MGM film studios, and Lola (Moore) Watson, a real estate agent. She gained the name Brathwaite Burke through her two marriages—first to mathematician Louis Brathwaite and then, in 1972, to her present husband, Los Angeles businessman William Burke.

Yvonne Burke grew up on the East Side of Los Angeles and showed promise very early. The principal of her elementary school considered her so bright that she arranged for a transfer to a private school connected with the University of Southern California. Burke was the only black child at the school. Burke later attended Manual Arts High School, where she became vice-president of the student body. She had such high grades that her father's union provided her with a scholarship to attend the University of California at Berkeley.

Even with the scholarship, it was difficult to make ends meet, so Burke transferred to the Los Angeles campus of the University of California in order to cut costs by living at home. To help pay her college expenses she worked part time in a garment factory and in one of the college libraries. Graduating in 1953 with a B.A. in political science, she then entered University of Southern California School of Law. Here Burke paid part of her tuition by modeling for *Ebony* magazine. She applied to join the campus women's law society—but was told the society did not accept blacks or Jews. Burke and two Jewish students thereupon started a rival sorority.

Burke faced similar discrimination in 1956 when she qualified as a lawyer: "There were law school quotas against both blacks and women, and when you got out it was difficult to find work. Getting a job with a law firm was almost unheard of." Burke solved the problem by setting up her own practice, specializing in real estate law and civil law.

From time to time Burke obtained government work, as when she served as a hearing officer for the Los Angeles Police Commission. She also handled cases for the National Association for the Advancement of Colored People (NAACP), and in 1965, following the riots in the Watts section of Los Angeles, she organized a legal defense for the rioters. Burke's involvement in the case led to

Yvonne Brathwaite Burke

her appointment as legal attorney for the McCone Commission, which investigated the causes of the riots.

Begins political service

A longtime Democrat, Burke was first actively involved in politics in 1964 when she worked as a volunteer for President Lyndon Johnson's re-election campaign. Two years later she ran for a seat in the California legislature, winning the Democratic nomination against six male candidates in June 1966. However, Burke's Republican opponent, an ultraconservative white politician, mounted a bitter campaign against her. He accused her of being a communist, a black militant, a subversive, a danger to society. Despite this onslaught, Burke emerged victorious to take her seat as the first black woman in the California General Assembly.

Twice re-elected, Burke served in the assembly until she ran for Congress in 1972.

During these years she supported legislation that was designed to improve social conditions, especially programs that helped the poor and gave women more opportunities. Because of her involvement in social issues, she was chosen to be chairperson of the assembly's committee on housing and urban development in 1971–72.

Nevertheless, Burke's life as a politician was not easy. Her concern for the poor and disadvantaged brought renewed accusations that she was a black militant, even though she believed very strongly in the rule of law. "I am more interested in effectiveness than in being a firebrand," she has said. Burke remembers 1968 as a particularly bad year: "For two weeks I was in Chicago, where the police did everything but put me in jail. I mean I was harassed and subject to just tremendous pressures.… It was terrible."

When a new congressional district was formed in Los Angeles in 1972, Burke took the opportunity to move on to federal politics. That summer, having won the Democratic nomination for the seat, she was chosen vice-chairperson of the Democratic National Convention in Miami Beach, where she gained great prestige for the confident way she handled a heated eleven-hour meeting on policy changes. Burke then won the congressional seat in the November elections and so became the first black woman from California to be a member of the U.S. House of Representatives. The following year, when her daughter Autumn Roxanne was born, she became the first member of Congress to become a mother.

Burke promoted social reforms during her years in Congress, just as she had done in the

California legislature. She was re-elected in 1976 but resigned in 1978 to run for the position of attorney general of California. Here, for the first time, she failed to achieve her aims. But she was compensated for the loss in 1979 when Governor Jerry Brown appointed her to fill a vacancy on the Los Angeles Board of Supervisors after one of the board members died.

Burke was the the first woman ever to serve on this powerful five-person board. However, it was a brief triumph, for she was defeated in the 1980 elections. But twelve years later she made a comeback, winning election to the board after a fierce contest with Diane Watson, who like Burke was a black liberal Democrat. This 1992 victory made Burke the first black person ever elected to the Los Angeles County Board of Supervisors.

When not serving in government, Burke has practiced as a lawyer. She has always worked within the system, even though she regards the system as inadequate. Nevertheless, through her contribution both as a lawyer and as a legislator she has achieved a number of reforms that will open the way for other black women to play a role in guiding the nation's affairs.

Octavia E. Butler

Science fiction writer
Born June 22, 1947, Pasadena, California

"I don't write utopian science fiction because I don't believe that imperfect humans can form a perfect society."

Octavia E. Butler is the first African American woman to gain fame as a science fiction writer. Her nine novels and many short stories have brought her a large following of readers, as well as winning her some of the top science fiction awards. She won the Hugo Award in 1984 for her short story "Speech Sounds" and the Hugo, Nebula, and Locus awards in 1985 for her novelette *Bloodchild*.

Bloodchild is typical of Butler's approach to science fiction in that it focuses on human relationships rather than on futuristic technology. *Bloodchild* is about men who can become pregnant and are used by an alien race to bear their children. By reversing the sexual roles of men and women, Butler is showing how women have been misused throughout the centuries. All Butler's books have some such statement to make as she explores such issues as racism, sexism, power, and the abuse of power. Yet her books are never "preachy." Butler writes about thoroughly believable characters, many of whom are black women— and she always tells a rattling good story.

Began writing science fiction in junior high

Octavia Estelle Butler was the only child of Laurice and Octavia (Guy) Butler. Her father died when she was still a baby, and she was brought up by her mother and grandmother in one of the poorer parts of Pasadena. Like many people in the neighborhood, Butler's mother took in boarders to help make ends meet. She also worked as a maid.

Lacking brothers and sisters, Butler was a shy child who did not mix easily with others.

She was exceptionally tall—she grew to be six feet—which made her feel different, as did her upbringing as a strict Baptist. She was happier reading by herself than joining in activities with other children.

Like many lonely children, Butler expressed her feelings in writing: "I began writing," she said, "when I was about ten years old.... I didn't realize then that writing was supposed to be work. It was too much fun." By the age of thirteen she was composing science fiction stories, which she worked on with the help of one of her high school teachers. At elementary school, Butler had been considered slow and stupid, largely because of her shyness and her awkwardness about reading or speaking in public. But at McKinley Junior High there were sympathetic teachers who understood her problems and helped her cope with them. Butler's grades improved, and she decided she was not stupid after all.

After graduating from John Muir High School in 1965, Butler studied at Pasadena City College, where she earned an A.A. degree in 1968. She then enrolled at California State University, Los Angeles, but left after a year because the courses did not include sufficient instruction in creative writing. Working at temporary jobs to support herself, she signed up for a course with the Writers Guild of America, West, which she found very helpful, and she followed up in 1970 with a six-week course at the Clarion Science Fiction Writers Workshop. In 1971 one of her short stories was published in the Clarion anthology.

Butler then embarked on her life as a writer, but five years passed before she had a book accepted by a publisher. Despite this discouragement, she kept on writing and sending in manuscripts to publishers. She supported herself by taking a series of odd jobs, though friends and relatives kept telling her to settle down and get a "real" job. But the only real job Butler wanted was the job of science fiction author. Even when her first novel was published she could not immediately afford to give up her other work. But before long the good sales of her books allowed her to be a full-time author, and she produced one blockbuster after another.

Explores prejudice and racism in her books

Five of Butler's first six novels are part of the "Patternist" saga—a series of stories about a group of specially bred people who are able to communicate with one another by mental telepathy. All the Patternists are related and are descendants of the evil Doro, a 4,000-year-old

Octavia E. Butler

Nubian who has survived through the ages by moving into one human body after another. When Doro moves into a new body, he kills the one he is leaving behind. Indeed, he kills whenever it suits his purpose.

The first novel in the series, *Patternmaster* (1976), is set in the future in the region that was once California. There the members of the Pattern live in communities called Houses and are served by slaves called "mutes" who are not capable of telepathy. The Houses are under constant attack by nomadic tribes called Clayarks. The main story in this book is the struggle for power between two brothers who are senior members of the Pattern.

The second novel, *Mind of My Mind* (1977), is set in Los Angeles in the near future and is told by light-skinned Mary Larkin, a daughter of Doro. In a story that examines the handling of power, Mary struggles to break free from Doro's control. Next comes *Survivor* (1978), which features Afro-Asian Alanna, who is taken to another planet to escape a virulent disease that is killing earthlings. This novel explores the issues of color and class with its description of the two races on the alien planet, where the most prestigious leaders are able to change their color to blue. Color prejudice is again a theme in the fourth novel, *Wild Seed* (1980), which is set in the era of American slavery. The fifth novel, *Clay's Ark* (1984), returns to the future with a story about a black astronaut named Eli.

One of Butler's most powerful novels is *Kindred* (1979), which is not part of the Patternist saga but incorporates many of the same themes. The heroine is Dana, a black woman in twentieth-century Los Angeles who is summoned back in time to a Maryland plantation to save the life of the white plantation owner's son. This obnoxious young man calls her back to the past on more than one occasion—a dangerous experience for Dana, since she has to pose as a slave. But she has to help him because he is an ancestor. If he does not survive to bear children, Dana herself will not exist several generations later.

Butler has also written a series of novels about a black woman, Lilith Iyapo, who is forced to breed with an alien from another planet after earth has been conquered by these extraterrestrials. The novels in this series are *Dawn: Xenogenesis* (1987), *Adulthood Rites: Xenogenesis* (1988), and *Imago:Xenogenesis* (1989).

Breeding patterns and genetics are featured in many of Butler's books as she explores the issues of prejudice and racism. "When I began reading science fiction," she says, "I was disappointed at how little this creativity and freedom was used to portray the many racial, ethnic, and class variations. Also, I could not help noticing how few significant women characters there were in science fiction." In the past fifteen years Butler has helped make up for this deficiency, thus giving her own special slant to the literature of science fiction.

Cab Calloway

Singer, bandleader
Born December 25, 1907, Rochester, New York

"My heroes are the notes, man. The music itself. You understand what I'm saying? I love the music. The music is my hero."

Although his family assumed he would become a lawyer, Cab Calloway had other plans. With a burning desire to become a musician, Calloway hopped the train in the early 1920s to become a singer in Chicago. Once dubbed the Dean of American Jive, Calloway became a fixture at the famous Cotton Club, before touring with his orchestra across the United States and Europe. Calloway has also appeared in numerous films and Broadway productions, and even wrote a best-selling book. Now at a time when most people retire, Calloway is trying to bring the joys of the jazzy, big-band sound to a new generation.

Sisters gets him singing job in Chicago

Calloway was born on Christmas Day, 1907, as Cabell Calloway III in Rochester, New York, to Cabell, a lawyer and real estate broker, and Eulalia Calloway. The family moved to Baltimore, Maryland, when he was six. Calloway enjoyed singing solos at the Bethlehem Methodist Episcopal Church, but his family assumed he would follow in his father's footsteps towards a law career. His older sister found work as a singer with a show in Chicago and Calloway appealed to her for advice. She sent him a train ticket, and set the teenager up as a singer with a quartet when he arrived.

By 1925 he had become a talented drummer and was performing with the Sunset Cafe orchestra in Chicago. Two years later he organized his own orchestra and was singing lead vocals. He dubbed the group Cab Calloway and his Alabamians, and they became quite popular in the city. As word spread, they soon appeared at the Savoy Ballroom in New York City. When that engagement flopped, Calloway disbanded the group, and was about to return to Chicago when he received a part in a Broadway comedy, *Connie's Hot Chocolates*. The show was an all-black revue, and Calloway was a hit with the audience for his rendition of "Ain't Misbehavin'."

Irving Mills, a Broadway manager, convinced Calloway to organize another band, so he formed the Cab Calloway Orchestra, which found work in Harlem speakeasies and nightclubs. In 1929 he filled in for Duke Ellington at the Cotton Club, and afterwards the two alternated engagements. During his time at the Cotton Club, Calloway developed his crisp, jazzy song-and-dance style that would be his hallmark for years to come. He was one of the first performers to make use of scat singing—random use of nonsense syllables—when he forgot a song's lyrics. Audiences loved the sound, so he began to write songs with scat choruses. His legendary "Minnie the Moocher" song, which debuted at the Cotton Club, is one such composition. Its refrain—hi de hi de hi de ho—invites the audience to sing along in the old call-and-response style. Recordings of this song have sold in the millions worldwide, and at least one version is still available for sale.

During the 1930s and 1940s, Calloway's popularity was at its peak. He appeared in several films including: *Hi De Ho, Cab's Jitterbug Party* in 1932; *The Big Broadcast*, 1932; *International House*, 1933; *Roadshow*,

Cab Calloway

1941; *Stormy Weather,* 1943; and *Sensations of 1944,* 1944. Calloway also helped to popularize the jitterbug with songs like "Jumpin' Jive," "Reefer Man," "It Ain't Necessarily So," and "If This Isn't Love." He also wrote a book, *Hepster's Dictionary,* which sold two million copies and ran into six editions. He also began touring extensively throughout the United States and Europe.

Calloway paid top salaries

Although many do not associate Calloway with the big band era, he did front a fine ensemble during that time. His ability to pay top salaries attracted a brilliant array of talent including sax players Chu Berry, Ben Webster and Hilton Jefferson; trumpeters Dizzy Gillespie and Jonah Jones; bassist Milt Hinton; and drummer Cozy Cole. George T. Simon noted in his book, *The Big Bands,* "the esprit de corps of the Calloway band was tremendous, and the great pride that the musicians possessed as individuals and as a group paid off handsomely in the music they created."

During World War II Calloway entertained troops in the United States and Canada. When the war ended, he returned to club work and the Broadway stage—most notably as Sportin' Life in the George Gershwin operetta *Porgy and Bess.* In the late 1960s Calloway took another important Broadway role by becoming Horace Vandergelder in the all-black version of *Hello, Dolly!* Despite his age (he was 60), Calloway never missed a step in the strenuous show.

Calloway continued performing throughout the 1970s and was introduced to a new audience in the 1980 film *The Blues Brothers.* The movie, which starred John Belushi and Dan Aykroyd, gave him the opportunity to perform "Minnie the Moocher." Clad in a snazzy white zoot suit with tails, Calloway made the number the highlight of the film. Critics who panned *The Blues Brothers* usually singled Calloway out for praise.

Despite being well into his eighties, Calloway is still performing, occasionally with his daughter Chris. The *Philadelphia Inquirer* stated that his "moves have slowed a bit since the '30s, a time when Calloway could have danced Michael Jackson or Mick Jagger into the ground. The hair is white and thinner now, the midsection thicker, and that classically handsome face lined and puffy after eight decades of full-throttle living. But every bit of his voice is still there—and every bit of the style and grace that made the legend."

Calloway, who lives in White Plains, New York, denies that he ever had any idols in the music business. He does not look up to

Ellington, Webster, or Gillespie simply because he ranks up there with them. Indeed, he was with them when the new music was being created. "I'll tell you who my heroes are," he once said in an interview. "My heroes are the notes, man. The music itself. You understand what I'm saying? I love the music. The music is my hero."

Roy Campanella

Baseball player
Born November 19, 1921, Homestead,
   Pennsylvania
Died June 26, 1993, Woodland Hills,
   California

"Down there I put on my baseball shirt and cap, and I'm in this wheelchair, and I'm going all over the place. I get out early and work with the catchers, even the veterans. I don't care how old you are, you'll see something in this game you've never seen before."

S hortly before the 1946 season, Branch Rickey, the owner of the Brooklyn Dodgers, decided to take a chance on five baseball players from the Negro leagues. One of them was Roy Campanella. The short, stocky catcher played for nine years in the National Negro League, the winter leagues, and in Mexico. In ten major league seasons, Campanella was one of the game's most popular players, earning the most valuable player award three times and leading the Brooklyn Dodgers to their only World Series championship.

A teenage catcher in the Negro leagues

Campanella was born in Homestead, Pennsylvania, to an African American mother and an Italian father. He started his baseball career when he was fifteen with the Bacharach Giants, a hometown semipro team. His catcher's skills soon came to the attention of officials with the Baltimore Elite Giants of the Negro National League. They were so impressed that they offered him a spot on the lineup, despite his age. Since Campanella was still in school, he played only on weekends and provided relief for veteran Biz Mackey. In 1938, he quit school and joined the team full time. The next year he became the first-string catcher and led the team to playoff victories over the Newark Eagles and the Homestead Grays. Campanella collected five hits, including one home room, and drove in seven runs in only four games.

With Josh Gibson on the downswing of his career, Campanella became the league's dominant catcher. In the 1941 East-West all-star game, he was voted the most valuable player (MVP). After a dispute with Baltimore owner Tom Wilson, Campanella jumped to the Mexican League for part of 1942 and all of 1943. He came back to the Giants the next year and led the league in doubles in 1944 and in runs batted in (RBIs) in 1945.

In October 1945, Campanella caught for a black all-star team in a five-game exhibition series against a squad of white major leaguers. The latter team was managed by Charlie Dressen, who had orders to arrange an appointment for Campanella with the Brooklyn Dodgers. The Dodgers later signed Campanella to their Nashua, New Hampshire,

Roy Campanella

Class B farm team (Eastern League), which was run by Buzzie Bavasi and managed by Walter Alston. Campanella was one of five black players signed by the Dodgers before the 1946 season.

Campanella roomed with pitcher Don Newcombe and hit a respectable .290 in 1946. He lead the league in putouts, assists, and errors, and won the MVP award. In 1947, he advanced to Montreal, the Dodgers' International League team, and was again named MVP, despite a late-season slump that saw his average plummet to .273.

In 1948 Campanella made the Dodger's roster, but owner Branch Rickey delayed promoting him because he wanted to integrate the minor league American Association first. When Campanella was finally called to the major leagues, Rickey told manager Leo Durocher to play him in the outfield. Playing an unfamiliar position, Campanella disappointed the team and was sent down in May to

their AA team in St. Paul. He made the most of his demotion with forty hits (half for extra bases), thirty-nine RBIs, and a .325 batting average in thirty-five games. He was recalled to the big league near the end of the season.

A member of "The Boys of Summer"

This time Campanella was there to stay. For the next nine years he caught for an outstanding Brooklyn team, whose members were often referred to as "the Boys of Summer." They won the National League pennant in 1949, 1952, 1953, 1955, and 1956. They narrowly missed two others and achieved Brooklyn's only World Series championship in 1955. On a team of stars, Campanella still stood out. He won the MVP award three times in five years. He played on seven consecutive National League all-star teams from 1949 to 1955. His best season was in 1953 when he batted .312 and scored 103 runs. He also set major league records for catchers with 41 home runs and 142 RBIs. Campanella was a strong performer in the field and handled a predominately white pitching staff with distinction.

Like many catchers, Campanella suffered from injuries. During spring training in 1954, he chipped a bone in his heel and damaged a nerve. He was limited to only 111 games, and his batting suffered. After undergoing surgery, Campanella performed better the next year, but the problem returned in 1956.

Campanella's playing days came to an end in January 1958. While returning home from a liquor store he owned, Campanella lost control of his car on an icy street. The car slammed into a telephone pole, flipped over, and pinned him behind the steering wheel. The crash fractured his fifth cervical vertebra and damaged his spinal cord. He survived, undergoing years of therapy, but remained a quadriplegic.

On May 7, 1959, the largest crowd in baseball history, 93,103 fans, attended Roy Campanella Night at the Los Angeles Coliseum. In the middle of the fifth inning of the game, Campanella was wheeled out to second base, and the coliseum's lights were extinguished. The crowd was asked to light matches for him, and Campanella looked up as thousands of lights flickered around him. "I'll never forget this as long as I live," he told *Sports Illustrated*.

A few years after the accident, Campanella separated from his wife, Ruthe, and moved into an apartment building near his liquor store. He later met Roxie Doles, and she became his nurse. On May 5, 1964, the two married and moved into a sixteen-room house in Hartsdale in Westchester County. In 1969, he was voted to the Baseball Hall of Fame, and six years later he was inducted into the Black Athletes Hall of Fame. Campanella suffered from a variety of illnesses stemming from his paralysis, and the New York winters became uncomfortable. In the spring of 1978, he moved to Los Angeles and became an executive with the Dodgers' community relations program.

Campanella visited the clubhouse before almost every game, offering counsel and encouragement. "When he speaks everyone listens," catcher Mike Scioscia told *Sports Illustrated*. "He doesn't miss a thing. He'll come in the day after a game and ask me, 'Now why did you call for that pitch when the count was two and two?' What an amazing individual! He's gone through a life that none of us, hopefully, will have to endure, but he's come out of it so strong he makes all the rest of us look like wimps. I just thank God I've had the chance to know him." Campanella died at his home in California in 1993.

Naomi Campbell

Model, singer, actress
Born May 22, 1970, London, England

"They used to call up asking for a beautiful white model or a beautiful black model. Now they just ask for a beautiful model. It just doesn't matter what color you are anymore."

F ashion model Naomi Campbell has been hailed as one of the world's most beautiful women. Tall, lithe, and elegant, she has an irrestistible charm that adds a unique quality to her dazzling good looks. "She doesn't realize how wonderful she is," enthused fashion coordinator Audrey Smaltz. "She has terrific body language—most models don't—and can translate this into whatever she's wearing."

Campbell has worked with some of the biggest names in the fashion industry and has become a familiar figure on the runways of North America and Europe. She has been featured in all the major fashion magazines, including *Vogue*, *Cosmopolitan*, and *Elle*, and was the first ethnic woman ever to appear on the cover of the French edition of *Vogue*.

As one of the world's top models, Campbell can command more than $10,000 for a single day's work. She brings in earnings of more than $1 million a year. Yet people who know Campbell find her wonderfully unspoiled and natural. "She's one of the most delightful girls I've ever worked with," said fashion photographer Francesco Scavullo. "One of my favorite models."

Photographed in school uniform for first modeling job

Although Naomi Campbell was born in England and spent her childhood there, she comes from a family of Jamaicans. It is from a Chinese grandmother in Jamaica that she inherited the slightly Oriental look that gives her beauty its special quality.

Campbell's family moved to England before she was born, and she grew up in London, where her mother was a dancer in contemporary ballet. Thinking she might follow her mother with a career on the stage, Campbell attended the Academy of Performing Arts. But when she was fifteen an incident happened that changed her life.

It was late afternoon, and with her school day over Campbell was wandering through a shopping arcade in the Covent Garden district of London. Her stunning looks attracted the attention of a top London agent, who was also window shopping in the arcade. "I was just hanging out," Campbell told George Wayne of *Interview* magazine, "and this woman comes up to me and says, 'I'm a modelling agent. I took her card home and gave it to my mother. And then I saw an interview of her in the *Tatler,* so I knew she was legitimate. After

that I started pleading with my mother to let me go see her."

Campbell's mother eventually agreed, and Campbell went to meet the agent—wearing her school uniform. "After she took a couple of pictures of me in my school uniform, I got my first job," Campbell remembers. Her first job was with a photographer who was working on an assignment in New Orleans for the British edition of *Elle*. So began the career of the young woman soon to be hailed as "the hottest black model of the era."

"It doesn't matter what color you are anymore"

Campbell rapidly became a familiar face in a wide range of fashion magazines. From her base in the United States she flew to locations throughout the world. The location shooting brought Campbell some exciting experiences, such as the time she was photographed stand-

Naomi Campbell

ing precariously at the mouth of a volcano in Spain.

The fashion photographers have been profuse in their praise of Campbell. "No one else has such an amazing body. She makes clothes come alive," says photographer Francesco Scavullo. Campbell returns the compliment: "I do very much like working with Scavullo. He makes me feel like a woman." As well as being on such good terms with the world's top fashion photographers, Campbell has friends in show business, many of whom, including Madonna, attended her twenty-first birthday party in New York in 1988. Campbell's boyfriends have included champion boxer Mike Tyson, actor Robert De Niro, and other high-profile celebrities. In May 1993 she became engaged to the Irish rock musician Adam Clayton of the band U2. The couple met on a flight to the Grammy Award ceremonies in Los Angeles earlier in the year.

Shortly before meeting Clayton, Campbell made her own mark on the music world by releasing her first record album. However, this was not her first performance as a singer. In 1992 Campbell had recorded a duet with rapper Vanilla Ice for his *Cool as Ice* movie soundtrack.

The versatile Campbell has also revealed considerable talent as an actress. Her theatrical experience goes back to the days before she took up modeling, when she was a student at the Academy of Performing Arts in London. During that period she appeared on the stage in *The King and I,* and she has since performed in the movies *Quest for Fire* (1982) and Pink Floyd's *The Wall* (1992). Campbell has television experience too: in 1988 she was cast as Julia, the girlfriend of Theo's friend Howard in "The Cosby Show."

While Campbell foresees a career that will cover many areas, for the time being her prime focus is modeling. With her stunning looks and come-hither pout, she remains one of the most sought-after models in the fashion world. It pleases Campbell that she is no longer categorized as a "black model." She is sought after simply as a model, one of the very best. "They used to call up asking for a beautiful white model or a beautiful black model," she says. "Now they just ask for a beautiful model. It just doesn't matter what color you are anymore. If I've had something to do with that change, then I'm really proud."

Stokely Carmichael

Writer, political activist
Born June 29, 1941, Port-of-Spain, Trinidad and Tobago

"The alliances being formed by the party are alliances which I cannot politically agree with, because the history of Africans living in the United States has shown that any premature alliance with white radicals has led to complete subversion of the blacks by the whites, through their direct or indirect control of the black organization."

Gifted, handsome, and articulate, Stokely Carmichael rose to fame as the chairman of the Student Nonviolent Coordinating Committee. In contrast to civil rights leader Martin Luther King, Jr. and his nonviolent approach, Carmichael became known for his use of the dynamic phrase "black power," which advocates violence to liberate blacks from their white oppressors. He later became prime minister of the militant Black Panthers and then an organizer for the All Afrikan People's Revolutionary Party.

Although Carmichael was a controversial factor in the civil rights movement, he served as chief spokesman for the black power concept and became a symbol of violence at the time of uprisings in several American cities.

Rejected scholarships to white universities

Carmichael was born on June 29, 1941, at Port-of-Spain in Trinidad. His father, Adolphus, was a carpenter, and his mother, Mabel, was a housewife. Carmichael came to the United States when he was eleven. The transition from Trinidad to an American ghetto was difficult for him. He came to believe that "black" and "impotent" represented the same things. When he was later admitted to the Bronx High School of Science, where he befriended white liberals, he came to feel that the whites had adopted him as a "mascot."

In 1960, Carmichael joined the Congress of Racial Equality (CORE), which aimed to integrate public accommodations in the South. Founded in 1942 by James Farmer as the result of a campaign protesting discrimination at a Chicago restaurant, CORE was an interracial passive-resistance organization committed to confronting racism and discrimination with direct action.

The same year Carmichael entered Howard University, rejecting scholarship offers from white universities. He graduated in 1964 and joined the Student Nonviolent Coordinating Committee (SNCC). This group was formed in 1960 to co-ordinate the activities of students engaged in direct action protest, such as sit-ins and jail-ins in the South. SNCC achieved great results in desegregating public facilities and earned respect from the country for its determination to act peacefully, no matter how violent or demeaning the provocation.

Caused controversy with cry for black power

Carmichael was elected SNCC leader during the 1964 Democratic Convention. By this time he felt the American system could not be turned around without being threatened by violence and disruption. Believing that peaceful integration could not occur, he thought black liberation could only be achieved through violent means.

Carmichael's attitude drove a wedge between those who believed in peaceful solutions and those who wanted guerilla warfare. In June 1966 Carmichael used the phrase "black power" in Greenville, Mississippi, to describe a new black nationalism that advocated violence. Carmichael and other civil rights leaders had come to the state after James Meredith, the first black admitted to the University of Mississippi, had been shot during a protest march across the state.

Carmichael explained: "Black power seems to me a number of things. Number one, that black people in this country are oppressed for one reason—and that's because of their color, and that's what this country has to face....

Their rally cry must be the issue around which they are oppressed, as it was for unions. The workers came together, they were oppressed because they were workers. And we must come together around the issue that oppressed us—which is our blackness. Unions—they needed power to stop their oppression. We need power to stop ours. So it's black power. And black power just means black people coming together and getting people to represent their needs and to stop that oppression."

In the days following Carmichael's first use of the term black power, many civil rights leaders analyzed and condemned the concept. Martin Luther King, Jr., for example, said he thought black supremacy was as bad as white supremacy. "I don't think that anything can be more tragic than the attitude that the Black Man can solve his problems by himself."

Joined Black Panthers

In 1967 Carmichael joined the Black Panther Party, a group created in 1966 by Huey P. Newton and Bobby Seale that departed from the platform and tactics of established civil rights organizations. The Black Panthers condemned institutional structure, which they viewed as corrupt. They believed established channels of authority and operation either oppressed or overlooked significant portions of the black community.

Carmichael initially believed the Black Panthers were in the forefront of the black liberation movement, but soon after joining he clashed with Eldridge Cleaver, the Black Panthers' minister of information. He disagreed with Cleaver's belief that coalitions could be formed with white radicals.

Stokely Carmichael

Carmichael also coauthored his first book in 1967. Entitled *Black Power: The Politics of Liberation in America,* the book detailed his belief that violence was necessary to free the black man from his white oppressors.

Moved to Guinea

When he left the Black Panthers, Carmichael soon found himself without a platform from which to speak. In 1969 he and his wife, Mariam Makaba, a South African singer he had married the year before, moved to Guinea, where he still resides. In 1971 he released the book *Stokely Speaks: Black Power Back to Pan-Africanism,* which details his new Pan-African ideology, focusing on an increased awareness and acceptance by American blacks of the culture, heritage, and ideals of Africans. Carmichael stressed that this is not a new course but the ultimate extension of black power. He returned briefly to the United States in 1972 to lecture on this ideology, but his activities as a civil rights leader have decreased since that time.

Benjamin Carson

Neurosurgeon
Born September 18, 1951, Detroit, Michigan

"Think big! Set your sights as high as Mount Everest. Nobody was born to be a failure. If you feel you're going to succeed—and you work your tail off—you will succeed."

Reader's Digest has called him a miracle worker of modern medicine. As the director of pediatric neurosurgery at Johns Hopkins Hospital in Baltimore, Maryland, Benjamin Carson has received recognition throughout the medical community for his surgical skills. He has undertaken many high-risk operations, primarily on children, involving complex and delicate neurosurgical procedures. In 1987, he gained international acclaim for leading a team of seventy medical personnel that separated a pair of Siamese twins who were joined at the backs of their heads. Carson continues his miracle work at Johns Hopkins University.

A childhood of fighting and poor grades

Carson was born on September 18, 1951, in Detroit, Michigan, to Robert and Sonya Carson. His parents divorced when he was eight years old, and he lived with his mother. Although Carson dreamed of becoming a doctor, he was a poor student who had a tendency to get into a lot of fights. Whites taunted and threatened him because he was black. "He had no hope," his mother told *People*. "He just felt there was no way out, and so why should he try? He was just really at the point of no return."

Finally at age ten, his mother cut back his television viewing to three shows a week and forced him to read two books weekly and submit written book reports to her. Carson became an avid reader, and his grades steadily improved until he was near the top of his class. "Once I discovered that between the pages of those books ... we could go anywhere and we could meet anybody and we could do anything, that's when it really started to hit me," he told *People*.

Although he began to improve academically, Carson still ran into racial prejudice. Once he was confronted by a group of boys armed with sticks who threatened to kill him for going to school. When he joined a neighborhood football league, a group of white adults warned him to stay away, and he did. His most humiliating experienced took place in eighth grade when a teacher berated his white classmates for letting Carson, a black student, win the outstanding student award. These episodes only served to heat up his temper. He once opened a three-inch gash in the forehead of a schoolmate who teased him. He also broke the nose of another boy with a rock.

After graduating third in his high school class, he received offers from several Ivy League universities. Carson accepted a scholarship to Yale University and then went on to study medicine at the University of Michigan.

His original intention was to become a psychotherapist, but after his first year of medical school, he discovered neurosurgery. "I loved dissecting things," Carson said in an *Ebony* interview. "And I always felt that I was very good with my hands. Neurosurgery was a natural for me."

Australia provides valuable experience

Carson did his internship in general surgery and residency in neurosurgery at Johns Hopkins Hospital, one of the top medical centers in the country. After graduating he became the hospital's first-ever black neurosurgery resident. In 1983 he moved with his wife, Lacena (known as Candy), to Perth, Australia, to become the senior neurosurgery resident at Queen Elizabeth Medical Centre, one of that country's leading centers for brain surgery.

Due to a lack of qualified neurosurgeons in Australia and Carson's advanced medical skills, he quickly obtained valuable work experience. "I was operating so much," he told *Ebony,* "I was able to concentrate several years of experience into one year."

In 1984 Carson returned to Johns Hopkins and soon became one of the hospital's leading surgeons. He was promoted to director of pediatric neurosurgery within the year, becoming at the age of thirty-four the youngest director of a surgical division in the United States.

Carson's skills became known throughout the medical community. He was especially adept at safely performing operations that were usually considered high-risk proce-

Benjamin Carson

dures. He gained renown for dealing with hemispherectomies (a complex operation in which a portion of the brain of a critically ill seizure victim or other neurologically diseased patient is removed to restore normal functioning) and for separating Siamese twins.

One of his most difficult cases took place in 1985 when he operated on Christopher Pylant, a four-year-old from Atlanta, Georgia, with a malignant tumor of the brain stem. Other physicians had pronounced the cancer inoperable, but Carson told the boy's father he could save him. When he operated, Carson could not even see the brain stem; it apparently had been destroyed by cancer. Carson removed what he safely could and then delivered the sad news to the parents. But over the next few weeks, Pylant improved, and a brain scan indicated a brain stem still existed. Three weeks later Carson operated again, removed the tumor, and Pylant eventually made a complete recovery.

Another controversial case involved four-year-old Maranda Francisco of Denver, Colorado, who suffered up to 120 seizures a day. Her right side was paralyzed, and she had a rare brain sickness that, if unchecked, would have left her with serious neurological damage. Carson removed the diseased left hemisphere of Francisco's brain during a ten-hour operation. Six months later she had regained nearly complete use of her right arm and leg and was free of seizures. The right side of her brain had taken over functions of the left.

The ultimate test

Carson's most famous medical operation occurred in 1987, when he led a surgical team of doctors, nurses, and technicians to separate a pair of West German twins, who were congenitally joined at the back of their heads. The twins shared a blood vessel in the back of their heads, and Carson devised a plan to separate the twins by completely shutting down their blood flow, severing their common blood vessel, and then restoring their individual vessel systems. The entire operation lasted twenty-two hours, but Carson and another surgeon only had one hour to conduct the actual surgery and restoration. The operation went smoothly until Carson noticed the vessels that carried blood from the brain of each child were more entangled than had been expected. Twenty minutes after stopping the twins' circulation, Carson made the final cut. He then had forty minutes to reconstruct the severed blood vessels and close. Just a few minutes before the hour limit, the twins were separated, and the operating tables were wheeled apart. Carson told *Ebony*, "Not only was it

exciting to be part of a history-making event, but the significant fact is that we put together an incredibly complex scene with a team of incredibly competent people who submerged their egos and pulled off what was perhaps the most complex surgical feat in the history of mankind."

Carson is a contributor to numerous journals including the *Journal of the American Medical Association*. In 1987 he wrote the book, *Pediatric Neuroncology*, and followed it with *Achondroplasia*, the next year. He co-authored *Gifted Hands: The Ben Carson Story* in 1990 with Cecil Murphey, and in 1992 published *Think Big*.

Carson has received numerous awards and honors for his efforts. He received a cum laude award from the American Radiological Society in 1982; was named a Paul Harris fellow from Rotary International in 1988; received an American Black Achievement Award from *Ebony* in 1988; and was given a Candle Award from Morehouse University in 1989. He has received honorary doctorates of science from Gettysburg College, North Carolina Agricultural and Technical State University, Andrews University, Sojourner Douglas College, and Shippensburg University.

Despite the accolades thrown his way, Carson has remained modest about his accomplishments. A devout Seventh Day Adventist, Carson places his achievements in a religious context. "God created the body. He knows more about it than anybody else and can heal virtually every problem. It's only a matter of whether we're willing to let Him work through us," he told *Ebony*. He also credits his mother for helping him with his success. In an article he wrote for *Ebony,* he credited her philosophy of "no excuses for anything" and "if anybody can do something, you can do it better" with motivating him.

Carson and his wife, Candy, live in Columbia, Maryland, with their three children, Murray Nedlands, Benjamin Solomon, Jr., and Rhoeyce Harrington. He raises his children on the two books a week rule and speaks to other kids about staying away from drugs and violence. "It doesn't matter if you come from the inner city. People who fail in life are people who find lots of excuses," he told *People.* "It's never too late for a person to recognize that they have potential themselves."

George Washington Carver

Agricultural scientist
Born 1864 near Diamond, Missouri
Died January 5, 1943, Tuskegee, Alabama

"It has always been the one great ideal of my life to be of the greatest good to the greatest number of my people."

Peanut butter, peanut oil, and many other products are common today largely because of the genius of George Washington Carver. Through his painstaking research and innovative thinking, he found ways of making more than 300 products from peanuts. Before Carver began his work, peanuts were not considered an important crop. By the time of his death, they had become a $200 million industry and were the chief product of Alabama.

George Washington Carver

Carver also found hundreds of uses for sweet potatoes and soybeans, and he encouraged Southern farmers to grow these crops instead of relying solely on cotton. A skilled teacher, he devoted his life to improving farming throughout the South and raising the standard of living of the farming families, especially poor black families.

Struggled to get his education

George Washington Carver knew first-hand what it was like to be poor. He was the son of a slave called Mary, who was bought by struggling homesteaders in Missouri a few years before slavery was abolished. George's father, who died around the time of his birth, is thought to have been a slave on a neighboring homestead. Born during the Civil War, George Carver was only a few months old when the homestead was attacked by raiders, who kidnapped him and his mother. A man hired to trace them managed to find the young boy and rescue him, but Mary was never heard from again.

Left an orphan before he was a year old, Carver was raised by Moses and Susan Carver, the white homesteaders who had been the owners of his mother. They also raised his brother Jim, who was a few years older than George and had avoided capture by the raiders. The Carvers were stern but kindly people who did their best for the boys, despite their limited means. As Carver grew older, he helped his foster mother with household chores such as cleaning and sewing, for he was too frail to do heavy farmwork like his brother.

The local school did not take black children—and Carver desperately wanted to read and write—so he left his foster parents when he was ten to attend the black school at Neosho. There the small boy stayed with a black midwife, for whom he did odd jobs to pay for his schooling and his room and board. This was to be the pattern of Carver's life for the next ten years as he wandered back and forth across the midwestern states, going to school whenever possible and earning what he could by cooking, sewing, gardening, scrubbing clothes, picking fruit, or doing whatever was needed. Often he went hungry and sometimes he had no place to sleep, but that didn't worry him so long as he could find the money to buy the textbooks he needed.

George W. Carver (as he was now calling himself) was over twenty years old when he graduated from high school in 1885. That same year, he was accepted as a student at Highland College in northeastern Kansas, but when he arrived there, he was told, "I'm sorry, Highland College does not take Negroes." George slept that night in a barn. Disillusioned, poor, and hopeless, he found work in a nearby fruit farm, mending fences and picking fruit.

Earned bachelor's and master's degrees

Since it looked as if he would never get to college, Carver decided to try his hand at homesteading, and as soon as he had saved enough money he claimed a homestead on the prairie in western Kansas. He endured two years of fierce winter blizzards and burning summer sun, yet this proved to be a healing time, for he gradually began to get over his bitterness, take up reading again, and do some sketching.

In 1888 he left the homestead and worked his way east to Iowa, where a Baptist minister and his wife, encouraged him to apply to Simpson College at Indianola. They assured him he would not be turned down because of his color, because the school already had one black student there. Carver enrolled at Simpson in 1890, having saved the twelve dollar tuition fee, and he planned to study painting, but the painting teacher—who recognized his talent—foresaw the difficulty he would have pursuing a career as a painter. "You should study something more practical," she said. Her father was a professor at Iowa Agricultural College at Ames, and through him Carver was admitted to Ames in 1891.

As the first black student at the agricultural college, Carver had a difficult time to begin with. He was not given a room of his own—until the dean of agriculture moved out of an office to make space for the new student. Nor was he allowed to eat in the dining room with the other students, though this was soon rectified. It was typical of Carver to put up with the slights without making a fuss. His quiet dignity impressed people, and gradually he became popular with students and staff alike. Far older than most of the students, he was about thirty years old when he earned his B.S. in 1894.

An exceptionally intelligent student, he worked as an assistant botanist at the college's experimental station while he studied for his master's degree in agriculture and bacterial botany. Carver's research into fungi brought him considerable fame in agricultural circles, and when he received his M.S. in 1896, he accepted the offer of black educator Booker T. Washington to become director of agriculture at Tuskegee Institute in Alabama. The institute had been established by Washington in the 1880s as an industrial and agricultural school for blacks, and Carver felt that this was where he was most needed.

Taught and researched at Tuskegee

Today Tuskegee Institute has more than 150 well-equipped buildings, but when Carver arrived, it was little more than a collection of shacks. He had no proper laboratory, and he had to make his own equipment out of bits of wire, old bottles, or whatever he could lay his hands on. Carver enjoyed these challenges to his ingenuity. Indeed, the lack of money led to many of his inventions, for it made him find ways of improving the local agriculture in practical, uncostly ways—for instance, by using green manure instead of expensive fertilizer.

Carver was shocked when he first saw the local farms—they were desperately poor and run down—so in addition to his teaching and research at Tuskegee, he wrote instructional pamphlets on farming, and he set up a movable school which traveled around the South to instruct the farmers. When the movable school was started in 1906, it was no more than a mule-drawn cart, but before long Carver had a large motor truck that traveled from place to place with tools and exhibits. One of his aims was to persuade the farmers to give up growing cotton (which was depleting the soil and bringing in very little money) and to diversify by growing vegetables, peanuts, and soybeans.

Over the years Carver concentrated increasingly on research, especially on the peanut. Having promoted it as an excellent plant to grow, he realized that he must find uses for it so that the farmers could sell their crop easily. The many products Carver developed from peanuts included soap, face powder, mayonnaise, shampoo, metal polish, adhesives, and many other things. He also thought up more than 100 recipes using peanuts. Carver's peanut research became widely known when he appeared before a congressional committee to promote the plant in 1921. From then on he was frequently invited to lecture to scientific groups, and as his fame spread, he became known internationally, too, and people such as Mahatma Gandhi of India consulted him about their diet.

Carver never married. All his energies were devoted to his research and to helping others help themselves. Of his many inventions, he patented only three, saying that "God gave them to me, so how could I sell them to someone else?" In 1938 he donated $30,000 (most of his life savings) to establish the George Washington Carver Foundation for agricultural research at Tuskegee. When he died, the following words were inscribed on his tombstone: "He could have added fortune to fame, but caring for neither, he found happiness and honor in being helpful to the world." In his memory, the George Washington Carver National Monument was established in 1951 on the farm on which he had been born.

Wilt Chamberlain

Basketball player
Born August 21, 1936, Philadelphia,
   Pennsylvania

"For a long time, fans of mine had to put up with people saying Wilt couldn't win the big ones. Now maybe they'll have a chance to walk in peace, like I do."

B asketball legend Wilt Chamberlain trained for his sport on the playgrounds of Philadelphia. From the street corners of Philly to the famous Harlem Globetrotters and then the National Basketball Association, Wilt "the Stilt" dominated whatever league he played, and to a generation of young black men, he symbolizes where hard work, determination, and skill can lead.

The greatest offensive player in professional basketball during the 1960s and 1970s,

Wilt Chamberlain

Chamberlain led the NBA in scoring from 1959 to 1967 and held the single game record of 100 points, a feat he accomplished twice. By the time he retired from the game in 1974, Chamberlain held most of the major basketball records.

Opted to attend University of Kansas

Chamberlain was born in Philadelphia, Pennsylvania, on August 21, 1936. His family lived in a racially mixed middle-class neighborhood. When he entered Shoemaker Junior High School, Chamberlain was already 6 ft. 11 in.—only two inches short of his present height. Despite his height, he was strong, agile, and fast. At Overbrook High School he could run a 47-second quarter mile, put a 16-pound shotput 55 feet, and high jump 6 ft. 10 in.

But basketball was his true love. Chamberlain played on the school team, where he scored more than 2,200 points in three sea-

127

sons. He also went to the playgrounds, where he learned a lot from older players. He once said, "I still think you could pick up a team from the street corners of Philly that would give most colleges a hard time."

After graduating from school he was recruited by 77 major colleges and 125 smaller ones. Chamberlain decided to stay away from the larger cities and play in the Midwest. He seriously considered Dayton, Michigan, Indiana, and Kansas universities, before being pursuaded by Hall of Fame coach Phog Allen to attend the University of Kansas.

Played with the Globetrotters for one year

At Kansas Chamberlain continued to out-score the other players. In his first game he scored 52 points. He led his team to the finals of the National Collegiate Athletic Association tournament, but they lost to North Carolina in double overtime. During his college career he averaged over 30 points per game and was twice selected to All-American teams. After his junior year he decided to quit college and become a professional because, he said, "The game I was forced to play at (Kansas) wasn't basketball. It was hurting my chances of ever developing into a successful professional player."

Without completing his college degree, Chamberlain was not eligible to play in the National Basketball Association for one more year. He joined the Harlem Globetrotters, a group of basketball players who travel around the world entertaining audiences with their superior skills. Chamberlain claimed this year was one of the most enjoyable he ever spent.

Joined the NBA

In 1959 he joined the Philadelphia Warriors of the NBA. He made an immediate impact on the league despite the abundance of good centers such as Clyde Lovellette, Johnny Kerr, Johnny Green, and Bill Russell. Chamberlain became a terror on the court, and he seemed to be able to score at will. Other teams gave up trying to stop him and instead concentrated on trying to contain him. His scoring average in his rookie season was 37.9 points—more than 8 points per game higher than anyone else had ever scored in the history of the league. He was named the Rookie of the Year and the Most Valuable Player, the first person to receive both awards in the same season.

For the next six seasons, Chamberlain was the league's scoring leader. In 1961–62 he averaged 50.4 points and scored 100 points in a game. In 1962–63 he averaged 44.8 points. Chamberlain was simply the greatest scorer in NBA history.

Despite these achievements, Chamberlain still had not won a NBA championship. The Boston Celtics had established a dynasty with center Bill Russell leading the charge. Russell was noted for his defense, just as Chamberlain was known for his offense. Russell also had great teammates, notably Bob Cousy, Bill Sharman, John Havlicek, and Sam Jones. Chamberlain also had great teammates, but they couldn't seem to beat the Celtics when it mattered most.

Grueling haul to first championship

In 1967 the tables turned. The Warriors moved to San Francisco, but Chamberlain was traded back to the newly formed Philadelphia 76ers.

Supported by Chet Walker, Luke Johnson, Hal Greer, Wally Jones, and Bill Cunningham, Chamberlain's team finished the regular season with the best record in league history. They defeated the San Francisco Warriors to win the world title.

In 1968 Chamberlain was traded to the Los Angeles Lakers. The Lakers had many great players throughout their history, including Elgin Baylor and Jerry West, but they had not won a championship since the team moved to Los Angeles from Minneapolis in 1960. They lost the championship series seven times between 1962 and 1970. The 1969 loss was especially bitter for Chamberlain since it was to Russell and the Celtics again. In the final game Chamberlain was injured and played very little. Russell later criticized Chamberlain for not playing, creating a permanent rift between the two men. The Lakers lost the championship series again in 1970.

In 1972 the Lakers seemed finally ready to win. They finished the year with the best regular season record in history, breaking the mark set by Chamberlain and the 76ers in 1967. Besides Chamberlain, the team featured other stars, including Happy Hairston, Gail Goodrich, Jim McMillan, and Jerry West. In their first playoff game the Lakers defeated the Milwaukee Bucks, with Chamberlain outplaying their highly talented center Kareem Abdul-Jabbar.

In the championship series the Lakers played against the New York Knickerbockers, led by Willis Reed, Dave DeBusschere, Bill Bradley, and Walt Frazier. Chamberlain suffered a fractured wrist in the fourth game. The Lakers were leading the series three games to one, but the overall outcome was in doubt because of Chamberlain's injury. Chamberlain put football linemen's pads on both hands and played despite the pain. He scored 24 points, grabbed 29 rebounds, and blocked 10 shots, giving Los Angeles its first world championship.

Post-NBA career activities

After the 1973 season Chamberlain left the Lakers to become the player-coach of the San Diego Conquistadors of the now-defunct American Basketball Association (ABA). The contract was worth a reported $500,000. The ABA was an unusual challenge for Chamberlain, since the players were not nearly as good as those in the NBA and he had no coaching experience. The Conquistadors were a poor team and Chamberlain soon retired.

Nevertheless Chamberlain had left his mark on the sport. He left the NBA as its all-time leading scorer with 31,419 points and rebound leader with 23,924. He won four Most Valuable Player awards and held more than 40 league records. In 1979 he was voted to the Basketball Hall of Fame, and in 1991 the Philadelphia Sports Writers Association presented him with a Living Legend Award.

Recently Chamberlain has been involved in a variety of activities, including sponsorship of several amateur athletic groups, especially volleyball and track teams. Wealthy because of his wise investments, he has also kept in shape and is the owner of Wilt's Athletic Club and Big Wilt's Smalls Paradise Niteclub. Chamberlain has also appeared in several television commercials and movies, including *Conan the Destroyer* in 1982.

Ray Charles

Singer, pianist, songwriter
Born September 23, 1930, Albany, Georgia

"I've always sung music I've liked, and I've always sung it the way I feel tonight; tomorrow it may be something else altogether."

With his gritty, husky voice and his talent for making each song uniquely personal, Ray Charles has gathered millions of fans throughout the world. He is best known as the Genius of Soul, the man who almost single-handedly created soul music by blending gospel music and blues, yet his repertoire also includes country music and pop songs—in fact, anything he feels like singing.

In a career spanning more than four decades, Charles has been an enormous influence on other musicians, including such well-known artists as Aretha Franklin and Stevie Wonder. As well as performing as a singer, he has been a composer, arranger, recording executive, bandleader, saxophone player, and especially a pianist.

Rather than singing with a band, Charles usually prefers to accompany himself on the piano. With his hands pounding the keys and his head thrown back, he injects a depth of emotion into such songs as "Georgia on My Mind," conjuring up all the richness and suffering of the black experience in America. Charles has had his own share of suffering, having lost his sight as a child, though he did not allow this disaster to block his ambitions.

Nor did he let it limit his personal life; he has been twice married and has three children.

Overcoming adversity

"I was born with music inside me," Charles wrote in his autobiography, *Brother Ray* (1978). "From the moment I learned that there were piano keys to be mashed, I started mashing 'em." Charles's mother, Aretha, took in washing in her efforts to support her two boys, since she was not married to their father, Bailey Robinson. Charles's full name was Ray Charles Robinson, but he dropped the Robinson when he became a performer, because his name was so often confused with that of Sugar Ray Robinson, the boxer. Charles taught himself the piano at the age of three, trying to copy the boogie-woogie played at the local café. Two years later, this carefree stage of his life came to an end when his younger brother George fell into a large washtub and drowned despite Charles's efforts to save him.

Soon after the death of his brother, Charles began to go blind, and by the time he was seven he could not see at all. His mother sent him to the St. Augustine School for Deaf and Blind Children in Florida, and there he was given a thorough grounding in music. He was taught the piano, clarinet, alto saxophone, organ, and trumpet, and also learned how to compose musical scores in braille, the raised-character writing system for vision-impaired people.

When Charles was fifteen his mother died of food poisoning, and while he was home attending her funeral he decided not to go back to St. Augustine's. He wanted to be independent, to earn his living as a musician, so he went to stay with friends in Jacksonville, Florida, where he obtained occasional jobs as a pianist with local bands. The following year Charles moved to Orlando, where he was entirely on his own. When short of work he often went hungry, but he was determined not to live on charity or accept money simply because of his blindness. Adopting the motto "No dog, no cane, no guitar," he moved on to Tampa, where he obtained his first steady job, playing the piano with a white country-and-western band.

The Father of Soul Music

When Charles was seventeen, he boarded a bus for Seattle, Washington, where he landed a job as pianist of the McSon Trio. During the next couple of years he played in small clubs in Seattle and Los Angeles, modeling his style on that of pianist-singer Nat King Cole and rhythm-and-blues singer Charles Brown. In 1950 he scored a national hit among the black community with "Baby, Let Me Hold Your Hand," a rhythm-and-blues song he had written.

In the early 1950s Charles was almost constantly on tour, travelling with the blues band of Lowell Fulsom as well as performing on his own. Meantime, he recorded a number of singles and scored a number of hits, including his 1954 number, "It Should Have Been Me." During these years, Charles was developing his own special style, and in 1955 he made recording history with his smash hit "I Got a Woman." Combining the emotionalism of gospel music and the earthy sexuality of blues, this was the first recording in the style that came to be called "soul music."

Although some people found this new style shockingly sacrilegious, it quickly gathered a large following, and Charles scored hit after hit with his soul songs, which he wrote as well as performed. His 1950s hit singles included "Hallelujah, I Love Her So, "Lonely Avenue," "Night Time Is the Right Time," "This Little Girl of Mine," and "What'd I Say." The latter sold over a million copies and made a breakthrough by attracting a large white audience in addition to Charles's many black fans. This opened the door to concert performances at such prestigious locations as Carnegie Hall, where he first performed in 1959.

In 1960 Charles had his biggest hit to date with his recording of Hoagy Carmichael's

Ray Charles

"Georgia On My Mind" in his album *The Genius Hits the Road*. The album had outstanding sales and brought Charles the first two of his many Grammy awards. He won another Grammy in 1961 with his version of Percy Mayfield's rhythm-and-blues single, "Hit the Road, Jack."

By this time Charles was recording many songs written by other musicians. This was especially the case with his excursion into country-and-western music. In 1961 and 1962 he released the two-volume *Modern Sounds in Country & Western Music*, which contained his own versions of songs popularized by such singers as Hank Williams. A spinoff from this highly successful album was the hit single "I Can't Stop Loving You," which sold 2.5 million copies. Charles was the first black performer to achieve stardom as a country-and-western singer, though "I Can't Stop Loving You" was also a major hit with pop and rhythm-and-blues audiences. It was at the top of the charts among all three groups for fourteen weeks.

International fame

Each year from 1961 to 1965 *Downbeat* magazine's poll of international jazz critics named Ray Charles the top male American vocalist. He began touring abroad in the mid-1960s, traveling to New Zealand, Japan, and many other countries, where his performances consistently attracted huge crowds.

In 1963 Charles established his own recording, publishing, and management company, RPM International, and in 1965 he started producing his own records. His hits continued in the 1970s when he added to his many types of music by recording the album *A Message from the People* (1972), which included his powerful rendition of "America the Beautiful." Later released as a single, this became yet another hit. Meanwhile, Charles won yet another Grammy with his 1975 version of Stevie Wonder's "Living for the City."

During the 1980s and on into the 1990s, Charles continued his familiar pattern of touring for the major part of each year and of recording numbers that very often became hits. His albums from this period include *My Kind of Jazz* (1975) and *Brother Ray Is at It Again* (1980). Always ready to try something new, he used synthesizers and drum machines for the first time in his 1990 album *Would You Believe?*

By 1993 Charles had won eleven Grammy awards as well as numerous other honors, and though approaching his mid-sixties, he had no intention of retiring. "I would play music for nothing," he told an interviewer. "It just so happens that people want to pay me. I look at music the same as I look at my bloodstream, my respiratory system, my lungs. It's something I have to do."

Charles Waddell Chesnutt

Writer
Born June 20, 1858, Cleveland, Ohio
Died November 15, 1932, Cleveland, Ohio

"The object of my writing would not be so much the elevation of the colored people as the elevation of the whites.... The Negro's part is to prepare himself for recognition and equality, and it is the province of literature to open the way for him to get it—to accustom the public mind to the idea; to lead people on, imperceptibly, unconsciously, step by step, to the desired state of feeling."

Charles Waddell Chesnutt

As the first black author to write about race from an African American viewpoint, Charles Waddell Chesnutt holds an important place in American literature. His aim was to change the attitude of whites—to bring about a "moral revolution"—by influencing them through his writings so that they would gradually drop their prejudices and thus end discrimination and racism. "If I can do anything to further this work, and can see any likelihood of obtaining success in it, I would gladly devote my life to it," he said.

To some extent Chesnutt succeeded in his aims, for his realistic and sensitive portraits of African Americans drew considerable attention and were an eyeopener to many white readers. In his day, most black characters in books were portrayed as stereotypes, and they were written about in a very condescending way.

Chesnutt was the first African American to write about the difficulties that people of mixed blood had to overcome. This was of particular interest to him, since he had a fair complexion and was often taken to be white. Yet Chesnutt identified with his African American heritage; and it was as an African American that he informed his white audiences, in the hopes of lessening the racism that he so abhorred.

A writer in the making

When Charles Chesnutt was nine years old, he saw a sight he would never forget. Attracted by the sound of gunfire, he was just in time to witness the death of an African American who had been shot—while under arrest by the police. Chesnutt came across many other acts of racism during his childhood in Fayetteville, North Carolina. Because the city was so dangerous for free blacks, his parents, Andrew and Ann Chesnutt, had left Fayetteville two years before his birth, but they had returned after the Civil War, for this was their home. Charles's father ran a grocery store in Fayetteville, and Charles helped out when he wasn't at school. He attended the Howard School, which had been founded by the Freedman's Bureau after the Civil War, but he had to end his formal studies at the age of fourteen in order to earn money for his family. For a year, he was a pupil-teacher at Howard School, before moving on to be a full-time teacher at schools in the surrounding area and at Charlotte.

Around this time, Charles decided that he wanted to become a writer. When only fourteen, he had a serialized story published in the local newspaper, and when he was sixteen he began to keep a journal. But writing could be only a sideline while he had to earn his living as a teacher. He returned to Fayetteville in 1877 to be assistant principal of Howard School, and three years later he became principal. Meanwhile, in 1878, he married a fellow teacher, Susan Perry.

Stenographer, lawyer, and author

Chesnutt was determined to leave Fayetteville and escape the vicious racism of the South, so he taught himself shorthand, with the idea that it would qualify him for a good position in a northern city. Resigning from his school in 1883, he set off north, determined to find a well paying job. After working for a while in New York City, he moved to Cleveland, Ohio, where in 1884 he was hired as a clerk by the Nickel Plate Railroad Company. This brought in enough to support his wife and growing family, who soon joined him, and Cleveland became their permanent home. Meanwhile, Chesnutt had not given up his ambition to make his living as a writer. In 1885, he had the first of many stories published in the *Cleveland News and Herald.*

Before long, Chesnutt became legal secretary to Judge Samuel Williamson, the railway company's lawyer. Williamson encouraged him to study law, and in 1887 Chesnutt passed the Ohio Bar exams at the top of his class. Williamson then offered to help Chesnutt set up a practice in Europe, where he would find life easier because of the less racist atmosphere. But Chesnutt turned down the offer, for his ambition lay in other directions. In 1890, he established a court reporting business, which brought in a good income in the daytime and left his evenings free to concentrate on writing.

Chesnutt had been getting a heartening number of short stories published, and in 1887 he had made a breakthrough into the literary world by having a story accepted by *Atlantic Monthly.* This was a landmark event not only for the budding writer but also for the magazine; Chesnutt was the first African American to be published by this prestigious literary journal, though the editors of *Atlantic* did not know that he was African American.

In the limelight

Chesnutt's literary career was notable, though disappointingly brief. He started with a bang by having three books published in 1899. The first was *The Conjure Woman,* a collection of stories told by a fictional black gardener, Uncle Julius, to his northern employer. The second book, *The Wife of His Youth, and Other Stories of the Color Line,* also consisted of short stories. These were about the difficulties faced by people of mixed race, who were not fully accepted in either the black or white community. The third book was a biography of famous black abolitionist Frederick Douglass.

These books drew such praise and sold so well that Chesnutt closed down his court reporting business in 1900 so that he could give his full time to writing and lecturing—all sorts of groups now wanted him to give talks and readings. His success continued with the publication of his first novel, *The House Behind the Cedars* (1900), which was reprinted four times within the first six months. This novel explored the same racial themes as the stories in *The Wife of His Youth*.

It looked as if Chesnutt might indeed fulfill his aim of reducing racial prejudice by spreading understanding through his writings. But when he began to criticize prejudice more openly, his white audience turned against him. His second novel, *The Marrow of Tradition* (1901), attracted more controversy than sales. Based on the Wilmington Riot of 1898, it dealt with such taboo subjects as racial hatred. Suddenly, Chesnutt was no longer invited to speak to literary groups. He had more difficulty getting his writings published, and his book sales fell off so badly that he had to reopen his court-reporting business in order to support his family.

Chesnutt published one more novel, *The Colonel's Dream* (1905), but it did even worse than its predecessors. This did not stop him writing, and in the following years he occasionally had a short story accepted by a magazine or newspaper. But, for all intents, his literary career was over. In 1928, when the National Association for the Advancement of Colored People awarded him the Spingarn Medal for his "pioneer work as a literary art-

ist," he explained: "My books were written, from one point of view, a generation too soon.... I was writing against the trend of public opinion on the race question. And I had to sell my books chiefly to white readers."

Although Chesnutt's first collection of stories was reprinted in 1929, his other works remained out of print until 1960, when there was a resurgence of interest in him, partly as a result of the biography written by his daughter. Since then, he has gained increasing recognition. An extraordinarily gifted writer, Chesnutt helped establish an African American literary tradition in the short story and novel, and he made the literary world realize that virtually everything connected with African American life can be a suitable subject for fiction.

Alice Childress

Playwright, novelist, actress
Born October 12, 1920, Charleston, South
  Carolina

"The play form is the one most familiar to me and so influences all of my writing—I think in scenes."

Alice Childress has written a dozen plays, four screenplays, several novels, and numerous other works, including the young people's novel *A Hero Ain't Nothin' but a Sandwich* (1973) which was banned by a school library in Savannah, Georgia. Because Childress focuses on controversial subjects such as drug addiction and interracial marriage, several of her works have been banned at times in various locations. Some affiliated stations refused to carry her screenplays *Wine in the Wilderness* and *Wedding Band* when they were broadcast on national television, and *Wine in the Wilderness* was forbidden to be shown throughout the state of Alabama.

One of the reasons Childress causes offense is that she writes with such searing honesty about racism, poverty, and the treatment of women. She has made it her aim to break through stereotyping and show black people and their problems as they really are. She also consciously promotes black culture, and thus her works often incorporate aspects of black history.

Childress has won numerous awards, including an Obie Award in 1956 for her play *Trouble in the Mind*. She was the first African American woman to win an Obie.

Read avidly during her early years

"My young years were very old in feeling, I was shut out of so much for so long," Alice Childress has said. Born into a very poor family, she was brought up by her grandmother in Harlem, New York, because her parents divorced when she was five.

Childress's grandmother did her best to give the child a happy home. She told Childress stories, took her to museums and to the Wednesday night testimonials at Salem Church in Harlem. At these gatherings Childress heard about the many troubles of her low-income neighbors—the type of problems she would later write about in her plays and novels.

Alice Childress

As a teenager Childress became an eager client at the public library, sometimes reading as many as two books a day. At both Julia Ward Howe Junior High School and Wadleigh High School her teachers encouraged her to write, but she had to drop out of high school in the late 1930s when her grandmother died. Out on her own, Childress had a brief and unsuccessful first marriage and gave birth to her daughter Jean. To support herself and her child, she took a series of odd jobs—salesperson, maid, assistant machinist, insurance agent. Meanwhile, she also embarked on a career in the theater.

Caused controversy with her play *Wedding Band*

Childress began her acting career in 1940 in the play *On Strivers Row*. For eleven years she was associated with the American Negro Theater in Harlem, where she studied acting, performed in numerous plays, and also worked as a director. Childress both directed and acted in *Florence* (1949), the first of her own plays to be performed. It is about two women—one black and one white—in a segregated railway waiting room.

The first of Childress's works to attract attention was *Trouble in the Mind,* which was produced in 1955 at the Greenwich Mews Theater in New York and won an Obie Award the following year. A comment on racial attitudes, this is a play within a play. It features a group of black actors who are forced to rehearse stereotype roles for a play written, produced, and directed by whites who have no understanding of black life.

The next of Childress's plays to hit the headlines was *Wedding Band: A Love/Hate Story in Black and White.* As the title suggests, this is a drama about interracial love. But it is not about interracial marriage—and that is the whole point of the play, for it is set in the South Carolina of 1918, where marriages between blacks and whites were forbidden by law.

Wedding Band was first performed at the University of Michigan in 1966 and was later staged at an off-Broadway theater in New York in 1972 before gaining a wide audience—and causing considerably controversy—when it was broadcast on ABC television in 1973. Childress's other controversial television drama, *Wine in the Wilderness* (1969), was written as a screenplay for Boston WGBH-TV's series "On Being Black." It focuses on a painter who is trying to portray black womanhood.

Childress's dramatic works include a number of musicals, which she wrote in coop-

eration with her second husband, musician Nathan Woodard. She has also written two plays for young people: *When the Rattlesnake Sounds* (1975), about the heroine of the Underground Railroad, Harried Tubman; and *Let's Hear It for the Queen* (1976), which is based on the nursery rhyme about the Queen of Hearts. Childress wrote the play to celebrate the birthday of her granddaughter.

Wrote award-winning novels that were banned by schools

Childress was writing fiction at the same time as she was writing, directing, and acting in plays. Her first novel evolved from a column called "Here's Mildred" which she wrote for the paper *Freedom* in the early 1950s. Childress collected the best of these sketches and published them as *Like One of the Family: Conversations from a Domestic's Life* (1956). They are chatty pieces spoken by a black maid called Mildred who says just what she thinks—and tells her white employers what she thinks, especially when they do anything she disapproves of. Childress says she based the character of Mildred on her Aunt Lorraine, who worked as a domestic and "refused to exchange dignity for pay." Although her work was menial, she herself refused to be menial.

The best known of Childress's novels is *A Hero Ain't Nothin' but a Sandwich* (1973), a story about a teenager who is hooked on drugs. Despite being banned by a school in Georgia, the book drew wide praise and won several awards. Made into a movie, for which Childress wrote the screenplay, *Hero* won further awards, including the 1977 Paul Robeson

Award for Outstanding Contributions to the Performing Arts.

As Childress gained fame as a playwright and novelist, she was invited to appear on radio and television, and to take part in panel discussions and conferences. She has lectured at numerous schools and universities, including Fisk University in 1966, and from 1966 to 1968 she was visiting scholar at Radcliffe Institute for Independent Study in Cambridge, Massachusetts.

When asked about her various forms of writing, Childress says: "Books, plays, teleplays, motion picture scenarios, etc., I seem caught up in a fragmentation of writing skills. But an idea comes to me in a certain form and, if it stays with me, must be written out.... The play form is the one most familiar to me and so influences all of my writing—I think in scenes."

Shirley Chisholm

Politician, teacher
Born November 30, 1924, Brooklyn, New
  York

"I was the first American citizen to be elected to Congress in spite of the double drawbacks of being female and having skin darkened by melanin. When you put it that way, it sounds like a foolish reason for fame."

The first black woman elected to Congress, the feisty and clear-sighted Shirley Anita St. Hill Chisholm viewed her election not so much as a breakthrough but as a comment on the barriers that still had to be removed. "That I am a national figure," she said, "because I was the first person in 192 years to be at once a congressman, black, and a woman proves, I think, that our society is not yet either just or free."

Given a sound upbringing

Both of Shirley Chisholm's parents were immigrants to the United States. Her father, Charles St. Hill, was from British Guiana; her mother, Ruby (Seale) St. Hill, was from Barbados. Charles was a factory worker, and Ruby worked as a seamstress and domestic to help provide for the family. The young couple had a hard time making ends meet, and in the hopes of saving some of their sparse earnings, they sent their children back to the Caribbean. When Shirley was three, she and her two younger sisters, Muriel and Odessa, went to live with their grandmother in Barbados, where they stayed for seven years.

Education on the island was British-style and extremely thorough. "If I speak and write easily now," Chisholm once said, "that early education is the main reason." When she returned to New York at the age of ten, she found it difficult to adjust. To her annoyance, she was put into a class with children two years her junior, because she knew so little about American history or geography. Chisholm caught up in just over a year, and by the time she graduated from high school she was offered scholarships to Vassar and Oberlin colleges. But she enrolled at Brooklyn College, which was less costly.

At college, as at school, Chisholm was a hard worker. Her parents had brought up their children very strictly, emphasizing obedience and duty and taking the children to church three times each Sunday. But they were also warm and caring parents, providing plenty of encouragement and support. The household may have been short of money, but they were rich in the things that mattered.

Introduced to local politics

At Brooklyn College in the 1940s, Chisholm majored in psychology and planned to become a teacher, since teaching seemed to be the only profession open to black women.

Chisholm graduated with a B.A. with honors in 1946, then taught nursery school while studying for a master's degree in elementary education at Columbia University. During her college years, Chisholm joined the Harriet Tubman Society. "There," she said, "I first heard people other than my father talk about white oppression, black racial con-

Shirley Chisholm

sciousness, and black pride." She resolved to help change things for the better. In 1949 she married fellow Columbia student Conrad Chisholm, and in 1952 she graduated with her M.A.

While teaching and working as a New York City education consultant, Chisholm became involved in local politics, successfully campaigning to get black lawyer Lewis S. Flagg elected as a district court judge in New York in 1953. This was the boost Chisholm needed to seriously consider a career for herself in politics. When one of her teachers had suggested such a career years ago at Brooklyn College, Chisholm had pointed out, "I have two handicaps, I am black and I am a woman." A decade later such handicaps no longer seemed insuperable.

Shirley Chisholm went to Washington

In 1960 Chisholm helped form the Unity Democratic Club to get more black people elected to the 17th Assembly District of New York State, and in 1964 Chisholm offered herself as Democratic candidate for the Assembly. Despite some opposition, she was chosen as the candidate. Knowing that it would be a battle to win the election, she went all out, speaking on street corners and in neighborhood halls, talking to Puerto Ricans in Spanish (which she had learned at college), and successfully winning over the voters, especially the women. The result was a landslide victory for Chisholm. She won by a huge margin, gaining 18,151 votes against the Republican candidate's 1,893 votes and the Liberal's 913.

Chisholm served on the New York State Assembly for the next four years, gaining a reputation as a hard-working, no-nonsense legislator. She introduced more than fifty bills and was particularly pleased with two of those that were passed. One of them set up a program called SEEK, which sought out disadvantaged children in the schools in order to help them get to college. The other introduced the state's first unemployment insurance program for domestic workers.

Before the 1968 congressional elections, a new 12th District was created in New York, and since it had a large black population, Chisholm decided to contest the seat. She knew it would not be easy, for the Republican candidate was popular civil rights leader James Farmer, and he had far more campaign funds that she could hope to raise. Undaunted, she campaigned under the slogan "Fighting Shirley Chisholm: Unbought and Unbossed" and was elected to Congress by 34,885 votes to Farmer's 13,777.

Chisholm served in the House of Representatives from 1968 to 1983. As the first black congresswoman she made it her business to sponsor bills that helped the poor and disadvantaged and to push for equality for ethnic minorities and for women. Meanwhile, as "fighting Shirley Chisholm," she remained true to her beliefs, risking unpopularity for causes she believed in. In her first speech in the House she spoke out against the Vietnam War.

In 1972 she campaigned for the Democratic presidential nomination. Although it became clear, early on in the campaign, that she stood no chance of winning, she did not consider she had failed. As she said in her 1973 book, *The Good Fight,* "The mere fact that a black woman dared to run for President, *seriously,* not expecting to win but sincerely trying to, is what it was all about. 'It can be done.' That was what I was trying to say."

After being twice re-elected to Congress, Chisholm retired in 1983, because her second husband, Arthur Hardwick, was seriously ill. She then returned to teaching, serving as Purington Professor at Mount Holyoke College in Massachusetts for the next four years. Chisholm has said she does not want to be remembered as the first black congresswoman or even as the first black presidential candidate. She would rather be remembered "as a woman who had the perseverance to fight on behalf of the female population and the black population."

Joe Clark

High school principal
Born May 7, 1939, Rochelle, Georgia

"I've got the most orderly high school in America."

During the 1980s Joe Clark hit the headlines as the most famous high school principal in America—the controversial law-and-order principal at Eastside High School in Paterson, New Jersey. Carrying a bullhorn and baseball bat, Clark daily patrolled the corridors, establishing discipline in the problem school, which he transformed into one of the most orderly in the entire country.

Clark achieved his results partly by expelling unruly students, the ones he called "leeches, miscreants, and hoodlums." Such actions brought him into conflict with the school board and aroused criticism from other educators. However, many people approved of Clark's methods, including a large number of his students. Local newspapers named him "outstanding educator" and "New Jerseyan of the year," and in 1985 President Ronald Reagan personally honored Clark at a White House conference on academic and disciplinary excellence.

A "welfare kid" who beat the odds

Joe Clark has little sympathy for children at inner-city schools who turn to drugs and violence. He came from just as poor a home as they did. The son of Rhomie and Maggie (Majors) Clark, he has described himself as "a welfare kid" who worked hard at school, went on to college, and then married and successfully supported a family. Clark and his wife Hazel have three children—Joetta, Joe, Jr., and Hazel.

Willpower enabled Clark to pursue his education. In the 1950s he attended William Paterson College in Wayne, New Jersey, where he graduated with a bachelor's degree in 1960. He then worked as a grade school teacher in Paterson, New Jersey, until 1974, when he was appointed coordinator of language arts. During this period Clark studied for his M.A., which he received from Seton Hall University, South Orange, New Jersey, in 1974. His first appointment as a school principal came in 1979, when he took over PS 6 elementary school in Paterson. In 1982 Clark took on a

Joe Clark

big challenge when he was appointed principal of Eastside High School.

Eastside High had the reputation of being the worst school in New Jersey, reknowned for its violence and lack of discipline. Of the 3,200 students, most were African American or Hispanic, and they did whatever they wanted—they skipped school, scrawled on the walls, fought each other, attacked their teachers, and openly dealt in drugs. Education was not a priority in a school where the teachers were too scared to lay down the law.

Made the cover of *Time* magazine

Before assuming his duties as principal of Eastside High, Clark spent the summer vacation making changes. First, he spruced up the school buildings—grafitti was cleaned off the walls, fences and windows were mended, furniture was repaired, door locks were replaced. Then Clark drew up a list of new policies, which included identification tags for students, a sytem of suspensions for troublemakers, a dress code, and other new rules. He also organized security patrols of the school grounds. He was determined to keep the drug pushers out.

On the first day of school students learned that a big change was underway. On the steps of the school stood Joe Clark with his bullhorn, announcing, "I am your new principal, Joe Clark. Mr. Clark to you. This is the new Eastside High School. What was, exists no more. Go to your classrooms. Please walk to the right." Most students were so surprised that they obeyed the orders without argument. Those who did argue were given short shrift.

From the start, Clark showed that he meant business. In the first week alone he suspended 300 students. Some had merely been late for class or had broken one of the new rules, but others had been guilty of serious offenses such as attacking their teachers. The main lesson Clark was driving home was that every single one of his rules was to be obeyed. It was a case of "my way or the doorway." This applied to teachers as well as students. Those who didn't agree with his methods were dismissed or asked to leave.

During Clark's first five years at Eastside High, well over half the teachers left. Many objected to his habit of yelling at them in public—bawling them out in in front of the class. Others objected to his martial regime. Each day he walked nearly twenty miles as he patrolled the corridors. Students were made to feel they were under constant surveillance.

Clark succeeded in cleaning up the school and bringing order out of chaos, but he did so partly by expelling any students who caused trouble. As the expulsions continued, some members of the school board began to object, pointing out that Clark was depriving the expelled students of an education. Moreover, he was rejecting those who most needed help. When in 1987 Clark expelled sixty-six students, the school board decided to take action, charging him with insubordination. The intention was to dismiss him—but the board had not counted on Clark's supporters.

Many of Clark's students rallied to his defense, and early in 1988 they and their parents turned up at a school board meeting, shouting "Without no Joe, where will we go?" Clark's supporters included members of the Reagan administration, who offered him a post in the Office of Policy Development, which Clark turned down. In the end, Clark prevailed over the school board, but the controversy raged on, for it had attracted the attention of the media. Clark appeared regularly on television shows defending his law-and-order approach, and he became such a center of interest that in 1989 *Time* magazine did a cover story on him. That same year Warner Brothers made the film *Lean on Me* about Clark's principalship at Eastside High School. The role of Clark was played by actor Morgan Freeman.

In May 1989 Clark was swept up in a different type of drama when he had openheart surgery. Two months later he resigned from Eastside High, and soon thereafter he wrote the book *Laying Down the Law: Joe Clark's Strategy for Saving Our Schools* (1989). He has since been much in demand as a lecturer.

Although Clark is no longer a high school principal, the issues he raised continue to concern many people throughout the country. Clark succeeded in catalyzing people with his law-and-order approach as one possible answer to the growing problem of violence and crime in American schools.

Eldridge Cleaver

Writer, political activist
Born August 31, 1935, Wabbeseka,
  Arkansas

"I have, so to speak, washed my hands in the blood of the martyr, Malcolm X, whose retreat from the precipice of madness created new room for others to turn about in, and now I am caught up in that tiny space, attempting a maneuver of my own."

Best known for leading the civil rights movement down a more violent road, Eldridge Cleaver was minister of information for the militant Black Panthers Party. He wrote about the need for change, he advocated that blacks use arms in their struggle for liberation, and he felt a black socialist state was needed.

Cleaver had several confrontations with the law, including a shoot-out with Oakland police that caused him to flee the country. As the unofficial ambassador of the Black Panthers he visited many socialist countries, but he determined their methods would not work, either.

Disenchanted, he returned to the United States and worked out a deal with the government so he could avoid serving time in jail. He converted to Christianity and still seeks to improve the black position through nonviolent means.

Schooled in jail

Cleaver was born in Wabbeseka, Arkansas, on August 31, 1935, to Leroy, a dining car waiter, and Thelma, a janitor. Eighteen years later he was convicted of possessing marijuana, and in 1954 he began a twelve-year cycle that saw him in and out of prisons at Soledad, Folsom, and San Quentin. In Soledad, he earned his diploma from Bay View High School, and during his time in prison he also wrote *Soul on Ice,* a collection of essays about the situation of black people in America as well as Cleaver's own life. The book was published in 1968.

He received his inspiration for the book from several writers he read in prison, including Thomas Paine, Karl Marx, Nikolai Lenin, and James Baldwin. Cleaver was also influenced by Black Muslim leader Malcolm X, and he eventually converted to the Black Muslim faith.

Excerpts of Cleaver's book released before the book was published received a great deal of attention by the literary community, and several of the groups began petitioning the government for his release. Cleaver was paroled in 1966.

Wrote the acclaimed book *Soul on Ice*

When *Soul on Ice* was published, Gertrude Samuels in *Saturday Review* wrote the book is "an original and disturbing report on what a black man, reacting to a society he detests, reacting to life behind bars for nine years, finally becomes." Jervis Anderson of *Commentary* said that Cleaver expressed "the profound alienation from America which black nationalists feel and the extreme political and cultural view of its future which they take."

Cleaver became a staff writer for *Ramparts* magazine and a popular lecturer on college campuses after his release. He hoped to inspire and motivate black students, especially those from ghettos. When he was invited to address a group of Berkeley students as a black studies lecturer, California governor Ronald Reagan opposed the invitation.

Affiliated with the radical Panthers

A short time later Cleaver became the Black Panther Party's minister of information. The Black Panthers were founded by Huey P. Newton and Bobby Seale in October 1966 to condemn institutional structure, which in its view made American society corrupt. It also opposed established authority, which it felt either oppressed or overlooked the black community. As information minister Cleaver called for an armed insurrection to overthrow the existing government and the establishment of a black socialist one in its place. J. Edgar Hoover, director of the Federal Bureau of Investigations (FBI), is reported to have called the Panthers the nation's "greatest threat."

The Panthers ran free lunch programs for poor children and operated other service-oriented programs in several cities. But they were also heavily armed in the name of self defense and had a number of gun battles with the police. *Playboy* magazine reported: "[Cleaver] has been called the first black leader since Malcolm X with the potential to organize a militant mass movement of 'black liberation.' Whether he will succeed in forging it, and whether, if he does, it will be a force for racial reconciliation or division remains to be seen."

In 1968 Cleaver and several Panthers were involved in a gun fight with police in Oakland, California. One Panther was killed, and a police officer and Cleaver were wounded. His parole was revoked and he was charged with assault and attempted murder.

Support for Cleaver soon sprang up across the world. A demonstration was held in New York City on his behalf, which included writer Susan Sontag and actor Gary Merrill. In Europe French film director Jean-Luc Godard asked his audience to donate to Cleaver's defense fund. Later that year Cleaver's popularity became even more apparent when he was chosen as the presidential candidate of

Eldridge Cleaver

the Peace and Freedom Party, an organization of black and white radicals. In an interview with Nat Hentoff of *Playboy* magazine, Cleaver said, "I never exactly dreamed of waking up in the White House after the November election, but I took part in that campaign because I think it's necessary to pull a lot of people together, black and white."

Visited communist countries

In late 1968 Cleaver secretly fled the country rather than face charges over the gun battle with police and a prison sentence for violating his parole. Over the next seven years he lived in Cuba, Algeria, and France, and he was warmly welcomed on his visits to the Soviet Union, China, North Vietnam, and North Korea. It was said that an interview he granted while in the Soviet Union confirmed his connection with the spread of communism. *New Republic* writer Richard Gilman remarked that Cleaver "played a complicated role from afar in the troubled internal policies of the Black Panthers, served as an unofficial emissary of American radicalism to various communist regimes..., fathered two children with his wife Kathleen and found himself growing more and more disenchanted with both his life as an expatriate and his former political beliefs."

After visiting so many communist countries, Cleaver concluded that communism was not working as well as he thought. Cleaver wrote in his 1978 book *Soul on Fire,* "I had heard so much rhetoric about their glorious leaders and their incredible revolutionary spirit that even to this very angry and disgruntled American, it was absurd and unreal." He was reported to have said Cuba's communism was

"voodoo" socialism, and that North Korea and Algeria suffered the same problems, only longer. He became critical of both the Soviet Union and Red China for pursuing their own narrow interests, and that they should invest in their future by pooling their arsenals, supplying more generous arms supplies to fledgling liberation movements, and facing up to the imperialism of the United States.

Cleaver lost faith in communism as well as his belief in violence. He converted to Christianity after a dream in which he saw his own face on the moon, then the faces of his former heroes—Fidel Castro, Mao Tsetung, Karl Marx, Friedrich Engels—and finally, the image of Jesus Christ.

Although Cleaver said he was living happily in Algeria, a rift between him and his host country developed in 1972 over the issue of skyjacking ransom money. Contrary to Cleaver's desire, the Algerians wanted it returned to the airlines that had paid it. In 1973 it was reported that he was under house arrest in Algeria. Reports also began to circulate in California that Cleaver's former associates in the Black Panther Party, with whom he had broken, wanted to reconcile their differences with him.

Surrendered to the FBI

In 1975 Cleaver returned to the United States and surrendered to the FBI. Although he faced up to seventy-two years in prison, he struck a deal. By pleading guilty to the assault charge, the attempted murder charge was dropped, and he was placed on probation and sentenced to 1,200 hours of community service. One reason for the leniency was the feeling that

Cleaver's conversion to Christianity had changed him.

Since his return Cleaver has been involved in several ventures. In 1978 he opened a Hollywood boutique featuring men's trousers with a codpiece, his own design. The next year he founded the Eldridge Cleaver Crusades, an evangelical organization that planned to open headquarters in the Nevada desert. He visited many fundamentalist churches across the country to speak of his conversion and urged others to follow the same path. He returned to politics in 1984 as an independent conservative candidate for Congress, but his bid was unsuccessful. After spending almost his entire life criticizing the United States, Cleaver once told a group of students at Yale University that America was the "freest and most democratic country in the world."

George Clements

Roman Catholic priest and social activist
Born January 26, 1932, Chicago, Illinois

"I'm not going to stand by and watch my people die."

George Clements, best known as the Roman Catholic priest who adopted a child, was pastor of Holy Angels Church in Chicago for more than twenty years. A fervent activist, Clements encouraged families to adopt black youngsters, enforced discipline at the church school, fought against drug dealers, and was thrown in jail, and his style even ran him into trouble with church and city authorities.

Marched on Selma with Martin Luther King

Born on January 26, 1932, in Chicago, Illinois, to Samuel and Aldonia Clements, George Clements was the first black graduate of Quigley Seminary and, at the time of his ordination in 1957, one of only a handful of black Roman Catholic priests in the entire country. Service as associate pastor at several Chicago churches preceded his becoming pastor at Holy Angels in 1969. Active in the fight against racism, Clements marched on Selma, Alabama, with civil rights leader Martin Luther King, Jr. He later permitted members of the extremist Black Panther Party to use church facilities to hold meetings and other activities. When King was assassinated, Clements removed a statue of St. Anthony from the church and replaced it with an altar honoring King.

Clements made it clear to his parishioners from the beginning that the church would be their own church, not one that white people only allowed them to use. He was determined that they should be economically independent and not have to beg wealthy or white churches for support. In his first twelve years at Holy Angels membership doubled, and its budget nearly tripled.

Raises school standards

As pastor at Holy Angels, Clements was in charge of the largest black Catholic elementary school in the country. Under his leadership, the school acquired a national reputation for its high academic standards as well as strict discipline. Students falling below grade level were to come in on Saturdays. School starts at eight in the morning until four in the afternoon, and the year is twelve months.

The school also works closely with families. Tuition is kept low, but parents are required to take part in fund-raising activities. Parents must also pick up their children's report cards, and attend Sunday mass with their families. Clements's new policies were initially resisted, until 200 students were suspended when their parents failed to bring their families to mass. This provision is part of a contract that all parents whose children attend Holy Angels must sign.

Clements was especially concerned with the large number of black children growing up without traditional families and the bureaucratic red tape making it difficult for black parents to adopt. African Americans seeking to adopt often experience rejection because they lack homeowner status or do not meet income or educational requirements. To help cut through the red tape, Clements invited officials of the Illinois Department of Children and Family Services to a public meeting at Holy Angels to encourage adoption by black families. Only a handful of parishioners attended and none offered to adopt a child. Shocked by the lack of response, Clements announced from the pulpit three weeks later that he would adopt a child.

The black pastor's decision made headlines, and his superior, Cardinal John Cody, publicly disapproved. The church eventually permitted Clements to adopt Joey, a fourteen-year-old boy, which convinced others to adopt homeless black children. Clements told *Ebony* magazine: "The only reason black people don't adopt more often is because we aren't aware of the extent of the problem.... When we do find out, we take action."

Clements and other black clergymen formed One Church, One Child, an organization contending that if just one family in each black church in the country adopted a black child, the problem of homeless black children would be over. Wildly successful in Illinois, the program resulted in the adoption of more than 3,000 black children. The program won a Ford Foundation Innovations Award in 1986, and three years later there were chapters in twenty-nine other states.

Targets the drug dealers

Clements has expended significant energy toward eliminating drug abuse. In 1988 he and fellow priest Michael Pfleger began asking local grocery and convenience stores to stop carrying drug paraphernalia, such as cocaine spoons, crack pipes, and roach clips. After

George Clements

limited success, he organized a boycott of stores that continued to sell. More merchants stopped selling. When a wholesaler refused to let the pastor enter his building in June 1989, he pounded so hard on the glass door that it shattered, badly cutting him. He was arrested for trespassing and criminal damage to property, though the charges were later dropped. The *Chicago Tribune* stated: "You have to hand it to Rev. George Clements. His methods may be excessive, but it's easy to appreciate and admire his outrage.... Father Clements is unrepentant. 'I'm not going to stand by and watch my people die,' he said." Clements's tough stance angered local drug dealers, and he began receiving death threats. Continuous bodyguard protection couldn't prevent his car from being vandalized or a shot being fired through his rectory window. Eventually the Illinois legislature banned the sale of drug paraphernalia. In 1990 Clements increased his pressure on the dealers by videotaping drug deals and turning the tapes over to the police.

When Holy Angels Church burned to the ground in 1986, Clements set up a tent and told his parishioners that the church would be rebuilt without outside help. Asking each family to provide a 10 percent tithe, he received over $55,000 in donations the first week. Chicago architects Skidmore, Owings & Merrill offered their services free of charge, as did local construction firms. A modern, solar-powered church was dedicated on June 9, 1991.

Two weeks later Clements announced his retirement from Holy Angels. In a *Washington Post* interview, he explained: "I've loved this work, but it's past my time. I really haven't had an opportunity to do a lot of things priests do.... I've missed things like being able to do counselling, to do a lot more preaching.... I certainly want to get involved with meditation, contemplation and retreats—back into doing some of the things that inspired me to be a priest in the first place." He had an opportunity in 1987 to do missionary work in Nigeria, where the Yoruba tribe gave him the honorary title of "Chief Omowale." He took a short sabbatical before returning to priestly duties in the Bahamas.

Jewel Plummer Cobb

Cancer researcher, university president
Born January 17, 1924, Chicago, Illinois

"Women, who constitute 52 percent of the population, make up only 20 percent of the scientists."

A specialist in cell biology, Jewel Plummer Cobb has done important research into the treatment of cancer while also following an academic career both as a professor and administrator. She has served as dean at several universities and from 1981 to 1990 was president of California State University at Fullerton. Since 1990 Cobb has been trustee professor at California State College in Los Angeles.

Cobb is the author of some 37 scientific papers as well as a number of articles about minority groups and women. Of particular note is her "Filters for Women in Science," which was published in the *Annals of the New York Academy of Sciences* (1979). In this paper Cobb compared the situation of women in science to the type of filter found in the laboratory. She pointed out that the filter used for women had a far finer mesh than that used for men, and thus far fewer women were given the opportunity to become scientists. During her years in university administration, Cobb has attempted to rectify this situation. She has also tried to channel more black male students into the sciences.

Enjoyed an intellectual home life

Jewel Plummer Cobb is the third in a chain of four generations of scientists. Her grandfather, Robert Plummer, graduated from Howard University as a pharmacist in 1898; her father, Dr. Frank Plummer, practiced for years as a physician in Chicago; and her son, Jonathan Cobb, is a New Jersey radiologist. Jonathan is the only child of her marriage to Roy Cobb, which ended in divorce in 1967.

Although Jewel Cobb's mother, Carriebel (Cole) Plummer, was not a scientist, she too had an interesting profession. She taught interpretive dance at Chicago schools, having trained at Sargeants, a physical education college associated with Harvard University.

An only child, Cobb gained full benefit from her parents' cultural milieu, which included their many distinguished friends. Black writers, historians, and artists frequently visited their Chicago home, and Cobb grew up listening to their discussions about political and racial issues. Encouraged to read widely, she was given full use of her father's library, with its many scientific journals. She was also taken to the ballet and to other events in New York City.

Jewel Plummer Cobb

With such a home life, it is little wonder that Cobb was an honors student throughout her school years. In her second year at high school she had her first thrilling look into the lens of a microscope—an experience she credits with sparking her enthusiasm for biology. Having decided this would be her specialty, she took an extra year of biology before graduating from high school.

In 1941 Cobb enrolled at the University of Michigan. She chose Michigan because many of her friends were students there, but it was not the most suitable university for her personal needs, so at the end of her third semester she transferred to Talladega College in Alabama. There she majored in biology, earning a bachelor's degree in 1944. She then moved to New York University, where she was a graduate student and teaching fellow from 1944 to 1950. She specialized in cell biology, earning her master's degree in 1947 and her Ph.D. in 1950.

Teacher, administrator, cell biologist, and researcher

Cobb taught and conducted research at New York University until 1960, when she was appointed professor of biology at Sarah Lawrence College in Bronxville, New York. In 1969 she moved to Connecticut College, where she served as dean and professor of zoology until 1976.

Throughout these years Cobb combined her teaching and administrative responsibilities with research. However busy she was, she tried to devote several hours to her laboratory work each morning. As a cell biologist, she was interested in the behavior of living cells in the human body. One of her research projects involved growing cancer cells in test tubes and then testing a new type of chemotherapy drug on them to see its effect in controlling the cancer.

Cobb's particular area was pigment cell research—research into melanin, the brown or black pigment that colors the skin. She was interested in discovering how melanin shields the human skin from harmful ultraviolet rays, and she concentrated much of her research on melanoma, the most dangerous type of skin cancer.

Alongside her research, Cobb was fully occupied with her duties as professor and dean. At Connecticut College she instituted a premedical and predental program for students from minority groups. Privately funded, this program was most successful—about 90 percent of the students involved in it were accepted into medical or dental schools. Although the program was dropped after Cobb left Connecticut, it served as a model for similar programs in twenty other colleges.

In 1976 Cobb moved from Connecticut to Douglass College, where she served as dean and professor of biological sciences until 1981. Here the administrative and teaching duties proved so heavy that she had to give up her research work. Nor did she have time to conduct research during her years as president of California State University at Fullerton, 1981–90. However, she left her mark on these institutions in other ways. She had an especially strong impact at Fullerton, where she had a students' apartment complex built, thus transforming the Fullerton campus into a residential college. She also established an opportunity program for ethnic students.

Since becoming professor emeritus at the age of sixty-six, Cobb has continued to involve herself in the university's affairs as trustee professor for the entire California State University system. Based in Los Angeles, her work encompasses six colleges. One of her prime aims is to get more minority students studying science and engineering in these colleges—and, indeed, at all universities.

Cobb also wants to see more women qualifying in scientific subjects. "Women, who constitute 52 percent of the population, make up only 20 percent of the scientists but less than 1 percent of the engineers," she says. Cobb's aim is to start the process in the schools by making it easier for girls to specialize in the sciences and then to provide private grants and fellowships to help fund them through university. Her deep commitment to this cause is already showing positive results.

Johnnetta Betsch Cole

Educator and anthropologist
Born October 19, 1936, Jacksonville, Florida

"I have consciously lived and studied, taught and written, as an African American woman. The issues of race and gender have been central in my life."

Johnetta Betsch Cole

A s the first black woman president of Spelman College, the oldest college for black women in the United States, Johnnetta Betsch Cole is clear-sighted about her mission. In her acceptance statement in 1987, she said she aimed to make Spelman "a renowned center for scholarship by and about black women" and a place where "black women leaders of the world are nurtured, trained, and developed."

Since its founding in 1881, Spelman College has had seven presidents, yet it is doubtful if any has taken on the role with more zeal and excitement than Cole. Known as "sister president," she relates comfortably with her students, one of whom described her as "approachable, accessible, visible, and a real sister who cares about us." Above all, Cole has vision—a broad view that goes far beyond the Spelman campus and brings a balanced approach even to the most contentious issues.

Came from a family of achievers

Johnnetta Cole comes from a family of achievers. Her mother's grandfather was co-founder of the Afro-American Life Insurance Com-

pany of Jacksonville. Her father, John Betsch, worked for a rival insurance company, Atlantic Life, but moved to Afro-American Life after his marriage. Johnnetta's mother, Mary (Lewis) Betsch, is yet another achiever. A graduate of Wilberforce University, she taught English and served as registrar at Edward Waters College before joining Afro-American Life on her husband's death. Johnnetta's sister, Marvyne, is an Oberlin graduate, and her brother, John, is a jazz musician.

Johnnetta is the middle child in the family. She spent her early years in Jacksonville and did so well at school that in 1952, at the age of fifteen, she was able to enter Fisk University in Nashville, Tennessee, under its early admissions program. As a Fisk student, Johnnetta had daily contact with the college's famous librarian, the author Arna Bontemps.

After a year at Fisk, Johnnetta joined her sister at Oberlin College, where in her first

151

year she took a course on racial and cultural minorities. The subject so fascinated Johnnetta that she decided to major in sociology in preparation for a career in anthropology. This caused some consternation at home because she was expected to join the family business. When she told her grandfather she intended to be an anthropolgist, he expressed his disapproval by saying loudly, "What's THAT!" Nevertheless, Johnnetta persevered. After graduating from Oberlin in 1957, she did postgraduate studies at Northwestern University, where she obtained her master's degree in anthropology in 1959.

Established distinguished academic reputation

In 1960 Johnnetta married Robert Cole, a white economics graduate who had been a fellow student at Northwestern. When Robert came to Jacksonville to meet Cole's parents, members of the white community reacted by threatening to bomb the family business.

The young couple spent the first two years of their marriage in Liberia, where they conducted research for their doctoral theses and where the eldest of their three sons was born. On their return to the United States in 1962, Robert taught at Washington State University, and Johnnetta taught part time while completing her dissertation on "Traditional and Wage-Earning Labor in Liberia." In 1965 she was named Washington State University's Outstanding Faculty Member of the Year, and in 1967 she was awarded her Ph.D. in anthropology from Northwestern University.

For the next few years the Coles remained at Washington State, where Johnnetta initi-

ated and ran a program of black studies and served as assistant professor of anthropology. In 1970 the couple moved to the University of Massachusetts at Amherst where again Cole helped develop an African American studies program and taught anthropology. In 1983, the year after her divorce, she moved to Hunter College of the City University of New York, where she taught initially as Russell Sage Visiting Professor and was then appointed professor of anthropology. She also directed the college's Latin American and Caribbean Studies Program.

During these years Cole gained a powerful reputation as an anthropologist and wrote the textbook *Anthropology for the Eighties: Introductory Readings* (1982). While at Hunter she published her landmark study, *All American Women: Lines that Divide, Ties that Bind* (1986). The book broke new ground in women's studies because of its sensitivity to inequalities based on race, ethnic origin, class, and gender.

Cole's third book, *Anthropology for the Nineties,* was published in 1988, the year after her appointment as president of Spelman College. Her reputation as an anthropologist opened new possibilities for that venerable institution. Cole has made a particular study of cultural anthropology—her fieldwork ranges from racial and gender inequality in Cuba to research into female-headed households and the ways in which women age. Her research is especially concerned with women of African origin, whether in Africa itself or in the Caribbean and North America.

Cole has said: "I have *consciously* lived and studied, taught and written, as an African

American woman. The issues of race and gender have been central in my life, in my work as an anthropologist, and in my community activities. There is a fundamental question at the base of the work that I do: how can people of color, poor people, and women become full, productive, and equal members of the society in which they live?"

It is this question that Cole attempts to answer as she guides the students of Stelman College through the 1990s. Currently married to Arthur Robinson III, she faces the future with confidence. She looks forward to a time when "scholars, teachers, artists, policy analysts, and community leaders will turn to Spelman for comprehensive information on the rich and diverse history, struggles, conditions, and accomplishments of black women."

Nat King Cole

Singer, songwriter, pianist
Born March 17, 1919, Montgomery, Alabama
Died February 15, 1965, Santa Monica, California

"Nat's impeccable taste and vocal styling established him not only as one of the leading crooners of the day, but also as one of the best song salesmen in the business. He could take the most unlikely lyric and transform it to a hum or whistle on everybody's lips."

Although Nat King Cole was only forty-five when he died, he was already a legend—a crooner whose grainy baritone voice was one of the most popular on the airwaves. From the early days of his jazz trio and later as a soloist, he accumulated a long list of hit records, including "Sweet Lorraine," "Chestnuts Roasting on the Open Fire," "Nature Boy," "Ramblin' Rose," "Mona Lisa," "Too Young," "Those Lazy, Hazy, Crazy Days of Summer," and many others.

Because of his popularity with both black and white audiences, Cole became the first African American to host a TV variety show, "The Nat King Cole Show," which aired on NBC in 1956–57. He also appeared in several movies, playing a jazz musician and other roles.

Interested in a different kind of music

When Nat King Cole was about four years old, he was already strumming "Yes, We Have No Bananas!" on the family piano. Born Nathaniel Adams Coles, the "King" came later, as a nickname from the nursery rhyme "Old King Cole."

Cole's father, Edward Coles, was a Baptist minister who moved the family to Chicago in the 1920s and became pastor of the True Light Baptist Church. The Coles children took turns playing the organ at services. Cole and his three brothers and two sisters all showed musical talent, which their parents encouraged. Until the age of twelve Cole played by ear, but then his mother, Perlina, arranged for him to have formal lessons and learn pieces by Bach and other classical composers, intending for him to become a classical pianist.

This classical period lasted only a few years, until Cole was at Wendell Phillips High

153

School and formed his own twelve-piece band. He was about sixteen at the time, and although his father wasn't too pleased, his mother made the group uniform Cossack shirts so they could look more professional. Cole was the group's pianist, and they played at school and club dances for whatever payment they could get (often only hot dogs and hamburgers); occasionally they played at the Savoy for real money. As they became better known, Cole's brother Eddie, who had been playing with an orchestra, came home and formed a sextet with Cole and four others, and they began to play professionally.

Wrote his first hit, but no longer owned its copyright

In 1936, the year Cole graduated from high school, his group joined a company that was doing a revival of *Shuffle Along,* a black musical revue. His girlfriend, dancer Nadine Robinson (whom he married the following year), joined the revue too, and they went on tour with the show. All went well until they reached Long Beach, California, where the show closed, putting the newlyweds out of work.

Stranded, Cole managed to bring in a little money by playing in the clubs and bars around Los Angeles. His luck changed when club owner Bob Lewis asked him to form a quartet to play at his club. It is said to be Lewis who gave Nat Coles the nickname "King" and persuaded him to drop the "s" from his name. The group was to be called the King Cole Swingsters (and Cole was to wear a crown, which he disliked doing, so he managed to lose it after about three weeks). He

hired guitarist Oscar Moore and bass player Wesley Prince, but the drummer he chose failed to show up on opening night, so the quartet became a trio.

The trio featured no vocals at first, but one night a drunken customer demanded that Cole sing "Sweet Lorraine," so from then on he sang from time to time to provide a bit of variety. Gradually the King Cole Trio became well known in the Los Angeles area and began to appear on local radio and to make recordings.

In 1942 Cole signed a contract with Capitol Records, and the following year the trio recorded its first hit, "Straighten Up and Fly Right." The novelty of the tune, coupled with Cole's versatile piano playing, made the record a major hit in 1944, selling more then a million copies. However, Cole did not hold the copyright on the song even though he had written it, for he had sold it outright when he

Nat King Cole

was desperate for money in 1937. But although he didn't grow rich from this hit, he gained millions of fans who eagerly bought his next records.

Big band sound made him famous

By 1948, when Cole married his second wife, singer Maria Ellington, his recording of "Nature Boy" was being played in homes and on radio throughout the nation. Cole recorded this ballad as a solo vocalist with a big band rather than singing and playing with his trio. As time passed he realized his greatest successes came when he was accompanied by big bands, so he disbanded the trio in the 1950s and concentrated on solo performances.

During the late 1950s and early 1960s Cole was at the peak of his career, turning out one hit after another. He appeared at Carnegie Hall, performed for President Kennedy and other world leaders, went on tours overseas, and was featured frequently on television and radio.

He also tried to cultivate a movie career. Appearing as himself in the 1952 movie *The Nat King Cole Story* gave him a taste for filmwork and he dreamed of becoming a film star. Over the years he had small parts in several films, but he proved to have no great talent for acting. His starring role with Eartha Kitt in *St. Louis Blues* (1958) drew more criticism than praise, as did his one attempt at musical theater in the show *I'm with You* (1960). His final film was *Cat Ballou*, which was finished just before his death. Cole had been suffering from a cough and fierce chest pains, and he was found to have lung cancer.

Besides leaving behind a wealth of music, Cole passed on his talents to the next generation. One of his children, Natalie, has become a well-known singer, and in the early 1990s she recorded the duet "Unforgettable," singing alongside Cole's own rendition of the song. It was a touching homage from a daughter to her father.

Natalie Cole

Singer
Born February 6, 1950, Los Angeles, California

"I learned through my dad by osmosis because I traveled with him, and I'd see things and recall those things when I got older."

It can be a disadvantage to have a famous father. As the daughter of crooner Nat King Cole (1919–1965), Natalie Cole often felt she was riding on her father's fame rather than succeeding through her own talents. Despite six hit albums during the 1970s, she was plagued with self-doubts to such an extent that she became heavily dependent on drugs and alcohol.

With her career falling apart, Cole took hold of herself and fought her way out of her addictions, making a comeback in 1991 with her biggest hit, *Unforgettable*. When starting out as a singer, Cole had chosen a contemporary rhythm-and-blues style that was very different from her father's music. By contrast, *Unforgettable* was a collection of her father's songs, as was her 1993 album, *Take a Look*.

After so many years of trying to escape her father's shadow, Natalie Cole had at last united it with her own.

Nat King Cole's daughter

Natalie Maria Cole was the second of the five children of Nat King Cole and Maria (Hawkins) Cole, who had been a singer in the Duke Ellington Orchestra. During Natalie's childhood, her father was at the peak of his career, turning out hit after hit. Although he hated rock-and-roll music, he always brought home the pop records that Natalie asked for, though he usually added a few of his own choosing—records of Ella Fitzgerald, Sarah Vaughan, and other great jazz singers.

When Natalie was eleven, her father gave her a tape recorder, and one of the first songs she recorded was an Ella Fitzgerald number. When her father heard the tape, he told a friend, "She's got it! She's got the voice." Soon afterwards, he took Natalie on one of his concert tours, though with no real intention that she would choose music as career. At the time, he was encouraging her to aim for medicine or law. Natalie readily agreed with this choice of career, though she kept up her interest in music, and during her teen years she formed a short-lived jazz trio called the Malibu Music Men.

Natalie was a fifteen-year-old at prep school in Massachusetts when her happy world was shattered by her father's death from lung cancer. "All the excitement went out of my life," she said. On her mother's remarriage, the family moved to Massachusetts, where in 1968 Natalie enrolled at the University of Massachusetts at Amherst. As she later recalled, at college she "went wild and did a lot of crazy things that weren't healthy physically or mentally." This included experimenting with drugs, which were very much part of the "hippie" scene at the University of Southern California, where Natalie studied for much of her junior year.

Back in Amherst in 1970, Natalie took a summer job as a waitress, but this soon gave way to far more exciting work—singing in local clubs with a band called Black Magic. Here, Natalie had her first taste of what her life as a performer would be like, for the club owners insisted on billing her as Nat King Cole's daughter. While this was an obvious way for the clubs to attract clients, it upset Natalie. Did she really have talent, she wondered, or was she sought after only as the daughter of the legendary Nat King Cole?

The rising star

Natalie Cole's stint with Black Magic gave her a taste for showbiz. She graduated with a B.A. in child psychology from the University of Massachusetts in 1972, but she carried on as a solo singer. By 1973 she was singing in more prestigious clubs, such as Shepheard's in New York City. At first she sang many of her father's songs—largely because this was what her audiences expected—but gradually she developed her own rhythm-and-blues style, which combined rock, soul, and jazz.

Cole's big break came in 1974, when she teamed up with Chuck Jackson and Marvin Yancy, two Chicago-based songwriters and producers. They arranged to write songs especially for Cole and to sign her up with a suitable record company, but they were turned down by almost every major company except

Capitol Records. This was the one company Cole had hoped to avoid because it had been her father's recording company. She was still trying to move out of his shadow. Nevertheless, Cole proved to be her father's daughter in the way she had instant success recording with Capitol.

Cole's first album, *Inseparable* (1975), went gold, selling more than half a million copies, and it brought her two hit singles and two Grammy Awards (for best new artist of the year and best rhythm-and-blues female singer). Her next album, *Natalie* (1976), also went gold, while her third album, *Thankful* (1977), went platinum, selling more than a million copies. Of Cole's next three albums, two went gold and one went platinum, so that by the end of the 1970s she had achieved six major albums that had brought her a string of awards, including more Grammies. She had also married her producer Marvin Yancy, converting to the Baptist faith in the process, since he was a Baptist minister.

The popularity of Cole's recordings helped her career as a performer, and in 1978 she hosted an hour-long television special. Later in the year she gave a hugely successful concert at the Metropolitan Opera House in New York. Now that Cole had perfected her rhythm-and-blues style she was often compared to the Queen of Soul, Aretha Franklin. This led to a feud between the two singers, though Cole hoped to patch it up. As she explained, "I'm still looking very much to being on compatible and harmonious terms with Aretha, because I think she is a great lady.... She could sing circles around me, just from the experiences she's had. So I could never try to com-

Natalie Cole

pare or put myself on the same level, because I learned from her."

Unforgettable

By the end of the 1970s, Cole's life looked set for a continuing success story. As well as her thousands of fans, she had a loving husband and an infant son, a nice home, plenty of money … everything anyone could want. But in fact Cole was already on the downward path because of her addictions. By the early 1980s she was so heavily into drugs and alcohol that her live performances were often a disaster. Her marriage broke up, and it looked as if her career would soon end too.

In 1983 Cole entered the Hazelden Clinic for a six-month treatment that helped her overcome her addiction. She then began the long, slow climb back in the music business. Although Cole's next album sold badly compared with her former successes, she finally staged a comeback in 1987 with *Everlasting,* which produced three hit singles. Two years later she married record producer Andre Fisher. Although Cole has since divorced, the marriage represented a comeback in her personal life, matching that in her career.

Cole's greatest achievement in the late 1980s was the acceptance of her heritage as Nat King Cole's daughter. Instead of fighting, she decided to make a record composed entirely of her father's songs. The resulting album, *Unforgettable* (1991), was her first number one album. It contained twenty-two of her father's biggest hits, including the title number "Unforgettable," which Cole sang as a duet with her father by singing alongside his own recording of the song.

Unforgettable was a phenomenal success, winning seven Grammy Awards, three of which were for Cole herself. When in 1993 she brought out another album of her father's songs, *Take a Look,* she was asked whether the public could again expect an electronically fashioned duet with her late father. "No," said Cole, "the duet was magic. To try to do it again would have been like a trick.... We did it right the first time. There was no reason to repeat it." But Cole does see a reason to continue singing her father's songs. By doing so she is keeping alive the legend of Nat King Cole and bringing his music to a huge new audience.

Bessie Coleman

Aviator
Born January 26, 1893, Atlanta, Texas
Died April 30, 1926

During the early 1920s, a young black manager of a chili restaurant in Chicago, Illinois, decided she wanted more out of life. The papers were filled with stories of the latest exploits of a new group of adventurers known as aviators. Deciding that was the career for her, Bessie Coleman pursued her dream across the ocean and became the first black woman to receive a pilot's license. She soon became a popular stunt and exhibition flier, thrilling thousands with her daring stunts. Although she died in an accident when she was only thirty-three, Coleman became an inspiration for a generation of black aviators.

Father leaves for Indian Territory

Coleman's family moved to Waxahachie, near Dallas, while she was still a youngster. Her father was three-quarters Indian, and he moved back to Indian Territory when Coleman was only seven years old. Her mother, Susan, was left to look after the family—four daughters and a son—and supported them by picking cotton and doing laundry. The children also pitched in and helped whenever they could. Although Susan could not read or write at that time, she encouraged her children to get an education.

After finishing high school, Bessie Coleman wanted to go to college. Her mother let her keep the money she made from washing and ironing, so she could pay her college expenses. She enrolled at Langston Industrial College (now Langston University) in Oklahoma. College cost more than she expected, and Coleman was forced to drop out after one semester. She moved to Chicago, where she took a manicuring course. Coleman eventually found work at the White Sox Barber Shop on Thirty-fifth Street near State Street. Later she managed a chili restaurant on the same street.

Coleman had always been interested in reading, and she used her spare moments reading about current affairs. She also became interested in the new field of aviation. Looking for a new challenge, she decided to learn how to fly and get her pilot's license. Coleman was soon discouraged when all of her applications for entering aviation schools were rejected. A close friend, Robert S. Abbott, founder and editor of the *Chicago Defender* newspaper, encouraged her to learn French and study aviation overseas. She took his advice and took lessons from French and German pilots. Coleman also studied under the chief aviator for Anthony Fokker's aircraft corporation and learned to fly the highly regarded German Fokker airplane.

Receives her pilot's license

Coleman returned briefly to the United States in 1921 with her pilot's license. She made another trip to Europe before heading back to the United States in 1922 with her international pilot's license. It was a remarkable feat. Coleman was the first black woman to earn pilot's licenses, only ten years after the first American woman had earned a license and less than twenty years after Orville and Wilbur Wright made their historic flight in 1903.

With barnstorming a popular attraction in the United States and the main area of aviation open to women, Coleman decided to become a stunt and exhibition flier. During the Labor Day weekend in 1922, she made her

Bessie Coleman

first appearance in an air show at Curtiss Field near New York City, sponsored by her friend Abbott and the *Chicago Defender*. Coleman repeated her performance six weeks later at the Checkerboard Airdrome (now Midway Airport) in Chicago, again sponsored by Abbott. Her manager was David L. Behncke, founder and president of the International Airline Pilots Association.

Coleman soon became known as Brave Bessie for her aviation exploits. She participated in air shows across the country, including her hometown of Waxahachie. She gave lectures on the opportunities in aviation at schools and churches wherever she went. While in California, she did some aerial advertising for the Firestone Rubber Company.

One of Coleman's lifelong dreams was to establish her own aviation school, where young black Americans could learn to fly and prepare for aviation careers. She saved money from her barnstorming and lecturing jobs, and by early 1926, she wrote to her sister Elois that she was on the verge of reaching her dream.

Tragedy at the air show

At the end of April 1926, Coleman accepted an invitation from the Negro Welfare League to perform in a Memorial Day air show. On April 30, 1926, Coleman and her mechanic made a practice run with the mechanic piloting the plane. During one of the maneuvers the plane's controls jammed. Coleman was catapulted out of the plane and fell to her death. She was fortunate to have seen her longtime supporter Robert Abbott in Jacksonville shortly before the accident. She had chanced to meet him in a restaurant, and they had a reunion the day before her death. Her body was flown to Chicago and last rites were held at the Pilgrim Baptist Church at Thirty-third Street and Indiana Avenue. The burial was held at the Lincoln Cemetery in southwest Chicago.

Although gone, Coleman was by no means forgotten. A few years later, many black fliers belonged to the Bessie Coleman Aero Club. A monthly publication, the *Bessie Coleman Aero News,* was circulated to these clubs in May 1930, with William J. Powell as editor. Powell also wrote the book *Black Wings* in 1934, which looked at African American aviators. At the front of the book was a picture of Coleman in her flying uniform. Powell dedicated the book to "the memory of Bessie Coleman ... who although possessed of all the feminine charms that man admires in the opposite sex, also displayed courage equal to that of the most daring men."

Black aviators also paid tribute to Coleman by flying in formation over Lincoln Cemetery on Memorial Day and dropping flowers on her grave. In 1975 the Bessie Coleman Aviators organization was formed in the Chicago area by young African American women who were actively interested in aviation and aerospace.

In 1990 a fifty-one-foot-long mural was unveiled at Lambert-Saint Louis International Airport that recognized African Americans' achievements in aviation from 1917 to 1990. Titled "Black Americans in Flight" and painted by Spencer Taylor, it depicts seventy-five men and women pioneers in aviation, including Coleman.

Marva Collins

Teacher
Born August 31, 1936, Monroeville, Alabama

"Read. Read. Read. The key to all learning is read ... and then read some more."

Since founding Westside Preparatory School in Chicago in 1975, Marva Collins has become one of the best-known teachers in America. She founded Westside Prep in order to provide quality education for poor, inner-city children who were not getting the attention they needed in the public school system. Treated as inferiors by teachers who showed little dedication, these children seemed destined to become failures.

It was Collins's aim to turn this process around, not only by teaching the children to read and write, but by giving them a sense of pride and self-worth. "You are unique—there is no one else like you," she told her students. Stimulated by her encouragement, the children approached their studies with new confidence, and many of them made such good progress that Collins was hailed as a "miracle worker."

First girl at her high school to refuse to take home economics

Marva Collins was born into a well-to-do family, the daughter of Bessie Knight and Henry Knight, Jr., an Alabama businessman. Her father owned a grocery store, a cattle ranch, and a funeral parlor, and he is said to have bought a new Cadillac each year for his funeral business.

Marva's early childhood was secure and happy, but when she was twelve her parents divorced, which was a great blow because she adored her father. She was taken to Atmore to live with her mother, who later remarried and had a second daughter, Cynthia. Meanwhile, Marva's role model continued to be her father. She admired his determination and firmly held values, and she was especially impressed by his courage. She had seen him stand firm against a group of whites who were threatening to kill him. Another strong influence was Marva's grandmother, who read stories to her when she was little, inspiring a lifelong passion for books. Marva learned to read very early, and she read everything from fairy tales to Shakespeare plays.

Since Marva could read so young, she had a good start with her education. After completing elementary school at Bethlehem Academy, she attended high school in Atmore at Escambia County Training School. There she approached her studies the way she later approached her teaching—with a firm idea of just how she wanted to do things. Marva was the first girl at Escambia to refuse to take the home economics course. She objected on principle, pointing out that when black girls took the course it simply reinforced the white view that black women could only be domestics or homemakers. Instead of home economics, Marva therefore learned typing.

After graduating from Escambia in 1953, Marva attended Clark College in Atlanta, Georgia, where she gained a bachelor's degree in secretarial science. However, this did not lead to a career as a secretary. As a young black woman, Marva could not find a suitable secretarial job, despite her training. So she went to Monroe County Training School, where for two years she taught business courses while receiving her basic teacher training from the principal. She then moved to Chicago, where she met and married Clarence Collins and where her career as a teacher began.

Dissatisfied with public schools, Collins opened her own

Marva Collins's first teaching position was at Calhoun South Elementary School, where she stayed for a year. Later, after the birth of her first child, she taught at Delano Elementary School.

Even during that first year Collins became known as a trouble maker, for she found much to dislike in the public school system. She regarded many of the teachers as uncaring, and she objected to the way black children and children from poor homes were so often belittled or abused. They were treated as failures without being given the chance to succeed, she said. She also disliked the way the lessons were supposed to be taught. The attitude was "Learn this and do as you are told" and not "get the students to think creatively and work things out for themselves."

Collins refused to teach this way. Instead of following the curriculum guide, she added subjects that were not in the curriculum. She kept the lessons lively and interesting, and she made a point of encouraging the students and building up their self-esteem. Inevitably this led to quarrels with her fellow teachers, for it was not in her character to compromise. Like her father, if she believed something ought to be done, she carried it through regardless of threats of opposition.

Nevertheless, Collins became more and more frustrated with the public school system,

Marva Collins

and she eventually decided to open her own school so that she could teach "the Marva Collins way." She financed the school largely from her pension fund and from her husband's money. She did not seek federal funding because she did not want to be restricted by federal regulations, though she did accept some funds from the Alternative Schools Network.

From the very beginning Collins's teaching methods proved their worth. There were only 4 students when Westside Preparatory School opened in 1975. A few years later there were 200 students and a waiting list of 800. Parents were lining up to get their children taught by Collins when they heard of the results she was achieving. Children who had been given up by their public school teachers as hopeless seemed to take on a new life under Collins's care. Most impressive were the high test scores at Westside Prep. They were far above the public school average.

What was the secret of Collins's success? Partly it was the way she gave her students confidence, taking a hands-on approach, hugging them to show her affection, and consciously building up their self-esteem. By continually telling her students what great things she expected of them, Collins encouraged them to meet these expectations, and she promised she would not let them fail even if they had failed at previous schools. Another important factor was the wholeness of the education Collins provided, building up character and attitudes as well as imparting knowledge. Finally, she made the learning process exciting and interesting. Lessons taught by Collins and her staff were fun.

Her students' success brought awards and media attention

In 1979 Collins became famous throughout America when she was interviewed on the CBS television program "60 Minutes." The following year the newly elected President Ronald Reagan offered Collins the position of secretary of education, but she turned it down to continue teaching. Meanwhile, newspaper articles and television shows featured Collins the "miracle worker," and in 1981 the television movie *The Marva Collins Story* was made. The next year she published the book *Marva Collins' Way.*

All this publicity attracted critics as well as admirers. Collins had made enemies during her years as a public school teacher, and now they came forward with all sorts of accusations to prove she was not as wonderful as others claimed. A common complaint was that she was impossibly overbearing—that she behaved "like some kind of God." As the criticism grew, a disgruntled former teacher from Westside Prep stated that Collins had exaggerated the success rate of her students' test scores.

Collins appeared twice on the "Donahue Show" to comment publicly on the various charges. Among her defenders was the admissions director of a Chicago private school who had tested forty-five Westside students over a four-year period and who confirmed that the test results had been as high as Collins claimed.

As to whether or not Collins should be called a "miracle worker," she pointed out that she herself never claimed to be one. It was others who called her this. "I'm just a teacher," she said. Yet she has had great influence on American education. The recipient of many awards, including Educator of the Year awards, Collins has served on the National Advisory Board on Private Education and on many other committees and organizations. As she continues to exert an influence on education, more and more children are being taught in "the Marva Collins way."

John Coltrane

Jazz saxophonist
Born September 23, 1926, Hamlet, North Carolina
Died July 17, 1967, Long Island, New York

"I have to feel that I'm after something. If I make money, fine. But I'd rather be striving. It's the striving, man, it's that I want."

One of the major forces in modern jazz, saxophonist John Coltrane was constantly experimenting in his music. He was known especially for his "sheets of sound"—runs that were so rapid that the individual notes were barely distinguishable.

Because Coltrane's playing was so new and inventive, it aroused considerable controversy and turned off many listeners. They found his compositions too harsh and strange, and some even dubbed his playing noise rather than music. Yet the dissonance with which Coltrane experimented became a keynote of jazz throughout the 1960s, influencing many younger players.

While some observers still belittle Coltrane's playing, others have hailed him as a genius and a musician with a deep purpose. In the view of critic Edward Strickland, "Coltrane was attempting to raise jazz from the saloons to the heavens.... In his use of jazz as prayer and meditation Coltrane was beyond all doubt the principal spiritual force in music."

A background of gospel music

Known as Trane by his close friends, John William Coltrane was the son of John and Alice (Blair) Coltrane. Both his grandfathers were ministers, and he was raised in the religious atmosphere of the Southern church, with its wealth of gospel music. Coltrane's father, a tailor, was a keen amateur musician who played several instruments, and Coltrane was encouraged to learn to play too.

The family moved to High Point, in the northern part of North Carolina, when Coltrane was a boy, and at William Penn High

John Coltrane

School he started playing the horn and clarinet. After listening to the records of the legendary bandleader Count Basie, he persuaded his mother to buy him an alto saxophone, and this became his favorite instrument and the one he played in the school band.

After Coltrane graduated from high school in 1943, his family moved to Philadelphia, where he studied at the Granoff Studios and at the Ornstein School of Music. In 1945 he had his first work as a musician as a member of a cocktail lounge quartet, and he continued with his music during his military service, when he played with a U.S. Navy band in Hawaii (1945–47). Of necessity, Coltrane's playing during these years was quite orthodox—band music rather than avant-garde explorations.

The avant-garde musician

On leaving the navy, the twenty-one-year-old Coltrane landed a spot playing tenor saxophone with Eddie Vinson's band. Then, in 1948, he joined Dizzy Gillespie's group, with which he played for the next four years. This brought him into contact with many of the jazz greats, including Charlie Parker, Miles Davis, and Thelonious Monk, from whom he learned many tricks of phrasing and harmony.

The 1950s saw the release of a number of Coltrane records, some of which he dedicated to his first wife Naima Gibbs, whom he married in 1955. Early in the decade he worked with Earl Bostic and Johnny Hodges, and between 1955 and 1960 he played in Miles Davis's group and with Thelonious Monk at the Five Spot in Greenwich Village. With both groups he made some classic recordings, including Miles Davis's album *Kind of Blue*, on which Coltrane played tenor saxophone. It was during these years that Coltrane developed his unique style, with its "sheets of sound" and other innovations. While some members of the public found his music monotonous, most jazz musicians found it tremendously exciting.

In 1960 Coltrane formed his own group, with McCoy Tyner on piano, Elvin Jones on drums, and Jimmy Garrison on bass. Like Coltrane, they were all eager to explore in the free idiom, taking jazz to a higher creative level. This group was expanded on some recordings to include eleven men as well as pianist Alice McLeod, who became Coltrane's second wife after his divorce from Naima. Coltrane's best-known recording from this period is "My Favorite Things," a piece based on the song of the same name from the popular musical, *The Sound of Music.*

Now that Coltrane was in a position to play exactly as he wished, he gave full rein to his imagination. Often his solos went on and on as he experimented with the ideas that were bursting in his head. He encouraged the others in his group to do likewise. As one of them recalled, "Often there was no music. He'd just announce what key we'd be playing in, or that we'd be playing in twelve tones and we'd take it from there."

In 1965 *Downbeat* magazine's readers' poll voted Coltrane top tenor saxophonist of the year. He was also named jazzman of the year, and his album *A Love Supreme* was chosen as record of the year. By this time Coltrane was widely recognized as one of the most famous living jazz artists, the "father of avant-garde jazz." His reputation had spread not only to Europe but to Japan, where his music was extremely popular.

Unfortunately, Coltrane was not to be a living jazz artist for much longer, for he was suffering from liver cancer. Even though racked with pain, he continued to perform—and to experiment. "I have to feel that I'm after something," he said. "If I make money, fine. But I'd rather be striving. It's the striving, man, it's that I want."

Coltrane continued to strive right until the end. He made his last album, *Expression,* only a few months before his death. Although he lived only forty years, he profoundly influenced the jazz of an entire generation and left a legacy that will influence generations to come.

Anna J. Cooper

Teacher, scholar
Born August 10, 1858, Raleigh, North
    Carolina
Died February 27, 1964, Washington, D.C.

"If there is an amibitious girl with pluck and brain to take the higher education, encourage her.... Let there be the same flourish of trumpets and clapping of hands as when a boy announces his determination to enter the lists."

Anna Julia Cooper lived for well over 100 years: born in the last years of slavery, she died in the year of the 1964 Civil Rights Act. During her long life Annie Cooper achieved success in number of fields—as a school teacher, a writer, a scholar, and as one of the first African American women to gain a Ph.D. Fearless in her convictions, she was a vigorous campaigner against racism and for racial pride; against unfairness and for justice; against male chauvinism and for the equality of women. Despite being born in unpromising circumstances as the daughter of a slave in a small rural community, she became a public figure on an international stage.

Acquired two degrees

Cooper never knew for certain who her father was, though he was probably slave owner George Washington Haywood. Her mother, Hannah Stanley (Haywood), was one of his slaves. Slavery was abolished while Cooper was a small child, and she became a student at St. Augustine's Normal School, which opened in Raleigh in 1868.

Cooper did well at school and then stayed on to teach, and in 1877 she married fellow teacher, George Cooper. Only two years later her husband died, and though in her early twenties, Cooper never remarried.

She decided to study for a university degree, which was no easy ambition for any woman in the nineteenth century. Very few colleges admitted woman, and even fewer admitted African Americans, but Oberlin College in Ohio was one of the exceptions, so Cooper enrolled there in 1881. She received her bachelor's degree in 1884, then taught at Wilberforce University and at her old school in Raleigh while preparing for her master's degree in mathematics, which she earned in 1887.

Cooper then moved to Washington, D.C., to teach at the Preparatory High School for Colored Youth, which in 1891 became the M Street High School (and was later renamed Paul Laurence Dunbar High School). She spent most of the next fifty years at this school, with a brief stint as principal (1902–06), then disagreed with the Board of Education and was dismissed. Cooper went to Lincoln University in Jefferson City, Missouri, where she was professor of languages until 1910, when she returned to M Street School as a Latin teacher.

Held progressive views

Cooper's dismissal from the M Street School resulted from a quarrel over curriculum. The Board of Education wanted to reduce the education in "colored" schools, and Cooper objected strongly. She was determined to give her students as wide an education as possible so they would have a better chance in the world

By the early 1900s Cooper had the confidence to speak her mind over issues she cared about. She had been doing so at conferences for the past ten years. Many of these conferences focused on the problems of racism and of how to help people who until recently were slaves and how to make their lives both safe and satisfying. Others, such as the National Conference of Colored Women (1895), dealt with women's issues.

Cooper was especially concerned about the difficulties women faced and was a strong spokesperson for women's rights. This was made very clear in her first book, a collection

Anna J. Cooper

of essays and conference papers published in 1892 under the title *A Voice from the South: By a Black Woman from the South.* In this book Cooper hotly contested the popular argument that education was bad for women because it ruined their chances of marriage. Educated women, she said, not only lived far fuller lives but were a benefit to the world at large.

Earned her Ph.D. from the Sorbonne

Some conferences took Cooper overseas, and in the early 1900s she traveled through Europe, visiting the major sights, including the Paris Exposition in France. Partly as a result of her visit to France, she developed the ambition to gain a doctor's degree from the Sorbonne, the arts and letters school of the University of Paris. Since she was teaching in Washington at the time, it took her more than ten years, attending the Guide Internationale

in Paris during the summers of 1911, 1912, and 1913, and then studying at Columbia University in the summers of 1914–17. In 1925, when she was 66 years old, she was awarded her Ph.D. by the Sorbonne.

Cooper had completed two theses in order to get her doctorate. One was an edited version of a medieval tale about Charlemagne. The other was a historical work called *L'Attitude de la France a l'egard de l'esclavage pendant la Revolution* (France's attitude on slavery during the Revolution). Although the title mentions only French attitudes, the thesis dealt with slavery on both sides of the Atlantic. It examined how the slaves of Saint Dominique threw off their oppressors and formed an independent nation called Haiti, and compared the Haitian situation with that in the Bahamas and North Carolina.

The opening lines of the thesis stated: "Slavery in the European colonies of the Americas was an institution based solely on an abuse of force. Created by a short-sighted and barbarous policy and maintained by violence, we shall see that it could quickly be abolished by a simple legislative measure." As the work of an African American who was born into slavery, Cooper's thesis took a more sensitive approach than many studies have done, and it has been of great interest to scholars.

Although Cooper was past retirement age when her thesis was published, she was still hard at work promoting the causes she believed in. Late in life she became president of Frelinghuysen University, which provided adult education for African Americans.

Don Cornelius

Broadcasting executive
Born September 27, 1936, Chicago, Illinois

"Blacks have the option to listen to black radio stations or white radio stations. Read black magazines or white magazines.... But with television we're not able to choose the kind of television entertainment we see, except maybe once or twice a week."

The cameras come on, the lights flash on and off, and about forty dancers swing and bop to the music. Amid the revelry steps Don Cornelius in his flashy outfit, microphone ready to introduce his first guest performer. The show is called "Soul Train," the longest running music show in the history of television.

"Soul Train" is Cornelius's pet project. He came up with the idea in the late 1960s and was responsible for producing, hosting, and lining up the advertisers for the show. He overcame skeptical broadcasting and advertising executives to create a show that catered to a mainly black viewing audience. Cornelius was also instrumental in creating the first Soul Train Music Awards, which were dedicated exclusively to black musicians.

A radio career

Cornelius was born on September 27, 1936, and grew up on Chicago's South Side. He attended DuSable High School, where he studied art and drew cartoons for the school newspaper. After graduating in 1954, he joined the U.S. Marines and served eighteen months on a Korean airbase.

Cornelius returned to Chicago in 1956 and married his childhood sweetheart, Delores Harrison. Two years later, they had a son, Anthony, and in 1959 another son, Raymond. Cornelius did not have enough money for college, so he sold tires, cars, and insurance. By 1966 he was making $250 a week, but since he had always been interested in becoming a radio announcer, he spent $400 on a broadcasting course and landed a part-time job as an announcer with Chicago-based WVON. He was making only $100 a week, but he was doing what he wanted to do. "I started as a newsman, but I was also the swing [overnight] man," he told *Billboard*. "I filled in as an all-around substitute at WVON. I felt I had to justify my job there.... It was a very black station. I was sitting in for DJs and newspeople, doing public affairs outside the station, doing the talk show, and doing commercials."

In 1968 Roy Wood, Cornelius's boss, left WVON to join WCIU-TV, and Cornelius began to moonlight there as the sports anchor of "A Black View of the News." While working at WCIU, he started thinking about a new television show, "Soul Train." He took the name from a traveling music show he had hosted for WVON. The format was based on Dick Clark's "American Bandstand," which featured dancing teenagers and popular records. While "Bandstand" catered to a white audience, "Soul Train" followed a black music format. When Cornelius made his pitch, WCIU was interested in "ethnic" programming and agreed to give it a try.

Cornelius still needed a sponsor to make the program fly. His pitch fell on deaf ears until he met George O'Hare, a merchandise manager at Sears, Roebuck & Co. "George was a guy that ... was always receptive to new concepts," Cornelius said in *Billboard*. "When I went in I expected him to tell me what so many others had said about programming for Blacks. The theory that Blacks 'need' cultural or historical programs and not necessarily entertainment."

"Soul Train" makes its debut

"Soul Train" debuted on August 17, 1970, and featured dancers, a live appearance by singer Jerry Butler of the Impressions, and Cornelius in an outlandish outfit. Later shows featured guest artists performing in front of about forty dancing couples. The set featured flashing red and yellow train lights. Dancers also confronted guests such as Aretha Franklin, James Brown, and Al Green with blunt questions on their political views. If a performance was subpar, the dancers would show their displeasure by dancing right up on the stage.

Cornelius not only hosted the show, he also produced it and sold all the advertising. Within weeks, it was the number one show among blacks in Chicago, but many advertisers did not support the show. They felt they could get the same audience by advertising on general audience shows. Through a lot of hard work, Cornelius managed to win over a number of advertisers including Wate-On, Joe Louis Milk, and Coca-Cola.

Based on his success in Chicago, Cornelius decided to take "Soul Train" national. Sponsorship was again the key, but this time things

Don Cornelius

went more smoothly. George Johnson, president of Johnson Products, a black-owned manufacturer of hair and facial cosmetics, signed on. "Soul Train" was directed at Johnson's target audience—young blacks.

"Soul Train" went nationwide on a weekly basis on October 2, 1971. It was produced at Hollywood's Metromedia Studios and was slicker and more colorful than the original show. Cornelius was confident of success, but he had many doubters. The syndicating agency was able to debut the show in only seven of the twenty-five areas Cornelius had targeted, but within eight months, all twenty-five stations had signed on. The big payoff occurred in August 1972, when Johnson Products signed a $1 million advertising deal.

Much of the show's success came at the expense of "American Bandstand." Clark tried to fight back with a copy cat show "Soul Unlimited," which was backed by the ABC-TV network, while "Soul Train" had no network affiliation. Before the controversy got out of hand, Cornelius and Clark worked out an agreement. Clark dropped "Soul Unlimited" and offered to coproduce some black specials with Cornelius for ABC. By 1974 "Soul Train" had attracted ninety-five stations.

"I'd like to say it was a struggle," Cornelius told *Billboard*, "but it really wasn't; it just was a thing that was so long overdue that it caught on instantaneously. The point is that there should be far more than just one hour of Black-oriented entertainment. Anybody could see that there was a market there, but it's so difficult to get something like that started unless you get ... money and some kind of reputation."

Soul Train Records

With the television show doing well, Cornelius turned his attention toward records. He teamed up with Dick Griffey, a promoter and talent coordinator for "Soul Train," to form Soul Train Records. They released only twelve albums per year, with RCA handling distribution. Among the early albums was *Soul Train '75*, which featured participants from the television show, as well as an album by the Whispers—a group that included Jody Watley, a former "Soul Train" dancer and later a popular solo recording artist. The company lasted for three years, after which Cornelius and Griffey went separate ways.

"Soul Train" continued to be popular and even spun off a British version called "6:20 Soul Train." The only trouble Cornelius ran into was scheduling. Many stations put "Soul Train" on late at night, rather than keeping it in its regular Saturday morning slot. "There was and still is," Cornelius commented in *Billboard,* "a trend towards putting all music shows on at night or in the middle of the night.... I disagreed with it because so many young people watch our show and they obviously can't see it at 2 o'clock in the morning."

Cornelius took a six-month leave of absence at the end of 1982 following life-threatening brain surgery. The operation lasted twenty-one hours and was performed to prevent the risk of possible leakage or hemorrhaging of blood vessels in the brain. He returned to work in March 1983.

Three years later, Cornelius established the Soul Train Music Awards, the first music awards show dedicated to black musicians. The show attracted a wide following and big name advertisers such as Chrysler Corporation in 1990. "We were stereotyped to where we weren't supposed to sell anything but black hair-care products and records. Of course, now it's known that we buy tires and shoes and houses too."

In 1992 "Soul Train" became the longest-running music program in syndication. "Twenty years ago every region of the country had its own style," Cornelius told *Interview.* "But now dancing—at least street dancing—has become a universal language, and I think that's due to television in general and 'Soul Train' in particular."

Bill Cosby

Actor, philanthropist
Born July 12, 1937, Philadelphia,
    Pennsylvania

"I'm trying to reach all people. I want to play Joe Q. Public."

The famous and wildly successful Bill Cosby is well known as Dr. Cliff Huxtable on his recent television series *The Cosby Show*. He broke into television when he landed a major role in the 1965 show *I Spy*. Co-starring with Robert Culp, Cosby played a globe-trotting secret agent who defended American rights. He won three consecutive Emmy awards as outstanding actor in a dramatic series for this role.

Afterwards Cosby became a popular comedian who played to sold-out performances. He produced twenty-seven comedy records, and it was reported that he sold more records than any entertainer except Herb Alpert. He landed roles in a variety of television shows and in 1984 created *The Cosby Show*, which remained the number one show for several years.

Much of Cosby's widespread appeal can be traced to his early efforts to de-emphasize race. He did not tell racist jokes, and his television shows have always aimed to depict real people, not stereotypes.

Had a knack for making people laugh

Cosby was born in an all-black ghetto in north Philadelphia on July 12, 1937. His father, William Cosby, was a mess steward for the U.S. Navy; and his mother, Anna, was a domestic worker. As a youngster, Cosby became known for his athletic skill and sense of humor. He paid close attention to the way advertising salesmen sold their products on television and

began mimicking their style in his school yard comedy routines. Young Cosby did well on standardized testing, but his grades were poor. While attending Germantown High School, he was captain of both the track and football teams, but after failing grade ten, he dropped out and joined the Navy.

Cosby spent four years in the Navy and was assigned to land and sea duty. He also earned a high school diploma through correspondence courses. After leaving the Navy, he entered Temple University in Philadelphia on a track scholarship. He majored in physical education and played on the track and football teams. He spent his off-hours as a bartender, where he entertained the customers with his comedy routines. Encouraged by their reception, he left Temple in 1962 to pursue a career in show business.

First black to star in a television series

Cosby's early days as a comedian were similar to any other comics, except that his humor was a gentle middle-class variety that did not feature racial or sexual jokes, but rather focused on everyday family situations. He began playing small clubs around Philadelphia and New York's Greenwich Village, and within two years he was performing in clubs across the United States, sharing the stage with Woody Allen and other well-known comedians. He got his first big break in 1965 during an appearance on the popular television program *The Tonight Show*. Producer Sheldon Leonard offered him a part in his new television series, *I Spy*. The story was about the adventures of two American secret agents who traveled disguised as a tennis player and his trainer. Despite the serious nature of the show, the scripts allowed Cosby and co-star Robert Culp to develop a humorous style, and the show attracted a large following.

This was the first time a black person had been offered a starring role in a television series. Although the program was well received, Cosby was criticized by some of the militant members of the civil rights movement who said his character was too dull and not a proper representation of black people. Cosby replied that the series was not about the problems of black Americans; he was simply portraying an average human being, without regard to race.

Established a successful performing career

After *I Spy* was canceled in 1968, Cosby starred in another series, *The Bill Cosby Show,* about a physical education teacher at a Los Angeles high school. The high school was in a lower-middle-class neighborhood, and the show focused on Cosby's relationships with students, family, and other teachers. It received high ratings its first year but was canceled during its second.

At the same time he was on television, Cosby was also performing at Las Vegas clubs and making comedy records. *Life* magazine reported that Cosby was making about $50,000 per show. By the time he was in his early thirties, he was a multimillionaire.

In 1972 Cosby started a Saturday morning children's program entitled *Fat Albert and the Cosby Kids*. This cartoon show featured

characters based on real-life people Cosby knew during his childhood. That same year he co-starred with Culp in the movie *Hickey and Boggs*. He followed with several other films including *Uptown Saturday Night, Mother, Jugs and Speed*, and *Leonard Part VI*. He also made numerous commercials for such products as Jell-O pudding, Coca-Cola, and Kodak film.

Cosby also became interested in furthering his education, so he enrolled in a part-time doctoral program in education at the University of Massachusetts at Amherst. He received his doctorate in 1977.

Cosby appeared in two other television series during the 1970s. The unsuccessful variety programs featured him with several guests, but they both ended after one season. In 1984 he approached the networks to try another series about a New York family simi-

Bill Cosby

lar to Cosby's real-life family. Only the third-rated network, NBC, was willing to take a chance.

Created television family that broke audience records

The new *Cosby Show* began in September 1984 and focused on the adventures of the Huxtable family. Just like Cosby's real-life family, with four girls and a son, the television series featured Cosby as Cliff Huxtable, an obstetrician, who lived with his wife and five children. *The Cosby Show* became a surprise hit, achieving audience levels that had not been reached for years. It became the number one ranked show with an estimated audience of 60 million Americans.

The show continued Cosby's particular brand of humor, in which sexual and racial humor were avoided, and the show represented the adventures and experiences of a typical family. Some critics said the program was not very realistic for American blacks, but Cosby replied that the show was meant to reach all the peoples of the world, not just blacks. The program reflected human values and was intended to speak to human beings no matter what race.

The Cosby Show provided even greater financial rewards for Cosby. Syndication (or rebroadcasting) rights for the program set monetary records and may eventually reach $1 billion. Cosby owns one-third of those rights. He also wrote the book *Fatherhood* in 1986, which was well received by the public, and his fees for appearances and commercials are also at all-time highs.

Endowed Spelman College with largest gift in its history

In 1988 he donated $20 million to Spelman College, the school for African American women in Atlanta, Georgia. The contribution was the largest individual gift the college had received in its 107 year history, and the largest such gift ever made by an African American.

Elizabeth Cotten

Folksinger
Born January 1892, Chapel Hill, North
 Carolina
Died June 29, 1987, Syracuse, New York

"I banged that guitar all day and I banged it all night so nobody could sleep. Nobody helped me. I give myself credit for everything I learned."

Elizabeth "Libba" Cotten first started on her career when she was sixty-seven. Between then and her death at the age of ninety-five, she became famous across the world as a folksinger and composer, and as the guitar player who introduced the "Cotten style" of guitar picking.

Although Cotten had taught herself the guitar when she was a child, she spent most of her life working as a domestic. Her song "Freight Train," which became so popular in the 1960s, was composed when she was eleven. Even more extraordinary is the fact that it was purely by chance that her talent was discovered—and that although this happened

Elizabeth Cotten

so very late in life, she still enjoyed a thirty-year career.

Dropped out of school to earn money for her first guitar

Libba Cotten was the youngest of the five children of George Nevills, an iron miner, and his wife Louisa (Price) Nevills. Chapel Hill in the North Carolina Piedmont, where she spent her childhood, had a strong blues tradition, and both blues and rags were played at local gatherings. The Nevills family were all very musical, playing a variety of instruments and singing in the local church, though most of them could not read music. Like the others, Cotten harmonized instinctively, knowing from the melody when to go up or down. Eager to learn to play an instrument, she taught herself by practicing on her brother's banjo when he was out at work.

When Cotten was eleven, she dropped out of school to earn money to buy a guitar.

Going from house to house, she announced, "I can scrub the floor and wash clothes and dust the furniture and carry in the wood and chips." This sales pitch landed her a job at 75 cents a month, and a few months later she was able to buy her first guitar, which cost all of $3.75. She then settled down to teach herself how to play it.

Cotten had a unique playing style because she was left-handed and had first learned on a banjo strung for right-handed players. When she started with the guitar, she found she couldn't play it when it was strung for a left-handed player. She had to play it the way she had taught herself on her brother's banjo—holding it upside down, with the bass strings on the bottom. As a result, she played the bass strings with her fingers and the treble with her thumb, achieving a different rhythmic effect than other musicians. The two-finger and banjo stylings she developed became known as "Cotton picking" or "Cotten style."

With her new guitar and her original style of playing, Cotten seemed all set to follow a musical career, writing such songs as "Freight Train." But at fifteen she eloped with her boyfriend, Frank Cotten, and at sixteen she gave birth to a daughter, Lillie. She then did what her elders expected her to do—she settled down to be a wife and mother.

Discovered by the Seeger family

Cotten's husband was a chauffeur who eventually opened his own business in New York, where he settled his wife and daughter. Meanwhile Cotten herself took a variety of jobs, usually as a domestic servant. Since this occupied most of her time and energy, she let her guitar playing lapse. After her divorce in the late 1940s she moved to Washington, D.C., where her daughter was then living, but she still could not concentrate on her music, because she had to earn a living. She found a job in the toy department of Lansburgh's Department Store.

It was in Lansburgh's that a small incident changed Cotten's life. A little girl had wandered off by herself and was lost, and Cotten comforted the child and took her by the hand to find her mother. The mother turned out to be the composer and music teacher Ruth Seeger, wife of musicologist Charles Seeger.

While chatting with Cotten and thanking her for finding little Peggy, Ruth Seeger told her that if she ever wanted to leave Lansburgh's, she would be welcome to come and work for them in Chevy Chase, Maryland. Cotten took up the offer, and a short while later she was "discovered" by the Seegers, who overheard her practicing in the kitchen on young Peggy's guitar. Ruth Seeger was fascinated to hear the songs Cotten played, for she was compiling a folksong collection at the time.

Cotten could hardly have found a more suitable family to launch her on her musical career. Ruth Seeger's stepson was folksinger Pete Seeger, and her daughter Peggy and son Mike followed in Pete's footsteps as soon as they were old enough. Cotten's first professional performance, in 1959, was with Mike Seeger at a concert at Swarthmore College in Pennsylvania.

From then on, Cotten was a regular performer at folk festivals, in concert halls, and on college campuses, where she always attracted large crowds. Pete Seeger has described how, in 1968, "Libba Cotten, 72 years old and black, got a standing ovation from 3000 white students at Duke University." Many of the songs she sang were her own compositions, including the popular "Washington Blues," a ragtime piece she had written many years earlier.

In 1982, at the age of ninety, Cotten toured Europe and America with Taj Mahal. The year afterwards she toured on her own for four months, and she did so again the year after that. As always, she opened her concerts by chatting informally with the audience, strumming lightly on the guitar while she told them a little about herself or discussed the songs she was going to sing. She kept the same intimate style on some of her records. Cotten made four records: *Negro Folk Songs and Tunes* (1957), *Shake Sugaree* (1967), *When I'm Gone* (1975), and *Elizabeth Cotton Live!* (1983). She won several awards, including a Grammy, and the National Folk Festival Association honored her with the Burl Ives Award for her "unique contribution to folk music."

Ellen Craft

Abolitionist and school founder
Born c. 1826, Clinton, Georgia
Died c. 1897, Charleston, South Carolina

"I would much rather starve in England, a free woman, than be a slave for the best man that ever breathed upon the American continent."

Born a slave on a Georgia plantation, Ellen Craft is famous for her daring escape with her husband, William. The story of their getaway is recounted in their book, *Running a Thousand Miles for Freedom* (1860).

After the Crafts gained their freedom, they joined the abolitionists in giving lectures against slavery and working to get the practice abolished. They lived for several years in England, where they attracted great publicity with the stories of their adventures. On returning to the United States after the Civil War, they settled in Georgia, where they opened an industrial school.

Born to slavery and determined to escape it

Ellen Craft was the daughter of a slave known as Maria. Her father was white plantation owner Major James Smith—her mother's master. As a child growing up on the plantation, Ellen was so pale skinned and looked so much like the Smith children that she was often taken to be a member of the family. This so annoyed Mrs. Smith that she took the first opportunity to rid herself of the child. She gave Ellen away as a wedding present when her eldest daughter married and went to live in Macon, Georgia.

Ellen was eleven at the time, and although she was treated well as a favorite house servant, she missed her mother. In time she found a friend in William Craft, one of the male slaves. As Ellen grew older, William asked her to marry him, but she refused, because she did not want to bear children who would grow up in slavery. Only after she and William had

hatched a plan of escape did she change her mind and marry him—having first, of course, obtained permission from her owners.

During this time William was carefully saving money for their flight north. He was able to earn money because he was hired out to a cabinetmaker. Meanwhile Ellen was making her disguise. Since she was so pale skinned, they decided that she should pose as a young white man traveling with his black servant. (She could not pose as a white woman, because a white woman would not travel alone with a male slave.) However, there were two problems with this scheme: first, a white man would have a beard; second, he would be required to sign hotel registers and other documents. Ellen did not have a beard, and she had never been taught to write. She solved both problems by swathing herself in bandages, thus appearing to be a sickly young man with a bandage round part of his face and his right arm in a sling.

Surprisingly, this subterfuge worked. The couple took off in December 1848, just before Christmas. Ellen dressed herself in the men's clothes she had made, cut her hair short, wrapped herself in bandages, and wore a pair of eyeglasses with green shades. She did indeed pass as a young man. Traveling by train the first day, she found herself sitting next to an elderly white man who had dined with her owners the previous evening. Yet he did not recognize her, and Ellen avoided speaking to him by turning her back and staring fixedly out of the window.

William had obtained permission for a few days' leave over the Christmas holiday, so the couple hoped to be a long way north by the

Ellen Craft

time they were missed. They traveled by train and steamer and had few problems until they reached Baltimore, Maryland. Since this was the last stop before the train entered the free state of Pennsylvania, officials were on the lookout for runaway slaves. A railroad agent demanded to know why William was traveling without papers—why did he not have the documents required of all slaves traveling north? William explained that this was an emergency—his "master" was extremely sick and desperately in need of medical care. When the other passengers backed him up, the agent let the couple continue their journey. It had been a close call.

Ku Klux Klan torched their school

When they arrived in Philadelphia the next day, Ellen was happy to be able to abandon her disguise. It was wonderful to be in a free state. They were befriended by white Quakers and free blacks, and they stayed for several weeks with a Quaker family, who began to teach them to read and write.

The Crafts then moved on to Boston, another center of abolitionist activity, where they lived for the next two years. William worked as a cabinetmaker while Ellen trained to be an upholsterer, and both appeared from time to time at abolitionist meetings to give an account of their escape or to describe the miseries of slavery.

This period of their life changed when the Fugitive Slave Law was passed in 1850. The law allowed slaveowners in the South to send agents into the northern states to catch escaped slaves and bring them back, which meant that no escaped slave was safe anywhere in the Union. Because of the Crafts' activities with the abolitionists, their former owners knew they were in Boston and sent two agents to arrest them. But the Crafts escaped to Nova Scotia before they could be captured. From there, with the help of the abolitionists, they traveled to England, where the law protected them from capture.

In England the Crafts were again looked after by abolitionists. They went on speaking tours with another former slave, William Welles Brown, and appeared at the 1851 Great Exhibition at the Crystal Palace in London. But even though slavery was outlawed in England, there was still racial prejudice, and the story went round that Ellen wanted to leave William and return to the security of being a slave. Ellen responded to the outrageous suggestion in a letter she wrote to the paper, saying she "would much rather starve in England, a free woman, than be a slave for the best man that ever breathed upon the American continent."

The Crafts had five children during their years in England. They supported themselves by teaching manual crafts at a school in Surrey, and during the Civil War they volunteered in the British and Foreign Freedmen's Aid Society. Returning to the United States in 1868, they lived in Boston for a while and then settled in Georgia, where they founded an industrial school to teach farming to young African Americans. Recalling her slave days, Ellen forbade any whippings in the school. The school was succeeding until the place was destroyed by a fire set by the Ku Klux Klan. But the Crafts had surmounted worse difficulties than this during their lives, and they simply started over again on land they bought near Savannah.

They were a remarkable couple, and their children followed in their footsteps. One of their daughters married William Demos Crum, a physician who served as United States minister to Liberia. Ellen was staying with the Crums in Charleston at the time of her death. In accordance with her wishes, she was buried under her favorite tree on her Georgia plantation. Three years later William joined her there.

Countee Cullen

Poet
Born May 30, 1903, Louisville, Kentucky
Died January 9, 1946, New York, New York

"To read Countee Cullen's work is to hear a voice as representative of the Harlem Renaissance as it is possible to find."

A leading figure in the Harlem Renaissance, Countee Cullen is considered to be the writer who best represents that vigorous flowering of black culture in the 1920s. The Harlem Renaissance grew out of the frustrated expectations the black community experienced following World War I. Black soldiers who had risked their lives in the war could not even find jobs. They thronged the cities looking for work, and the injustice was expressed by the intellectuals, many of whom voiced their protest through their art. Harlem and other large black communities became vibrant centers of culture, with writers and artists producing fresh new works about black life, often harking back to their African roots.

Thrived in his adopted home

Little is known about Countee Cullen before his adoption in 1918. Even his place of birth is uncertain, though it is generally considered to be Louisville, Kentucky. The boy's mother, Elizabeth Lucas, named him Countee LeRoy Porter and then passed him over to his grandmother, who looked after him until her death. The fifteen-year-old Countee Porter was then adopted by a minister and his wife, Frederick and Carolyn Cullen of the Salem Methodist Episcopal Church in Harlem.

In his adopted father's home Cullen came under the influences that would shape his poetry, for the Salem Methodist Episcopal Church was a nerve center of local action. Here he heard discussions about racial injustice and the many other problems concerning the black community. His adopted father, Reverend Cullen, was an active member of the

Countee Cullen

Harlem chapter of the National Association for the Advancement of Colored People (NAACP) and later served as its chapter president.

Already writing some poetry before being adopted, Cullen was encouraged to develop his talent. At the largely white De Witt Clinton High School in New York he joined the local poetry group and was treasurer of the Inter-High School Poetry Society. He also edited the school magazine, which in 1921 published his poem "I Have a Rendezvous with Life." Like several of his early efforts, this poem won a prize. He graduated from high school in 1922.

Cullen won other prizes during college years. In 1923 his "Ballad of the Brown Girl" won second prize in the national Witter Bynner Poetry Contest, and in 1925 he won first prize in the Witter Bynner and won several other important awards as well. Twenty-two years old, the somewhat cocky young man had a succession of other accomplishments that year: he graduated with a B.A. from New York University, was accepted to a master's degree program at Harvard, and had his first book of poems published by the well-known trade publisher Harper & Row. The book was called *Color*.

Critically acclaimed for his first book

Many of Cullen's best-known poems appeared in *Color*. The book collected 73 poems arranged in three sections—"Color," "Epitaphs," and "Varia"—and it dealt with the major themes that were to dominate his work. The theme of racial injustice was movingly expressed in such poems as "Incident" and "Atlantic City Waiter." "Atlantic City Waiter" also emphasized African origins and a romantic nostalgia for the old days in Africa, a theme repeated in "Heritage" and many other poems in *Color*.

Despite the racial themes in the books, Cullen desired to be known as a poet, not as a black poet. His success in a largely white culture at school and university made him resent being later classified by color. This was his theme in his well-known poem "Yet Do I Marvel":

> Yet do I marvel at this curious thing:
> To make a poet black, and bid him sing!

Because Cullen was determined to bridge the gap between black and white writers, he did not find it inconsistent to take the English poet John Keats as his model. The "Epitaphs" section of *Color* contains poems on Keats as well as on the nineteenth-century African American writer Paul Laurence Dunbar, while the "Varia" section includes the well-known poem "To John Keats, Poet. At Springtime."

Cullen enjoyed great success with *Color,* which received excellent reviews and was awarded the Harmon Foundation's first gold medal for literature two years later.

Wrote his major works from France

After completing his master's degree from Harvard in 1926, Cullen worked as assistant editor at *Opportunity* magazine, for which he wrote a column called "The Dark Tower." In 1928 he won a Guggenheim fellowship, allowing him to travel, and he spent much of the next six years in France. Prior to leaving, he married Nina DuBois, the daughter of W. E. B. DuBois, the well-known leader of the African American intellectual community. The wedding was Harlem's social event of the year, though the marriage failed almost immediately. Cullen had a happier second marriage, in 1940, to Ida Robertson.

By the end of the 1920s Cullen published three more poetry collections, *The Ballad of the Brown Girl* (1927), *Copper Sun* (1927), and *The Black Christ and Other Poems* (1929). Although he later published several more collections, Cullens is remembered for these earlier works.

In 1932 Cullen published his only novel, *One Way to Heaven,* but he was more successful with his stories for children. After returning from France in 1934, he taught at Frederick Douglass Junior High School in New York,

and to help inspire sound values in young people he wrote two collections of stories: *The Lost Zoo* (1940) and *My Lives and How I Lost Them* (1942).

Cullen had also been trying his hand at writing for the theater, his most noted effort being the musical "St. Louis Woman," based on Arna Bontemps's first novel. Objections raised about it being demeaning to blacks delayed the show's production, but Cullen never lived to see it staged. He died of uremic poisoning three months before it opened in New York.

Angela Davis

Social activist, educator
Born January 26, 1944, Birmingham, Alabama

After growing up in a racist-filled area and attending universities that discussed class struggles, Angela Davis grew up with a determination to improve black rights. She was a member of many influential black rights groups and the Communist Party.

She was a popular lecturer at the University of California, but she was fired twice for her beliefs. Davis rose to national prominence after a gun she had purchased was used in a murder. She was placed on the FBI's most wanted list in connection with this crime, and attracted a huge following that staged protests around the world to free her. She was eventually acquitted.

Her supporters eventually formed the National Alliance Against Racist and Political

Angela Davis

Repression, which now has over 20 chapters. She has written numerous essays on her social and political beliefs, and is in high demand as a university lecturer.

Lived on Dynamite Hill

Davis was born on January 26, 1944, in Birmingham, Alabama. Her father, B. Frank, owned a gas station and worked as a mechanic after having been a teacher, a profession he quit because of its low pay. Her mother, Sallye, also a teacher, taught Davis to read and write before she started school. The family lived in a middle-class area of Birmingham called "Dynamite Hill" because the Ku Klux Klan frequently bombed the area.

At the segregated Carrie A. Tuggle Elementary School Davis learned about such famous black Americans as Frederick Douglass, Sojourner Truth, and Harriet Tubman, as well as traditional black music and customs, all of which instilled a sense of pride within her. However, the black teachers also stressed that blacks would amount to nothing if they did not work hard. The barrier of race was hardly mentioned.

Transferred to a New York school

At Parker High School Davis became dissatisfied with the teachers and found the courses unstimulating. In her junior year she was accepted to the Elizabeth Irwin High School on a scholarship from the American Friends Service Committee. She stayed with the family of William Howard Melish, an Episcopalian minister and winner of the 1956 Stockholm peace prize. While in New York, Davis was introduced to socialist ideology and joined Advance, a Marxist-Leninist group.

In 1961 Davis entered Brandeis University in Waltham, Massachusetts, spending her junior year at the Sorbonne in Paris.

Educated abroad

In Paris Davis studied under the philosopher Herbert Marcuse in 1964–65, which made her feel even more resistant toward a system that had made blacks subservient.

After graduating, Davis studied with the philosophy faculty at the University of Frankfurt. The professors felt she was one of the best students they had ever taught, and she had mastered French and German in the process.

Joined radical organizations

Davis completed her master's degree in philosophy in 1969 at the University of California at San Diego under the tutellage of Marcuse, who came to San Diego after his retirement from Brandeis. By the end of the next year she finished all the requirements for her doctorate except her dissertation. Davis became involved in civil rights by assisting the Black Students Council, developing a program for an experimental college for minorities, and supporting the San Diego Black Conference.

In 1968 she moved to Los Angeles and joined the Student Nonviolent Coordinating Committee and the Black Panthers, both were dedicated to black liberation. However, she became frustrated with these male-dominated groups, so, after studying the groups similar to her own political and social philosophy, she joined the Communist party on June 22, 1968.

Regents plot to get her fired

Davis joined the faculty of the department of philosophy at the University of California at Los Angeles in spring 1969 and taught four courses, "Dialectical Materialism," "Kant," "Existentialism," and "Recurring Political Themes in Black Literature." Although her courses were popular, she ran into trouble with the board of regents because of her Communist party membership. When her membership became public, the board of regents— under pressure from California governor Ronald Reagan—fired her, though eventually the courts overturned the action as a violation of her constitutional rights.

The board of regents looked for other ways to have her fired. At the end of the 1969–70 academic year they refused to renew her contract because she lacked a doctorate and allegedly made controversial statements in the community. The statements the regents

referred to were made in speeches on behalf of prison inmates George Jackson and W.L. Nolen, both communists. In 1970 Nolen and two prisoners got into a fight and were killed by shots from the guard tower. When a white guard was found murdered, Jackson and two other prisoners were indicted for his murder.

Davis took up the prisoners' cause by organizing, picketing, and making speeches to raise defense funds. Without ever having seen Jackson, she fell in love with him through a series of secret letters. He was killed by the guards during an alleged escape attempt, although charges against him had been dropped.

Went underground, until arrested by FBI

Davis herself had been getting death threats, so she legally purchased guns to defend herself. But she was in big trouble when her guns were used in a murder. On August 7, 1970, Jonathan Jackson, George's brother, took the guns to the Marion County Courthouse in San Rafad, where prisoner James McClain was on trial for stabbing an inmate at San Quentin. Jackson took out the guns, held hostages, and made a run for a van in the parking lot. Before the van could be driven away, Jackson, a judge, and two prisoners were killed.

When the guns were found to be registered in Davis's name, a federal warrant was issued for her arrest. Davis went into hiding, and on August 18, 1970, the Federal Bureau of Investigations (FBI) placed her on the Ten Most Wanted list for kidnapping, conspiracy, and murder. After a two-month search, the FBI tracked her down to a New York motel room. Arrested and transferred to California, she remained in jail without bail until the call for her release developed into a world-wide protest. Rallies took place everywhere from Los Angeles to Paris to Sri Lanka. Finally on February 23, 1972, a judge released Davis on $102,000 bond.

At her trial her lawyer argued there was insufficient evidence to prove she was part of the murderers' plans. After deliberating for thirteen hours, the jury found her not guilty on all counts. She soon consolidated her supporters into a new organization to fight racism and sexism. This group became known as the Alliance Against Racism and Political Repression. She has spoken on behalf of the organization and has led demonstrations on various issues since 1972.

Barred from employment

The California state board of regents and Governor Reagan voted in 1972 that she could never again teach at a California State-supported university. Davis has been a lecturer since, speaking in 1975 on black studies at Claremont College in Claremont, California; in 1977 in philosophy and political science at Stanford University; and from 1978 to the present in women's and ethnic studies at the San Francisco Art Institute. Other lecturing positions include from 1983 to 1985 in ethnic studies at California College of the Arts and Crafts in Oakland, and in 1984 on the history of consciousness at University of California at Santa Cruz.

Her best-selling autobiography, *Angela Davis*, was published in 1984, and she has also published many essays on her beliefs. A documentary on Davis entitled "Portrait of a Revolutionary" was produced by one of her UCLA students. She is in high demand as a speaker and writer, so she has not had the time to finish her dissertation. She remains in the doctoral program in the department of philosophy at University of Berlin.

Benjamin O. Davis, Sr.

U.S. Army General
Born 1877, Washington, D.C.
Died 1970

When Benjamin O. Davis first entered the American armed forces, blacks were segregated into their own non-fighting units with little hope for career advancement. By the time he finished his career more than fifty years later, Davis had blazed a trail through the ranks, becoming the country's first black general and playing a major role in the desegregation of the armed forces. His perseverance in the face of racism enabled him to become a mentor to the troops during World War II. He visited overseas regiments to solve racial problems, advised General Dwight D. Eisenhower on integration, and trained black soldiers for new combat duties.

Army career over education

Davis was born in 1877 to Louis and Henrietta Davis. His parents were former slaves, but they learned to read and write, enabling Louis to find work as a government messenger and Henrietta as a nurse. They felt education was the key to success and encouraged their children to seek higher education. But Benjamin Davis spurned his parents' advice. He was captivated by soldiers' stories about the Civil War, and he became an enthusiastic cadet in high school. When the Spanish-American War broke out, he helped form a company of volunteers to participate. Davis accepted a temporary rank of lieutenant when he was twenty-one years old. He spent the following year in various army training camps.

In 1899 Davis enlisted as a private in the regular army's Ninth Cavalry. He was sent to the Island of Samar in the Philippines, where he eventually became a sergeant-major, the highest level an enlisted man could attain. Davis wanted more. He was determined to become an officer and took the examinations in 1901. His black colleagues, knowing the racism that existed in the army, predicted he would fail. He proved them wrong by becoming a second lieutenant in the Tenth Cavalry.

His next assignment was at Fort Washakie in Wyoming. He and his wife, Elnora, were the only black couple on the base and were often isolated from the other families. Davis persevered, rising to the duties of post quartermaster.

In 1905 Davis was assigned to teach military science at Wilberforce University in Ohio, an all- black institution, but he soon found himself dissatisfied with his new position. Wilberforce was a Christian school and Davis was not religious. His class lasted only three hours per week, students suffered from a lack of discipline, and the principal did not support his endeavors.

Four years later Davis became a military attaché in Monrovia, Liberia. He provided Washington with information on military events, estimated Liberian troop strength, and gauged the army's efficiency. Davis felt the Liberian forces were poorly trained and disorganized, and suggested they be completely reorganized with five American officers as administrators. Davis volunteered to stay in Liberia and participate in the reshuffling, but American law prohibited soldiers from serving in the armed forces of another nation. Dejected, he asked to be relieved of his assignment in 1911.

A return to active service

By 1915 Davis, now a captain, had finished a tour of duty on the Mexico-Arizona border. He was reassigned to Wilberforce University, which had had no military instructor for several years. The next year tragedy struck, when his wife died of an embolism during the birth of their third child. In 1917 Davis asked to be returned to active service, and he was again posted to the Philippines. He spent the rest of World War I as the commanding officer of a supply troop. Davis felt that he had earned the respect of his superior officers, but Colonel John Heard requested that Davis be replaced in 1920. Heard was against the racial mixing of officers.

Davis then was assigned a teaching post at Tuskegee Institute in Tuskegee, Alabama. He enjoyed his work at Tuskegee and settled down with Sadie Overton, whom he had married the year before. Davis became a lieutenant colonel, but his new assignment was not up to the standards of the new rank. He was also offended by the rampant racism they encountered. One night the Ku Klux Klan or-

Benjamin O. Davis, Sr.

ganized a march in support of a policy requiring an all-white medical staff at a nearby black veterans hospital. Although black residents were advised to remain indoors, Davis refused. He donned his white dress uniform, seated his entire family under a bright porch light and stood defiantly as the Klansmen—hooded and carrying flaming torches—passed within inches of him. Davis was glad to accept a new post as instructor to the Ohio National Guard in 1924.

He became a colonel in 1929 and returned to Tuskegee Institute the following year, against his wishes and those of the black press, which reported that a colonel with thirty-five years of experience should have more senior responsibilities. Seven years later Davis finally got his chance to lead. He was appointed commander of the 369th Cavalry New York National Guard, fulfilling the black community's wish that the regiment be commanded by black officers.

In 1940 President Franklin D. Roosevelt faced stiff critcism from the black community over discrimination in the armed forces. While campaigning for his third term in office, Roosevelt came under attack about restricting black army enlistees and the navy's policy of accepting blacks only for mess duty. Blacks were also being denied promotions unfairly.

The army's first black general

Roosevelt tried to calm the situation by promoting Davis, now sixty-three years old, to become the army's first black brigadier general. This command overrode the military law against promotions after the age of fifty-eight. Although Davis reached the official retirement age of sixty-four just a few months after his promotion, he was immediately reactived when the U.S. entered World War II. Based in Washington, he helped the inspector general coordinate the introduction of about one hundred thousand blacks into the army.

Davis traveled across the United States, guiding the troops, improving morale among black soldiers, settling disturbances, and helping to ease race relations. He also produced an educational film about black soldiers entitled *The Negro Soldier.* The film was designed to be a race relations tool for incoming white soldiers, but it was eventually distributed through Hollywood, generating a favorable public reaction.

In 1944 Davis toured the European war zone to calm rising tensions between whites and blacks. He suggested to General Eisenhower that many blacks who were in support roles be allowed to volunteer for the previously all-white combat replacement program. He also recommended that the men be assigned to units on the basis of need, without reference to color. Eisenhower modified Davis's recommendations so that black units were grouped together into platoons and placed into white companies to fill combat needs.

Davis retired from military service in a special retirement ceremony in the White House Rose Garden on July 20, 1948. Three years later he was sent to Liberia to represent the United States at the country's centennial celebrations. He later served as a member of the American Battle Monuments Commission. In 1960 he left the public stage, suffering from poor eyesight and other health problems. Davis died of leukemia in 1970.

Miles Davis

Jazz trumpeter, composer
Born May 25, 1926, Alton, Illinois
Died September 28, 1991, Santa Monica, California

"To be a great musician you've got to be open to what's new, what's happening at the moment. You have to be able to absorb it if you're going to continue to grow and communicate your music."

K nown especially for his muted, soulful playing, Miles Davis was a major force in modern jazz, from bebop to cool jazz and then on to other innovations. Every few years he changed his style, and each stage in his development inspired a fashion for that form of music.

Despite his wide influence Davis appeared to care little for his public. He would walk off the stage between choruses, and often he played with his back to the audience, for he liked to face the band. His sullen, brooding presence brought him the nickname Prince of Darkness, yet he had millions of fans. Some admirers attended his concerts just because of his cult reputation, but most came to hear the beautiful melodies he coaxed from his trumpet. Several of his records are regarded as classics, including *Tutu*, which won a Grammy award in 1986.

Played in clubs on New York's 52d Street

Unlike many jazz musicians, Miles Dewey Davis III was from a middle-class background. His father was a dentist, his mother a violin player, and they lived in a well-to-do part of East St. Louis. Davis's passion for music was encouraged by his parents, who gave him his first trumpet for his thirteenth birthday. Before long he was playing in his high school band, and when he was fifteen he joined a professional local band, Eddie Randall's Blue Devils, with whom he played for the next three years. Around this time he had the chance to sit in with two of his jazz heroes—Dizzy Gillespie and Charlie Parker, leaders of the bebop movement. Gillespie and Parker were visiting St. Louis with Billy Eckstine's band, and for three weeks Davis substituted for the third trumpet player, who was sick.

By the time Davis was eighteen he was already a husband and father. Soon after graduating from high school he took his wife and infant son to New York, where his parents had enrolled him at the Juilliard School of Music to study classical music, and although he did attend classes for a while, Davis was far more interested in the music in the clubs on 52d Street. He began to play regularly in jam sessions, sitting in with such players as Gillespie, Parker, and Coleman Hawkins, and as he absorbed their styles he evolved his own style of playing—lighter, voicelike, and without vibrato.

Evolved from bebop to cool jazz

In 1945 Davis was nineteen, and he made history performing on one of the first bebop recordings with Gillespie, Parker, and Max Roach, though his own performance was panned by the critics. Over the next few years, Davis toured with the bands of Billy Eckstine and Benny Carter, then formed a quintet in New York with Charlie Parker. In 1948 he organized his own nine-piece band.

Davis's nine-piece combo was not a commercial success—he only managed to get a two-week engagement at New York's Royal Roost club and one week at the Clique Club—but the band still made its mark. Between 1949 and 1950 they made eight records that have become classics, ushering in a lighter sound in jazz and paving the way for smaller groups. In 1957 they were released on one LP as *The Birth of Cool.*

Kicked heroin cold turkey

The early 1950s were a bad time for Davis. A chain smoker, he also became hooked on heroin and was arrested by the police, though the charges against him were dropped. His private life was a mess—all three of his marriages ended in divorce—and he was getting increasingly bad publicity in the press. It looked as if he were going to drop right out of sight, but with an incredible show of willpower he kicked the heroin habit and made a comeback. By 1954 he was leading his own group again, and in 1955 he was playing at the Newport Jazz Festival—once again drawing attention for his "different" sound, for he was already moving on from cool jazz to hard bop.

In late 1955 Davis formed a quintet that included John Coltrane on tenor sax. This proved to be a turning point in his career, for the group made five albums within a year, and the following year Davis made his first record with arranger Gil Evans, who had long admired his playing. This album, called *Miles Ahead,* featured Davis on the flugelhorn with orchestration by Evans, and when it was released in 1957 it was greeted with rave

Miles Davis

reviews. Davis and Evans collaborated on two more orchestral-jazz combinations: a version of George Gershwin's *Porgy and Bess* (1958) and *Sketches of Spain* (1960). Both are considered major landmarks in the development of jazz.

During this same period Davis was also playing with a sextet with whom he made the album *Kind of Blue* in 1959. This album moved his music in yet another direction, for it established modal improvisation in jazz, featuring modal scales rather than chords. It was a step on the way to further experimentation in the 1960s as Davis took advantage of the new electronics to blend together different styles of music and try out the genre known as fusion. The first album in this new style was *Bitches Brew* (1970).

Late life plagued by health problems

Davis kept out of the public eye during most of the 1970s, due primarily to health problems. In 1972 he broke both legs in a car accident, but he had never been strong. He suffered from diabetes and sickle-cell anemia, and vocal chord problems limited his speech to a husky whisper.

During the 1980s Davis was married for seven years to actress Cicely Tyson, and after the marriage ended he spent much of his time in Malibu, California, though he continued to tour and make records. His later recordings included rock music and pop songs, ensuring him a huge audience. Only a few years before he died, he won *Down Beat* magazine's readers' and critics' poll as the best electric jazz group.

Ossie Davis

Actor, writer, director, producer
Born December 18, 1917, Cogdell, Georgia

"That was the style of the times.... In New York City, you acted in the theater, and afterward, you went to a [civil rights movement] party for a lynching victim later that evening. [Actor Marlon] Brando was in one corner and [actor-director] Orson Welles was in the other corner. It was the same at home. I was born in the South, and my parents were always involved in something, raising money for this cause or that protest."

L ong before Bill Cosby and Danny Glover arrived to make their marks on the entertainment industry, there was Ossie Davis. Built like a football player, Davis is noted today for his performance as Ponder Blue on the television show "Evening Shade." He made his Broadway debut in 1946 and has had a career studded with accomplishments. He has starred in numerous plays and films and directed the landmark film *Cotton Comes to Harlem* in 1970. Davis also wrote and starred in *Purlie Victorious,* a 1962 play that was eventually revived as the smash Broadway musical *Purlie.* He certainly lives up to his billing as the grand old man of black theater.

Mentors and idols

Davis was born on December 18, 1917, in Cogdell, Georgia, to Charles and Laura Davis. His father was a construction worker and preacher. His parents were excellent storytellers, and their church activities provided the groundwork for his acting career. "Acting and preaching are essentially the same—unabashedly so," Davis said in a *Palm Beach Post* interview. "The theater is a church and I consider myself as part of an institution that has an obligation to teach about Americanism, our culture and morals."

Davis's parents never learned to read, but they stressed the importance of an education. He did well in school and found good role models. His mentors were his teachers, friends who could tell jokes faster than he could, and the fictional characters Brer Rabbit and High John the Conqueror. He also had idols in the entertainment industry—singers Paul Robeson and Lena Horne and trumpet player Louis Armstrong.

After graduating from high school, Davis received a scholarship to Tuskegee Institute in Alabama. But with no money to pay for living expenses, he had to turn it down. In 1935 two aunts in Washington, D.C., agreed to let him live with them while he attended Howard University. He hitchhiked his way there.

While at Howard, Davis met Alain Locke, a drama critic and professor of philosophy. Locke encouraged Davis to move to Harlem and join the Rose McClendon Players. He felt that since Davis had never seen live actors, he would benefit from acting and learning what it takes to put on a play. Davis never intended to become an actor; he thought the experience would help him as a writer.

The next few years were difficult as Davis worked odd jobs, studied acting, and sometimes had to sleep in the park and scrounge for food. In 1941 he made his acting debut in the McClendon Players presentation of *Joy Exceeding Glory*. His acting career was interrupted when the United States entered World War II. Davis joined the army and was assigned to Liberia, West Africa, as a surgical technician. He later transferred to the Special Services Department, where he wrote and produced stage works to entertain military personnel.

Broadway debut

When the war ended Davis returned to Georgia, where he was tracked down by Richard Campbell, McClendon's director. Campbell asked Davis to go to New York and audition for Richard Ardrey's *Jeb*. Davis won the lead role and made his first Broadway appearance. He portrayed a disabled veteran attempting to succeed as an adding-machine operator in racist Louisiana. Davis received good reviews, but the play was panned and only lasted nine performances. But there was some rewards. Davis met Ruby Ann Wallace, an actress whose stage name was Ruby Dee. The two became close friends, and they took roles with the touring company of *Anna Lucasta*. They were married on December 9, 1948.

Davis's acting career continued to prosper, and he started appearing in television and films, including *Stevedore, No Time for Sergeants, No Way Out, A Raisin in the Sun,* and *The Emperor Jones.* Despite his success, Davis was held back in the industry because he was black. He revealed in *Blacks in American Film and Television* that the "rejection did sting. In theater it took a peculiar form—of having to compete with your peers, like I did for *Green*

Pastures on Broadway, to fight to say words you were ashamed of. Ruby and I came along at a time when being black was not yet fashionable. There was little in the theatre for us except to carry silver trays."

Davis and his wife decided to create their own theater. They would entertain in the marketplace, churches, and schools. They also found time to be the official hosts for the civil rights march on Washington in 1963, and they stayed in contact with African American activists, such as Malcolm X and W.E.B. Du Bois. In 1970 they received the Frederick Douglass Award from the Urban League for their civil rights activities. Actors Equity presented them with the Paul Robeson Citation in 1975 "for outstanding creative contributions both in the performing arts and in society at large."

Writing career expands

Davis presented his plays and screenplays to producers throughout the 1950s and 1960s. He had some success pitching ideas. In 1952 his play *Alice in Wonder* appeared in New York. It was revised and expanded the next year as *The Big Deal,* but it was poorly received. It was not until 1961 when *Purlie Victorious* debuted that Davis's writing abilities were truly noticed. The play was a comedy about an itinerant black preacher who attempts to claim his inheritance and establish an integrated church. It ran for more than seven months in New York City and later became a movie called *Gone Are the Days.* It also became the Broadway musical *Purlie.*

The 1960s saw Davis perform in several television shows including: "The Defenders,"

Ossie Davis

"The Doctors," "The Fugitive," and "Bonanza." It was not the kind of work Davis wanted to do. He was a writer, but he needed the acting to pay the bills. As the 1960s progressed, he continued to build a reputation. In 1968 his play *Curtain Call, Mr. Aldridge, Sir* was produced at the University of California at Santa Barbara. The next year Davis received an Emmy nomination for his performance in the teleplay *Teacher Teacher.* By 1970 he was one of America's busiest black actors, and that year he made his debut as a film director with *Cotton Comes to Harlem.* It was one of the first black films to make money from a mainstream audience, and it opened the way for a series of pictures about blacks, which became known as "blaxploitation" films.

Through the mid-1970s Davis continued to direct. His films included *Black Girl, Gordon's War,* and *Countdown to Kusini,* but they never became blockbusters. Nevertheless, many critics felt his work was significant. *Blacks in American Film and Television* stated that "in a strange way ... Davis could be called one of the most serious black directors of his era; political undercurrents [ran] throughout much of his work. He ... never settled for simply making a standard action movie.... [He] hoped to take black American cinema into a new, more politically oriented direction ... for that he has to be commended."

For the rest of the 1970s, Davis spent his time on a several projects. From 1974 to 1978 he and Ruby Dee co-hosted the *Ossie Davis and Ruby Dee Story Hour* on radio. In 1976 he appeared in the film, *Let's Do It Again,* as well as in the play, *Escape to Freedom: A Play About Young Frederick Douglass.* In 1981 he and Dee appeared in *With Ossie and Ruby* on PBS. They also used their company, Emmalyn II Productions, to co-produce the show with two public television stations.

Emmalyn II produced several programs during the 1980s, including *Martin Luther King ... the Dream and the Drum* and *A Walk Through History* for PBS. Davis continued his acting career and starred in *I'm Not Rapaport* at Burt Reynolds's Jupiter Theater in Florida in 1986. Two years later he appeared in *School Daze* and in 1989 played the mayor in Spike Lee's controversial and acclaimed movie, *Do the Right Thing.*

Although past seventy, Davis has continued to remain in the public eye. He starred in the movie *Jungle Fever* and has a regular spot as Burt Reynolds's best friend in the television show, "Evening Shade." Davis is still a busy writer, and in 1992 published a story for young adults entitled *Just Like Martin,* about a small-town Alabama church congregation during the civil rights movement.

Davis seems to have no difficulty shifting directions as a writer, director, actor, and producer. He attributes his diverse skills to his storytelling abilities: "the story I want to tell is about black people. Sometimes I sing the story, sometimes I dance it, sometimes I tell tales about it, but I always want to share my great satisfaction at being a black man at this time in history."

Davis and Dee live in a large house in New Rochelle in New York's Westchester County. They have two daughters, a son, and a grandson.

Sammy Davis, Jr.

Entertainer, actor
Born December 8, 1925, New York, New York
Died May 16, 1990, Los Angeles, California

"An entertainer should entertain, babe."

A little man with a big heart and great talent, Sammy Davis, Jr., broke down racial barriers and opened the way for other black performers. As an entertainer he was brilliant. Called "Mr. Wonderful" and "the world's greatest entertainer," he could hold an audience spellbound for hours with a stream of comic patter and mimicry, and with bursts of singing and dancing.

Davis was also subjected to the ridicule of other comedians, who made fun of his flashy rings and bracelets. He was criticized by some

Sammy Davis, Jr.

blacks for living too much in the white world. And when he married his second wife, the Swedish actress May Britt, he received death threats from racist whites for daring to marry a white woman. But Davis managed to cope, because he was first and foremost an entertainer, and he was determined to be entertaining.

Doing his shtick on stage by two

Sammy Davis, Jr., was born into show business. His father was the lead dancer in Will Mastin's vaudeville troupe, and his mother was the lead chorus girl. They split up when Davis was two, and his father brought him on stage and had him performing his first song-and-dance acts by the time he was three.

At the age of six Davis starred in his first film, *Rufus Jones for President,* a sentimental movie about a boy who falls asleep in his mother's lap and dreams he is elected president. Shortly thereafter came another film role

in *Season's Greetings.* Meanwhile the boy toured with the Mastin group, featured as "Little Sammy" and then "Sammy Davis, Jr."

But all this time Davis had virtually no schooling. It was not until he was in the army that he taught himself to read. He was drafted into the U.S. Army when he was eighteen and experienced racism for the first time. He reacted to it boldly, defending himself with his fists, and he suffered a broken nose several times. He faced other indignities as well, such as being daubed with white paint and having foul words painted on his face and chest. He benefited from being transferred to Special Services to give shows in the camps across the country. These shows were immensely popular, and Davis quickly gained a huge following.

Broke into the big time

After the war Davis returned to vaudeville and the Will Mastin group, now reduced to the trio of Davis, his father, and Mastin. More and more the trio showcased Davis, with the two older men doing tap and softshoe dancing in the background.

During the late 1940s the Mastin trio appeared in shows with such stars as Mickey Rooney, Frank Sinatra, and Bob Hope. It also got a summer contract to appear on NBC television and a booking at Ciro's in Hollywood. As Davis moved into the "big time" as an entertainer, he also recorded his first Decca album of impersonations in 1954, *Starring Sammy Davis, Jr.,* which he followed up with an LP of songs, *Just for Lovers.*

That year Davis suffered a bad car crash in November and lost his left eye. The experience caused him to convert to Judaism, for he said he found an affinity between Jews and blacks, that both were oppressed peoples and both were trying to create a Godly kingdom on earth.

Never stopped performing

All the time Davis was lying in hospital he was given tremendous support by his fans, and when he was well enough to leave he had his pick of clubs throughout the country. He made his comeback at Ciro's, where he appeared with a patch over his eye and was given a ten-minute ovation. He later took to wearing a "glass eye" (actually made of plastic).

Two years later Davis scored his first hit on Broadway with the show "Mr. Wonderful," which ran for more than a year. He followed this up with appearances in a number of movies, including *Porgy and Bess* (1959) and *Robin and the Seven Hoods* (1964). He also had several roles in live theater and in 1964 starred in the musical "Golden Boy." Meanwhile he was making records and appearing frequently on television, and in 1965–66 he hosted his own television show, "The Sammy Davis, Jr., Show," one of the first TV shows ever to be hosted by a black person.

Along with all this theatrical activity, Davis threw himself into the civil rights movement and marched alongside Martin Luther King, Jr., in Montgomery, Alabama. He also contributed generously to black causes and gave benefit concerts for the family of Malcolm X and for jailed civil rights activist Angela Davis. His fans were shocked when in 1972 he publicly supported President Richard Nixon and was photographed with him at the Republican Convention in Miami Beach. But when Nixon failed to bring in the civil rights reforms he had promised, Davis turned away from him.

During the 1970s, Davis's jet-set life-style began to affect his health. He seemed to be always on the go, smoking and drinking too much, and partying late into the night. His third wife, Altovise Gore, whom he had married in 1970, helped him moderate his pace. Meanwhile, his performances continued to delight audiences, and his renditions of the songs "Mr. Bojangles" and "The Candy Man" were pop hits for years on end.

Davis never really stopped performing, despite increasing health problems. His final appearance was at a television special given in his honor, where, despite advanced cancer, he danced a brief softshoe, an entertainer to the end.

Juliette Derricotte

Educator
Born April 1, 1897, Athens, Georgia
Died November 7, 1931, Chattanooga,
  Tennessee

"Through the warmth and forcefulness of her personality, she succeeded in making people understand each other in the most practical manner."—Jean Elder Cazort

During her eleven-year career as an official with the Young Women's Christian Association (YWCA) and later as dean of women at Fisk University, Juliette Derricotte

Juliette Derricotte

strove to bring people together in friendship. She was convinced that barriers of race, religion, and nationality could be overcome if people would only drop their prejudices.

Derricotte made constant efforts to promote peace and harmony and had occasion to experience success at international conferences she attended in Europe and Asia. But when Derricotte was severely injured in a traffic accident, the only hospital in town, a white hospital, refused to admit her, and she died a victim of those very prejudices that she had spent her life trying to remove.

Developed career skills at Talladega College

Juliette Aline Derricotte was the fifth of nine children of Isaac and Laura (Hardwick) Derricotte. Her father was a cobbler and her mother a seamstress. Growing up in Georgia in the early years of this century, Derricotte learned very young about prejudice and rac-

ism. Like other southern towns, Athens was regulated by segregation laws forbidding African Americans to dine at most restaurants, stay at the best hotels, travel in the front seats of buses, use "white" washrooms.... There were even separate drinking fountains for blacks and whites.

Derricotte was educated at the town's black public schools, but after graduation she wanted to attend Lucy Cobb Institute, a college located in the tree-lined streets of the white section of Athens. It was a bitter disappointment when her mother explained Lucy Cobb did not accept black students.

In 1914 Derricotte enrolled at Talladega College in Alabama, where she entered enthusiastically into college life and took a leading role in student affairs. Her many activities included speaking on the debating team, organizing student events, and serving as president of the college's YWCA. As Derricotte performed these various roles she discovered that she was good at getting people to work together harmoniously, and on graduating in 1918 she chose a career that involved relating to people. She took a job with the YWCA because of her college experience with the association.

Traveled and made friends throughout the world

Derricotte took a summer course at the National YWCA Training School in New York, and in fall 1918 she was appointed secretary of the National Student Council of the YWCA. In this position she coordinated the activities of the various branches of the association. Her work involved visiting student groups throughout the country, organizing programs, planning conferences, and discussing new ideas and policies.

Derricotte enjoyed the job and performed her tasks enthusiastically. She is remembered particularly for the warmth of her personality—the pleasant yet practical way she dealt with problems and the friendly manner in which she could resolve disputes. Just as she had done at Tallageda, she helped people understand one another so that they dropped their animosities and worked together harmoniously. She is credited with making the National Student Council an interracial fellowship.

In 1924 Derricotte was one of the two black delegates sent to England to represent American college students at the meeting of the World's Student Christian Federation. Four years later she attended the World's Student Christian Federation in Mysore, India. Derricotte remained in India for seven weeks and came to understand many of the country's problems as she traveled around, living in YWCAs, student hostels, mission schools, Indian homes, and even in the furnished camp of a maharajah.

As Derricotte made friends with the other members of the general committee, with its ninety delegates from around the world, she realized that they were a form of United Nations. "This is what can happen to all the world," she said in one of her speeches. "With all the bitterness and prejudice and hatred that are true between any two or more of these countries, you are here friends working, thinking, playing, living together in the finest sort of fellowship."

On leaving India, Derricotte went on to China and Japan to meet with students there. On returning home, she wrote, "My head whirls, but every now and then I remember that there is so much more to know than I am accustomed to knowing and so much more love than I am accustomed to loving."

Fatal injuries

In 1927 Derricotte received a master's degree in religious education from Columbia University. Two years later she left the YWCA to become dean of women at Fisk University. She also served as a trustee at Talladega College—the only woman trustee the college had ever had.

At Fisk, the women students were calling for change, objecting angrily to the outdated rules limiting their activities. Derricotte moved in with her usual tact and before long had calmed the situation. She soon gained the students' trust and became one of the most popular members of staff.

Her promising future at Fisk was cut short tragically when Derricotte drove to Athens to visit her mother in November 1931. She had three students with her in the car, and after stopping for lunch in Chattanooga they headed south toward Atlanta. About a mile outside Dalton, Georgia, they had a head-on collision with a car containing a white couple.

Derricotte and one of the students were seriously injured, but they were refused admittance at Dalton's only hospital because it did not take black patients. Emergency treatment was provided in the private office of a white doctor, and they were then placed in the home of a black woman who had beds for black patients. The student died during the night. Next day Derricotte was taken by ambulance to Chattanooga's Walden hospital, where she died shortly after arrival.

When these details became public, there was a national outcry over hospital's refusal to treat Derricotte and the student. Spurred on by Fisk University and the National Association for the Advancement of Colored People, an investigation was conducted by Atlanta's Commission of Interracial Cooperation, which revealed many similar incidents of discrimination practiced in the South. Memorial services were held for Derricotte throughout the country, and she is still remembered as a woman of courage, kindness, and goodwill who strove to bring people of all races together in common understanding and friendship.

Irene Diggs

Anthropologist, professor
Born 1906, Monmouth, Illinois

"Basically, the differences between the 'problem of race' in the United States and Latin America is their different definitions of who is white."

As a youngster, Irene Diggs found great disparity in the way blacks and whites were treated. It was clear to her that economic prosperity had more to do with race than with hard work. Diggs's interest in race relations led her to devote most of her life to studying racial and cultural differences in North, South, and Latin America. A noted writer, her work

appeared in numerous publications, although time constraints prevented her from writing many book-length manuscripts. She also spent thirty years teaching sociology and anthropology at Morgan University.

An early interest in race relations

Diggs was born in 1906 in Monmouth, Illinois, a small college town located in the state's agricultural belt. Her parents were hard working and industrious, and she grew up in a supportive environment with her four siblings. At an early age, Diggs saw first hand the poverty that many blacks lived in. She realized that race played a role in economic inequality, and she was determined to obtain an education as a way out. Diggs spent a lot of time reading, and she soon wanted to travel to the countries she read about.

Since she had the highest average at the local school, she received a Chamber of Commerce scholarship to attend Monmouth College. After a year, Diggs transferred to the University of Minnesota because it offered more extensive courses. She majored in sociology and minored in psychology, graduating in 1928 with a bachelor of science degree. She then enrolled in Atlanta University (now Clark-Atlanta) for graduate work in sociology and received the university's first master's degree in 1933. She earned a doctorate in anthropology at the University of Havana in 1944.

Diggs met the noted activist and scholar W.E.B. Du Bois during her second semester as a graduate student at Atlanta University. Du Bois was a professor of economics, history, and sociology. Diggs registered for his course and did so well that Du Bois asked her to become his summer research assistant. The "summer job" lasted eleven years. During those years Diggs helped research five of Du Bois's books, including his social commentary *Black Folk Then and Now,* and founded with him the journal *Phylon: A Review of Race and Culture.*

In the early 1940s, Diggs spent time in Cuba before taking an intensive language course as a Roosevelt Fellow of the Institute of International Education at the University of Havana. She studied under Fernando Ortiz, a distinguished professor of ethnography and an expert on the African presence in Cuban culture. Diggs spent time collecting folklore, recording music, photographing festivals, and observing rituals and dances. She spent time in both cities and rural areas, writing on African culture, especially on Afro-Cuban descendants of Yoruban and Dahomean people.

For two years, Diggs studied the differences between race relations in the United States and in Latin America. In the *Negro History Bulletin* she wrote: "Basically, the differences between the 'problem of race' in the United States and Latin America is their different definitions of who is white."

An exchange student in Uruguay

After World War II, Diggs went to South America, where she spent almost a year in Montevideo, Uruguay, as an exchange student with the U.S. Department of State's Division of International Exchange of Persons. While in Montevideo, she conducted archival research and became a participant-observer in the Afro-Uruguayan and Afro-Argentinean (Buenos Aires) communities. Diggs developed an interest in fine art and wrote articles on the subject for several publications, including "Negro Painters in Uruguay" for *Crisis* and "The Negro in the Viceroyalty of Rio de la Plata" for *Journal of Negro History.* Diggs soon acquired a unique place among her African American colleagues as an expert on Afro-Latin American studies.

Diggs returned to the United States in 1947, and she was invited to join the faculty of Morgan State College (now University). With a heavy classroom commitment, Diggs had trouble writing book-length manuscripts. During the early 1950s, her work began appearing in a variety of publications. They included the *Journal of Negro History, Phylon,* several academic journals, and newspapers such as the *Baltimore Sun.* Some of her best-known works include: "Zumbi and the Republic of Os Palmares," *Phylon* 14; "Color in Colonial Spanish America," *Journal of Negro History* 38; "Legacy," *Freedomways* 5; "Cuba Before Castro," *The New American;* and "The Biological and Cultural Impact of Blacks on the United States," *Phylon* 41. Diggs was also co-editor of the *Encyclopedia of the Negro* (1945). Her last major project, *Black Chronology,* appeared in 1983.

Besides her professional affairs, Diggs has also been active in community organizations. She served on many civic and state-wide fact-finding commissions that focussed on the general population or issues relating to the African American community. She has participated on commissions regarding mental health, corrections, and family welfare. Diggs was a founding member of the Women's Committee of the Baltimore Art Museum and was on the board of the Peabody Conservatory. She was also a member of the American Anthropological Association and the American Sociological Association. In 1978, the Association of Black Anthropologists presented Diggs with the Distinguished Scholar Award for her outstanding achievement in the scholarship and research on peoples of African descent.

As an African American anthropologist, Diggs has made a major contribution to the profession through her work on Afro-Latin America, Afro-American history, African history, and black intellectual history. Her volume, *Black Chronology*, published in 1983, illustrates her view of culture and the use of historical research to document cultural change. The book is an excellent look at the African experience, both inside and outside of Africa, and focuses on the accomplishments of black peoples.

Diggs retired from Morgan University in 1976, after almost thirty years of service to the department of sociology and anthropology.

David Dinkins

Mayor of New York City
Born July 10, 1927, Trenton, New Jersey

"There's no need for you to agree with me. You have every right to prefer someone else. But understand this also. There will come a November 7 and then there'll be a November 8, and the people will have spoken. And after they've spoken, I'm equally confident that you're going to obey and abide by that judgment."

Ever since graduating from law school, David Dinkins has been groomed for a high-level politician's job. His life-long ambition finally came true in November 1989, when he was elected the first black mayor of New York City. Voters saw him as being calm, dignified, and deliberate, and he overcame fears of many white New Yorkers that he lacked leadership qualities. His success in the mayoral race was built on his other political victories, as a New York State assemblyman and Manhattan borough president.

Big man on campus

Dinkins was born in Trenton, New Jersey, and his parents separated while he was still a youngster. He and his younger sister went to live with their mother in Harlem, New York, but he later returned to Trenton to attend high school. After graduating he went to Howard University, but his studies were interrupted by World War II. His fellow students remembered him as a man with strong social skills, a fraternity man, popular on campus, and a ladies' man.

After graduating from Howard, he married Joyce Burrows and they settled down in Harlem. Since her family had political connections—her father was a former assemblyman and district leader—Dinkins was encouraged to pursue a career in politics. In 1953 he enrolled at Brooklyn Law School, where he could springboard into politics. His wife's family was ready to introduce him to those who could further his career.

Dinkins became friends with J. Raymond Jones (known as the Harlem Fox) and became involved with the Carver Club, a group that trained generations of young black business and political leaders and was well-known within the city's power structure. Dinkins started at the bottom, waking up at dawn to hang posters, helping to set up meetings, and doing most of the manual labor. His actions were noted, and Dinkins became friends with Basil Paterson, Charles Rangel, and Percy Sutton, three black city politicians whose power was to grow.

Although his associations cost him the support of some young black activists, many began to realize Dinkins could become the city's first black mayor. Whenever his limousine appeared in a black neighborhood, blacks would rush out to greet him. With the support of the community behind him, he successfully ran for the New York State Assembly in 1965. When his two-year term ended, his district was redrawn, and Dinkins decided not to seek re-election. He handled local political tasks until Mayor Abraham Beame offered him the post of deputy minister. Dinkins accepted, but then turned down the offer after it became public that he had not paid income taxes from 1969 to 1972. He paid back all of his taxes plus interest and was quickly appointed city clerk.

Manhattan borough president

In 1977 Percy Sutton resigned as Manhattan borough president and endorsed Dinkins as his replacement. Dinkins ran twice for the office and lost both times by large amounts. In 1985 he ran again and won. He now had a staff that numbered more than one hundred and an annual budget of nearly $5 million. As borough president he assembled task forces to

David Dinkins

look at a variety of issues including pedestrian safety and school decentralization. His strongest stance was probably in the area of supporting community-based AIDS services. The *Wall Street Journal* summed up his term by saying he "made little of the post, and was best known among city politicians for his problems making up his mind" on budget and land use issues. Dinkins would withhold his opinion or his vote until he could hold long meetings with aides and consultants. The public considered him deliberate and coolheaded, if a little vague.

In 1989 Dinkins decided to run for mayor of New York City. He would have to overcome incumbent mayor Edward I. Koch and popular district attorney Rudolph W. Giuliani. In announcing his candidacy, Dinkins said the city was ready for someone who was ready to "take the high road." His campaign was unimaginative, but his formal English pronunciation and calm tone won over voters. His best moment in the campaign probably took place in the summer, when the city was on edge. Tensions were running high after a white woman was raped and brutalized by black youths in Central Park, and a black youth was murdered in a white ethnic Brooklyn neighborhood. Dinkins emerged as a peacemaker during this volatile period. To appear cool and comfortable in the summer heat, his aides carried three or four identical linen suits, allowing for quick changes. In Bensonhurst, where black leaders had organized a march to protest the killing of Yusef Hawkins in August, Dinkins faced an angry crowd. After quieting the crowd, he got their respect with a short speech. The *New York Times* reported that Dinkins said, "Let's be clear on something. There's no need for you to agree with me. You have every right to prefer someone else. But understand this also. There will come a November 7 and then there'll be a November 8, and the people will have spoken. And after they've spoken, I'm equally confident that you're going to obey and abide by that judgment." An off-the-cuff speech like that was uncharacteristic for Dinkins. He rarely strayed from his prepared text.

The biggest hurdles Dinkins had to overcome were Jesse Jackson and his personal finances. Dinkins was a friend of Jackson, who once referred to New York as "Hymietown," a derogatory reference to its large Jewish population. Although many Jews refused to back Dinkins because of his association with Jackson, his campaign strategists managed to convince enough Jewish voters that Dinkins was his own man and repre-sented traditional Democratic party policies. The other hurdle involved Dinkins's failure to pay income taxes and his perceived unethical handling of his stock portfolio; Dinkins had transferred ownership of the portfolio to his son and substantially underreported its cash worth.

Ready for the mayor's chair

Despite the criticism, Dinkins appeared to be in control of the campaign. Shortly before the vote, the *New York Times* wrote that, "at 62, Mr. Dinkins' public persona fits neatly into a middle-of-the-road strategy that his campaign has pursued for the last nine months. He always appears poised, his tailored, double-breasted suits carefully pressed, and his syntax unfailingly correct; privately, his tastes are in the mainstream of his postwar generation. He loves the big, band tunes, Ella Fitzgerald, Billie Holiday and Frank Sinatra. He likes cowboy movies, holds Cary Grant in awe and admires the well-stitched quality of British television series like "Tinker, Tailor, Soldier, Spy."

In September 1989 Dinkins defeated Koch, and in the November general election was victorious over Giuliani. Dinkins and his wife currently live in a three-bedroom apartment on the eleventh floor of a high rise on Riverside Drive.

Sharon Pratt Dixon

See **Kelly, Sharon Pratt**

Thomas A. Dorsey

Creator of gospel music
Born July 1, 1899, Villa Rica, Georgia
Died January 23, 1993, Chicago, Illinois

"One day I got the idea that if I could get into church music the moans and feeling and pathos of blues, then I'd have something."

Thomas Dorsey is known as the father of gospel music, which he created in the 1920s by blending blues, ragtime, and church songs. During his lifetime, he composed about one thousand gospel songs, including such classics as "Take My Hand, Precious Lord," "The Lord Will Make a Way Somehow," "Peace in the Valley," and "Angels Watching Over Me."

Dorsey also wrote about two hundred blues songs. A passionate devotee of the blues, he began experimenting to try to bridge the gap between the emotional blues music and the conventional spirituals that were sung in church. As he explained, "I had been playing and writing blues for quite a while, but I always thought that someday I would bring my music back into the church, where I started. One day I got the idea that if I could get into church music the moans and feeling and pathos of blues, then I'd have something."

The moans and pathos caught on so quickly that within ten years gospel music had replaced spirituals in most black churches. Dorsey's songs were picked up later by pop stars, including Elvis Presley, who had a mil-lion-selling hit with "Peace in the Valley." Dorsey's gospel songs also spawned another form of music—soul, which emerged during the 1950s. Aretha Franklin and most other famous soul singers had their early training as gospel singers.

Singing the blues

Thomas Dorsey had both music and religion in his background. His father was a traveling Baptist preacher known for his revivalist sermons. His mother played the organ at the Baptist church in the small town of Villa Rica, where Dorsey and his four brothers and sisters spent their early years. Dorsey learned the organ and piano from his mother, and by 1910, when the family moved to Atlanta, eleven-year-old Dorsey could already play so well that he was considered a musical prodigy.

In Atlanta, Dorsey heard jazz for the first time, and he loved it. Although his parents followed a strict religious lifestyle, they did not prevent their children from listening to jazz. Dorsey made the most of this, as he later recalled: "When I was just a little fella I got a job selling pop at the old 91 Theater in Atlanta, because that was where some of the greatest musicians of the time played, including Ma Rainey, Bessie Smith, and Eddie Hayward. Even at that young age I knew I wanted to be playing that music someday, so I began asking performers to teach me whatever they could. I'd let them buy pop on credit and then have them teach me something in return."

By his early teens Dorsey was earning a small income by playing in the local bars and brothels, and at seventeen he moved to Chicago where blues music was developing among jazz circles. Unlike many of the jazz musicians, Dorsey could read and write music, and as a result he was hired by Paramount Records to write lead sheets for recording artists.

Calling himself Georgia Tom, Dorsey soon made a name for himself as a blues musician. Between 1922 and 1927 he toured with blues singer Ma Rainey, playing the piano and writing and arranging her songs. He then teamed up with another blues singer, Tampa Red, who gained fame largely through his association with Dorsey. For four years the two men toured together, achieving a number of hits, including "It's Tight Like That," which sold extremely well among white as well as black audiences.

By 1931 Dorsey had written some two hundred blues songs, which sold over half a

Thomas A. Dorsey

million records. But just when his career was heading for the top, he dropped out of the blues world. Some years earlier he had discovered a type of music that meant more to him, and it was this gospel music he wanted to devote himself to for the rest of his life.

The father of gospel music

Dorsey was in his early twenties when he first realized he wanted to write church music. It happened at a Baptist convention: "Some fellow got up and sang a beautiful song called 'I Do, Don't You?' and he blew the audience away with that song, including me. Then he passed around a collection plate that must have gathered in hundreds of dollars. I said to myself, 'That's where I ought to be,' and ever since then it never got off my mind."

Dorsey recognized that the song he had just heard had far more appeal to the crowd than the usual spirituals they heard in church. Spirituals such as "Swing Low, Sweet Chariot" were from another era and no longer touched the people deeply. By contrast, the blues songs of the bars and nightclubs expressed personal feelings. They evoked emotions that could easily be shared, and they had a familiar modern rhythm.

With Dorsey's strong religious beliefs and his love of blues music, it was natural for him to bring them together by writing emotional sacred music—the type of music that came to be known as gospel. He started doing so in the 1920s when traveling with Ma Rainey, and he had his first gospel hit during that period. Entitled "If You See My Savior," it was written in 1926 when Dorsey was recovering from a serious illness. He published the song at his own expense and sent copies of the sheet music to 250 black churches. Three years later, "If You See My Savior" brought the house down when a woman sang it at a Baptist convention.

As Dorsey became increasingly committed to writing gospel songs, he opened his own publishing house to print and distribute the sheet music, and he hired blues singer Sally Martin to perform the songs. The performances were held anywhere the two of them could gather an audience, whether in a church hall or on a street corner.

Most listeners were won over immediately, but their ministers were not. "A lot of them got angry at me," recalled Dorsey. "'You can't sing no gospel here,' they'd say, 'you can only preach the gospel.' I'd say, 'To me gospel means good news and it don't matter if you preach it or sing it, as long as it's for God.' Still, in those years I got kicked out of some of the best churches in town."

Despite the opposition, gospel music caught on quickly. Sally Martin criss crossed the country, teaching it to church choirs, and in the late 1930s Dorsey hired the then little-known singer Mahalia Jackson, who became world famous as "the queen of gospel" through her magnificent renditions of Dorsey's songs.

"Take My Hand, Precious Lord"

Even in the early 1930s gospel music was so popular that Dorsey decided to organize a National Convention of Gospel Choirs and Choruses. Meeting for the first time in 1932, the convention was marked by both triumph and tragedy. The conference itself was a success, but on the second day Dorsey learned that his wife had died in childbirth. A few weeks afterwards he wrote what is probably his most famous song, "Take My Hand, Precious Lord."

Recalling its creation many years later, Dorsey said, "Trying somehow to get over my grief, I began browsing along the keyboard of the piano, and something went off inside of me. I began playing a tune and singing words. I didn't write them, they just came to me. That week we taught the song to [Theodore] Frye's choir over at Ebenezer Baptist Church and they sang it at the Sunday morning service. That was the first time it was performed, and it tore up the church."

"Precious Lord" was later performed throughout the world. It has been translated into more than thirty-five languages and was sung frequently by Mahalia Jackson, as well as by the opera star Leontyne Price, who sang it at President Lyndon Johnson's funeral. "Precious Lord" was also a favorite of Martin Luther King, Jr., who asked for it to be sung during his visit to Memphis in 1968. Apparently he made the request just a few moments before he was assassinated.

The song was still at the height of its popularity when Dorsey married his second wife Kathryn, with whom he lived happily until his death at the age of ninety-three. During his last years, Dorsey liked to call himself the "grandfather" of gospel music. Not only did he have four grandchildren, but he was fondly referred to as "the professor" and was widely respected as a major figure in the music of his generation.

Dorsey received an increasing number of honors in his old age, including an invitation to the White House by President Ronald Reagan. He was elected to the Georgia Music Hall of Fame and to Nashville's previously all-white Gospel Music Association. In 1983 he was subject of the documentary film *Say Amen, Somebody,* and in 1992, shortly before his death, he was presented with a Grammy Award.

Frederick Douglass

Abolitionist
Born February 1817, Talbot County,
 Maryland
Died February 20, 1895, Washington, D.C.

"If there is no struggle, there is no progress. Those who profess to favor freedom and yet deprecate agitation are men who want crops without plowing up the ground, they want rain without thunder and lightning."

Born a slave of an unknown father, Frederick Douglass escaped to freedom and became an influential speaker and writer, the leading spokesman for black Americans in the nineteenth century. Knowing slavery himself, he devoted his life to abolishing the practice.

Douglass wrote three autobiographies: *Narrative of the Life of Frederick Douglass* (1845), *My Bondage and My Freedom* (1855), and his masterwork, *Life and Times of Frederick Douglass* (1881). These books had enormous impact, because they gave whites an insider's view of what it was like to be a slave. The vivid descriptions of the brutal treat-

ment and the terrible floggings shocked some white Americans into action and caused tens of thousands of people to call for the end of slavery.

Labeled a troublemaker

Douglass's original name was Frederick August Washington Bailey. He took the name Douglass to avoid capture when he was making his escape. Like many children born into slavery, he never knew who his father was, though he assumed it was the white slave owner. His mother was a slave called Harriet Bailey, but Douglass hardly knew her. When he was a baby, he was taken to a plantation twelve miles away, and after that he saw her only four or five times.

For the first few years of Douglass's life, he slept on the floor of a kitchen closet and, with the other slave children, was made to eat from a trough. If he ate too fast, he was whipped and deprived of food. At the age of eight he was sent to Baltimore to be a house servant to one of his master's relatives. Although this took Douglass away from his family, at least he found kindness. "I had been treated as a pig on the plantation," he wrote. "In this new house, I was treated as a child."

For seven years Douglass remained in Baltimore, living more like a servant than a slave. The white mistress of the house made sure that he had good food and clothing and, most important, she taught him to read. But this happy period ended when Douglass was fifteen and had to return to his former owners. Determined not to give in to despair, he tried to keep up the learning he had gained in Baltimore and to pass on his knowledge to his fellow slaves, but when he tried to start a Sunday school it was broken up by his master. A slave who could read and quote the Bible was considered dangerous, so Douglass was hired out to work for a farmer who had the reputation of being able to "break" even the most rebellious slaves.

Douglass was subjected to vicious floggings, but the farmer failed to break his spirit. Determined not to give in, Douglass surreptitiously kept up his learning and taught his fellow slaves to read. Because of his stubborn resistance he was labeled a troublemaker, and after he was jailed for organizing an escape, his master got rid of him, sending him to Baltimore to work in the shipyard. From there, disguised as a free black sailor, he escaped to New York in 1838.

Hired to lecture against slavery

Douglass was soon joined in New York by Anna Murray, a free black woman from Baltimore who became his wife. The couple moved to New Bedford, Massachusetts, where Douglass hoped to find work in the shipyard, caulking ships to make them watertight. But the white caulkers refused to work with him. For three years Douglass worked at such jobs as digging ditches and collecting garbage.

Yet he settled in happily at New Bedford, becoming a lay preacher at the local black church and going to antislavery meetings. In 1841 he attended a large meeting of the Massachusetts Anti-Slavery Society, held on Nantucket Island. He made his first major speech there, telling the crowd of thousands the story of his life as a slave and of his escape

to freedom. Douglass so impressed the audience that the famous abolitionist William Lloyd Garrison immediately hired him as a full-time lecturer for the Massachusetts Anti-Slavery Society. Douglass soon perfected his speaking style, building up the drama of his tale and adding humorous remarks when things got too serious.

During the next few years, Douglass also demonstrated against discrimination. He walked out of churches that would not allow blacks to take part in the services, and he walked into railway cars that were reserved for whites only. Meanwhile he was writing his *Narrative of the Life of Frederick Douglass.* When the book was published in 1845, it was immensely popular. There had already been many books on the horrors of slavery, but they had been written by white abolitionists and did not always ring true. Here at last was an eloquent story, told with great feeling, by

Frederick Douglass

someone who had actually experienced slavery.

However, the success of the book made life dangerous for Douglass, since it stated clearly that he was a runaway slave. With the possibility that someone might try and capture him to claim a reward from his owner, the antislavery society helped him escape to the British Isles, where for the next two years he traveled and lectured on slavery. This work enabled Douglass to raise enough money to buy his freedom from his former owner.

Parting ways with Garrison, Douglass urged revolt

Douglass's return to North America marked a turning point in his relationship with William Lloyd Garrison, for Douglass was no longer prepared to be treated as a protégé. With his lectures drawing larger crowds than Garrison's, he felt bold enough to speak out when he disagreed with the famous abolitionist. The two men now held opposing views on how slaves should gain their freedom. Douglass had concluded that the nonviolent "moral suasion" that Garrison advocated might not be enough, but that they should be prepared to resort to violence to bring an end to slavery. Douglass printed this view in the newspaper he founded in Rochester, N.Y., in 1847. Called the *North Star,* it became one of the most widely read papers in antislavery circles.

By this time Douglass was in touch with all the major people working to end slavery, including John Brown, and this put him in danger after Brown's raid on Harper's Ferry in 1859. Convinced that Douglass was involved in the revolt, the governor of Virginia swore out a warrant for his arrest, and Douglass had to take refuge in Canada until the crisis was over.

Douglass's conviction that violence was inevitable was proven by the outbreak of the Civil War. He threw himself wholeheartedly into the cause, and although he was too old to shoulder a musket himself, he urged younger men to do so, and he vigorously recruited black troops (including two of his sons) into the Union Army. Then, when the Emancipation Proclamation made it legal for slaves to fight for the Confederacy, he wrote editorials in his newspaper, calling on them to rise against the slaveholders.

Championed suffrage for women

After the war, during Reconstruction, Douglass was appointed to the legislature of the District of Columbia, and in 1872 he served as one of the presidential electors-at-large for New York. In 1877 President Rutherford B. Hayes made him marshal of the District of Columbia, though Hayes then removed many duties and privileges normally attached to the position, including the right to attend state receptions at the White House.

Douglass's wife died in 1882, and two years later he shocked many white people by marrying Helen Pitts, a white woman. For his part, though, Douglass saw this marriage as a blow against racism, and he tossed aside all criticism by pointing out, "My first wife was the color of my mother, and the second, the color of my father."

During his later years, Douglass continued to be appointed to high-profile positions, including consul general to the Republic of

Haiti (1889–91). He spent his final years in Washington, D.C., living in a large house called Cedar Hill and actively involved in many causes. On the day he died he had attended a convention for women's suffrage.

Charles Richard Drew

Surgeon
Born June 3, 1904, Washington, D.C.
Died April 1, 1950

"It's much more than a degree I'm after. There are those in high places who feel that Negroes have not yet reached intellectual levels which will permit their attempting the very high reaches."

When Allied casualities began to mount in the Second World War, a hunt took place for someone who could find a way to preserve blood for use in battlefield transfusions. That someone turned out to be Charles Drew. His dissertation on "banked blood" at Howard University made him an expert in new methods to separate and preserve blood. After contributing to the war effort, he later became chief surgeon at Freedmen's Hospital in Washington, as well as professor of surgery at Howard University Medical School.

A popular student and gifted athlete

Drew was born on June 3, 1904, in Washington, D.C., to a middle-class family. He was a hard-working youngster. When he was twelve years old, he sold newspapers; a year later he had six other boys working for him. In 1918, Drew entered Dunbar High School, long recognized as the best educational institution for black teenagers. He enjoyed the school's high academic standards and after-school sporting activities. By all accounts he was a popular student and a gifted athlete.

His athletic endeavors garnered him a scholarship to Amherst College in Massachusetts. Away from home for the first time, Drew eagerly began making new friendships and playing sports. His extracurricular activities took time away from his studies and his grades began to slip. He was called before the dean, who gave him a pep-talk on the importance of high marks. A friend of Drew, Hamilton Bims, said in an *Ebony* article that the dean told him, "Negro athletes are a dime a dozen. Good day." Drew did not let his grades slip again.

He decided to become a doctor and began studying for medical school. Since his parents were poor, he had to delay applying and looked for work to pay tuition costs. He worked as the athletics director at Morgan College in Baltimore, as a lifeguard, and as a teacher of biology and chemistry. By 1928 he had saved enough to pay tuition. He decided to apply to Howard University in Washington, D.C., so he could live at home. They rejected him because he lacked two English credits. Drew was then accepted by McGill University in Montreal, and he earned his degree there in 1933. After finishing his internship and residency two years later, Drew returned to Washington and became a pathology instructor at Howard University.

Drew's boss was Dr. Edward Lee Howes, who had been appointed specifically to train

Charles Richard Drew

upcoming black surgeons, and the dean instructed Howes to make sure his most promising student would follow in his footsteps. That promising student turned out to be Drew. Howes suggested that Drew set his sights toward a D.Sc. degree and advanced surgical training at Columbia University in New York. Howes also arranged for a two-year Rockefeller Foundation Fellowship for Drew.

A dissertation on banked blood

Blood transfusion and chemistry were Drew's two favorite subjects at Columbia. He gave his dissertation on banked blood and began the huge task it represented to complete. He also found himself with extra duties when he took over a vacancy in the residency program halfway though his first year. Drew worked at the new Presbyterian Hospital Blood Bank, which provided a base for his research. After a herculean effort, Drew presented a groundbreaking study that documented the history of

blood transfusions all the way back to the first recorded experiment in seventeenth-century France.

Drew graduated in 1940 when the number of casualties in the Second World War was taking its toll on the European armies. There was a desperate need for blood in quantities so large that the British Army Blood Transfusion Service turned to the United States for help. The Blood Transfusion Betterment Association, an affiliate of the New York Academy of Medicine, established a Blood for Britain program in association with the American Red Cross. Whole blood was deemed unsuitable for the program because its month-long shelf life could only be extended by freezing and storage in blood banks. This was not a practical solution under battlefield conditions. They believed the answer lay in the use of plasma, a yellow fluid that remains after the cells in blood have been removed by centrifuging. Plasma has a longer shelf life, is cheaper to handle, can be used by patients of all blood groups, and seldom produces serious reactions.

Plasma remained a mystery to most scientists, and the association decided to appoint a project supervisor to uncover its secrets. Their choice was Dr. Charles Drew. In September 1940, Howard University decided to release him for four months to work on the project. He instituted a system of rigorous processing in a central laboratory, so that the sterility of all donated blood could be controlled. Drew also relieved the community hospitals of their constant donor traffic by introducing refrigerated mobile blood banks. They would soon be a common sight across the country.

With Drew's help, Britain amassed a large supply of plasma. With the U.S. on the verge of entering the war, his talents were still needed. Howard University granted him a three-month extension on his leave of absence to work in New York. Segregating Negro blood became an important issue, and the Red Cross received specific instructions from the American military to accept only white donors, in the interests of "keeping the morale of white troops high." Although Drew knew that blood groups form the only medical basis for blood segregation, he met this ignorance with his usual calm and ensured that black donors were always as welcome as whites in his own Presbyterian Hospital blood bank.

In April 1941, a month before his leave was over, Drew left New York to return to Howard. Some say the segregation requirements angered him into leaving early, but it was probably due to the fact that he wanted to take the examinations required by the American Board of Surgery.

Setting standards of behavior

Drew had been at Howard for six years, and he started to spend more time teaching. He wanted the country's first black surgeons to stand proudly among America's best, so he set standards of behavior for study, neatness, and even recreational activities.

Although Drew's career featured many firsts in blood plasma research, he was denied membership in the American College of Surgeons. He was also barred from membership in the American Medical Association. In 1947 he decided to seek an AMA membership on behalf of other black physicians, whose lack of membership prevented them from admitting patients to hospitals, denied them official opinions about nationwide medical policies, and curbed their knowledge of new research.

Drew's attempt to receive a membership was never resolved. On April 1, 1950, he and three doctors drove out of Washington at about 2:15 A.M., bound for a free clinic for the poor in Tuskegee, Alabama. Drew had spent the previous day in surgery and had had only a few hours rest before setting out. Shortly before 8 A.M., the car he was driving swerved out of control and crashed; Drew died in the accident. The other three doctors escaped injury. A very promising career was tragically cut short.

William Edward Burghardt (W.E.B.) Du Bois

Social scientist, political activist, author, editor, educator
Born February 23, 1868, Great Barrington, Massachusetts
Died, 1963

"One never feels two-ness,—an American, a Negro; two souls, two thoughts, two unreconciled strivings; two warring ideals in one body, whose dogged strength alone keeps it from being torn asunder."

Years before the civil rights movement became popular in the United States, W.E.B. Du Bois was fighting for black rights.

As a social scientist, political activist, and writer, Du Bois actively campaigned that blacks should seek higher education so they could one day reach full-class citizenship.

His line of thinking was against the conventional wisdom of the day and he clashed with other black rights organizations. Du Bois organized the controversial "Niagara Movement" that wanted to end discrimination through protests.

Du Bois was also the editor of *Crisis*, the official publication of the National Association for the Advancement of Colored People, and it quickly became one of the most influential magazines amongst blacks in the country.

Du Bois backed his words with political action, and was a member of many organizations that were dedicated to helping blacks. After travelling overseas, he joined the Communist Party in 1961 and died at the age of 95 in Ghana, still protesting for black rights.

Pursued higher education

A descendant of French Huguenot, Dutch, and black forefathers, Du Bois (pronounced "du *boyce*") was born on February 23, 1868, in Great Barrington, Massachusetts. He took an early interest in writing, and by the age of fifteen he was covering local news for two black newspapers, the *Springfield Republican* and the *New York Globe*. After graduating from high school in 1884, he received a scholarship to Fisk University, an all-black college in Nashville, Tennessee. He studied classical literature, German, Greek, Latin, philosophy, chemistry, and physics. He earned a B.A. in 1888, then studied history and social sciences

at Harvard University. At his commencement in 1890, he was one of five students to deliver an address, and he spoke on Confederate president Jefferson Davis and on slavery in the United States.

Du Bois then pursued a graduate program in political science as Harvard's Henry Bromfield Rogers Fellow, writing on the suppression of the African slave trade for his dissertation. He received his master's degree in 1891, then received a Slater Fund grant to study overseas from 1892 to 1894. At the University of Berlin he completed a thesis on agricultural economics in the American South.

Vowed to make a name for himself

Traveling overseas made Du Bois more aware of the racism toward American blacks at home. The day before his twenty-fifth birthday he wrote in his diary that he would make a name for himself in science and literature to raise the status of his race.

Du Bois returned to the United States as professor of classics at Wilberforce University in Ohio, and he met his first wife, Nina Gomer. In 1895 he became the first black to receive a doctorate from Harvard. His thesis, *The Suppression of the African Slave-Trade to the United States of America, 1638–1870,* was published as the first volume in a series entitled the "Harvard Historical Monograph Series." In 1896 he worked as assistant professor of sociology at the University of Pennsylvania.

Adopted a militant view

Du Bois was a professor of economics and history at Atlanta University from 1897 to

1903. At the end of that period he published *The Souls of Black Folk,* a collection of fourteen essays exploring the effects of racism and the strength of black people to endure. Du Bois edited and annotated reports on a wide range of subjects between 1898 and 1915, but since they were mainly ignored, Du Bois began to believe the only way for real change to occur was through protests.

This view brought him in direct conflict with Booker T. Washington, a black leader of international recognition who supported technical training for blacks, rather than higher education. Washington felt blacks could assume full citizenship if they gradually assumed economic power, and his beliefs were widely supported by white philanthropists, political figures, and members of the black and white press. Their difference of opinion caused the black protest movement to split into two camps. Du Bois and Washington tried to reach an agreement at a conference at Carnegie Hall in New York City in 1904. They joined with Washington-supporter Hugh Browne to form the Committee of Twelve for the Advancement of the Negro Race. Du Bois later resigned from this group, because he said Washington tried to control it.

Founded the NAACP to sue and lobby for black rights

The next year Du Bois organized meetings of black leaders who shared his views. On July 11, 1905, his supporters met at Fort Erie, Ontario, to organize into what became known as the Niagara Movement. This group wanted to end all distinctions based on race, so blacks could enjoy full economic and political rights.

For the next five years the Niagara Movement held meetings across the country, blasting the white population for not dealing with racism.

The Niagara Movement face great opposition by Washington's Tuskegee Machine, a group that controlled the black press and was backed by white financiers. The Tuskegee Machine also did not engage in the infighting common within the Niagara Movement. Under pressure from Washington's supporters, the Niagara Movement ended in 1910.

The united black front made Du Bois sure of one thing: only a group of blacks and whites who disagreed with Washington's beliefs could bring about change. In 1910 he helped found the interracial National Association for the Advancement of Colored People (NAACP), which favored court litigation, political lobbying, and nationwide publicity to overcome racism. As director of publications

W.E.B DuBois

and research, Du Bois became editor of *Crisis,* the NAACP's official publication. During his twenty-five year stewardship, *Crisis* became widely influential among blacks.

Not an NAACP lackey, Du Bois was pressed to resign

Du Bois's editorial statements often conflicted with the official NAACP position. In 1934 he suggested that segregation allowed blacks to exert power in areas such as economics and education, a view contrary to the NAACP position that segregation be ended in all areas. Under intense pressure from the board, Du Bois resigned and worked at Atlanta University as chairman of the sociology department. He later returned to the NAACP until another rift developed between him and the organization's leaders in 1944.

During this time Du Bois produced several books on the history of the Negro race and racism. In *Black Reconstruction,* he wrote about the role blacks played in rebuilding the South after the Civil War. The history of the black race in Africa and America was outlined in *Black Folk: Then and Now.* He also wrote several novels, including *The Quest of the Silver Fleece* and *Dark Princess.*

In 1948 Du Bois campaigned for the Progressive party in national elections, and two years later he ran for senator from New York with the American Labor party. His work with the Peace Information Center, a group dedicated to banning nuclear weapons, also caused trouble. He and four other members were indicted for "failure to register as an agent of a foreign principal." The case came to trial in 1951, and they were acquitted.

Triumph over State Department's refusal to grant him a passport

When Du Bois wanted to travel overseas, he was denied a passport. Calling him a security risk, the State Department said they would issue the passport if he declared in writing that he was not a Communist party member. Du Bois refused, then he litigated. The Supreme Court ruled Du Bois free to leave the country, upon which he and his second wife, writer Shirley Graham, traveled to several communist countries.

Du Bois was so impressed with communism that he joined the Communist party in 1961, then was invited to move to Ghana by President Nkrumah. In August 1963 the ninety-five-year-old Du Bois inspired a sympathy march on the U.S. embassy in Accra to support the historic "March for Jobs and Freedom" taking place in Washington, D.C. Shortly afterwards Du Bois died. *Crisis* called him the "father of the Negro protest movement."

Paul Laurence Dunbar

Poet, writer
Born June 27, 1872, Dayton, Ohio
Died February 9, 1906, Dayton, Ohio

"There is no poet, black or nonblack, who measures his achievement. Even today. He wanted to be a writer and he wrote."—Nikki Giovanni

 ne of the most popular poets of his day, Paul Laurence Dunbar was the first important black poet in American literature. He was a master craftsman, not only in the dialect poems for which he was best known, but in the eloquent poetry he wrote in standard English.

In addition to his fourteen books of poetry, Dunbar wrote four novels and four books of short stories. His works gained immense popularity in the years immediately following his death, but then went through a period of being criticicized for giving stereotypical portraits of African Americans. However, Dunbar's work has since returned to popularity, and he is once again recognized as a poet of immense talent and deep feeling.

An exceptional student

Dunbar gained much of the material for his books from the stories told by his parents, both of whom had been slaves. His father, Joshua Dunbar, had escaped to Canada via the Underground Railroad and fought for the Union army during the Civil War, finally settling in Dayton, Ohio. There he met Dunbar's mother, Matilda, who had been a house servant on a Kentucky plantation and had made her way north after the war. She had two sons by a previous marriage.

Dunbar's mother was the main influence during his childhood, for his parents were divorced when he was four and his father died when he was twelve. His mother taught him to read and sent him to the local school, where he did extremely well. The only black student in his class, Dunbar was class president in his senior year, and he wrote the class poem, which he recited at the graduation ceremony in 1891. He had been writing poems for some

years and since 1888 had been getting them published in the *Dayton Herald.* As well, he published a small black newspaper during his last two years at school. Called the *Dayton Tattler,* it was printed by a classmate, Orville Wright—one of the Wright brothers who later gained fame as airplane inventors.

On leaving school, Dunbar longed to study at Harvard University, but he knew that his mother's earnings as a washerwoman were not nearly enough to cover the fees. Nevertheless, he had a good academic record and felt sure that he would get a job on a newspaper or in a law office. He was dead wrong. In the business world, his color proved to be more important than his abilities, and the only job he could get was as an elevator operator at four dollars a week.

The young poet

The elevator job gave Dunbar plenty of time to spare. When he had no customers, he read poetry and sometimes he wrote it too. During the next two years he had several poems and articles published in midwestern newspapers, though they brought in very little money. For his first short story, however, he was paid six dollars—more than a week's salary.

Dunbar's former English teacher had long recognized his talent, and in 1892 she asked him to give a welcoming address to the Western Association of Writers at its meeting in Dayton. Dunbar composed a poem for the occasion, which so impressed the audience that he was invited to join the association. Even more important, he met James Newton Matthews, who was to become a great admirer of his work and help promote it.

Encouraged by Matthews, Dunbar took a selection of his poems to a Dayton publisher, who agreed to print five hundred copies for the sum of $125. Dunbar did not, of course, have this much money, but he was allowed to delay payment until the book began to sell, and in fact he was able to repay the publisher within two weeks of publication. Titled *Oak and Ivy* (1893), this first collection of poems included two of his early dialect poems—"A Banjo Song" and "Goin' Back"—as well as "Sympathy," one of Dunbar's best-known poems.

During 1893 and 1894, Dunbar met a number of influential people, including lawyer Charles A. Thatcher and psychiatrist Henry A. Tobey. Both men were to be long-time patrons who promoted his work and helped him out when he was short of money—which he was quite often. In 1893, Dunbar also met a number of black writers and artists, for he spent the summer in Chicago, working for Frederick Douglass at the Haitian Pavilion at the World's Columbian Exposition.

Thatcher and Tobey arranged for the publication of Dunbar's second volume of poetry, *Majors and Minors* (1896), which gained more attention than the first. The poems in this book were divided into two sections. The majority, those which Dunbar considered most important, were grouped under the heading "Majors" and were written in standard English; then came the twenty-four "Minors" poems, which were written in dialect. Ironically, the Minors poems became most popular, and as Dunbar's reputation grew, he became known as a dialect poet.

Thatcher and Tobey also put Dunbar in contact with businessman James B. Pond, who became his manager in 1896. Pond organized public readings and tours for Dunbar, including appearances in a minstrel show. He also arranged a contract with the publisher Dodd, Mead, who undertook to publish Dunbar's future books and pay him a monthly salary. That same year, Dodd, Mead brought out *Lyrics of Lowly Life,* which became Dunbar's best-selling book and spread his reputation across the country.

The following year, Dunbar went to England on a lecture tour arranged by Pond. By this time he had many admirers, and on his return he was offered a well-paid job as assistant clerk in the Library of Congress in Washington, D.C. He held the position from 1897 until 1899, when he resigned in order to spend more time on his writing.

Established poet and fiction writer

During these years, Dunbar produced a large body of work—not only poetry, but novels, short stories, a musical, and various articles. As well, he gave poetry readings, received an honorary degree from Atlanta University, and married the writer and teacher Alice Moore.

Dunbar's first novel, *The Uncalled* (1898), was not well received, mainly because all of its characters were white, and his white readers found them unconvincing. On the other hand, his first two collections of short stories, *Folks from Dixie* (1898) and *The Strength of Gideon* (1900), were extremely popular, with their touching and often humorous accounts of daily life. The stories were set both before and after the abolition of slavery, and some of them were based on accounts told to Dunbar by his mother. Others—especially those deal-

Paul Laurence Dunbar

ing harshly with racism—were based more on his own observations and experiences; they were his way of protesting against the Jim Crow Laws that prevented free black people from becoming first-class citizens.

Dunbar's third collection of stories, *In Old Plantation Days* (1903), was equally popular with his white readers; but like his other plantation stories, it has been severely criticized by black scholars because of the portrayals of happy slaves and kindly white masters. Yet Dunbar was strongly concerned about racial injustice, as is clear from his last collection of stories, *The Heart of Happy Hollow* (1904).

In addition to several more poetry books during the early 1900s, Dunbar wrote three more novels. By far the most noteworthy was his last, *The Sport of the Gods* (1902), which dealt with the sufferings of African Americans in a white racist society. This is Dunbar's most significant fictional work, and it is widely regarded as the first major protest novel written by an African American.

Dunbar was not at all well during this period. He was slowly dying of tuberculosis and had taken to drinking heavily. His marriage was also falling apart. It had always been difficult because his wife's family objected to his darker complexion, and 1902 he and Alice finally separated. Dunbar then left Washington. He spent the last few years of his life in New York and Chicago, and in his home town of Dayton, where he died at the age of thirty-three.

Katherine Dunham

Dancer and anthropologist
Born June 22, 1910, Joliet, Illinois

"I would feel I'd failed miserably if I were doing dance confined to race, color, or creed. I don't think that would be art, which has to do with universal truths."

K atherine Dunham created a successful career treating black dance as an art as well as entertainment. Called the mother of Afro-American dance, she developed a new style of dance after visiting the Caribbean to study the culture, then combined aspects of ballet and modern dance with jazz rhythms and traditional styles of the West Indies.

Dunham promoted this new style in her own choreography and dancing as well as in the schools of dance and cultural arts she established in Chicago, New York, East St. Louis, Haiti, Sweden, and France. She per-

Katherine Dunham

formed in theater, opera, and musicals, and she appeared in several movies. Two of her best-known choreographic pieces are "Bhahiana" and "Burrell House."

Dashed hopes to dance ballet caused Dunham to study West Indian dance

Katherine Dunham's ancestors include Africans, Madagascans, American Indians, and French Canadians. Her interest in the theater dates from her very early years, when she and her brother, Albert, were sent to live with relatives after the death of their mother, Fanny (Taylor) Dunham. The relatives were in the midst of rehearsing a musical drama, which Dunham, then four, found exciting and longed to take part in. Her father, Albert Dunham, was then away working as a traveling salesman, but the following year he married former schoolteacher Annette Poindexter and again provided a home for his children. He settled

his family in Joliet, Illinois, where he opened a dry-cleaning store.

After graduating from high school in Joliet, Dunham attended Joliet Township Junior College, then studied dance at the University of Chicago. To support herself, she and some friends started a dance school, which staged its first dance, called "Negro Rhapsody," in 1931 at the Chicago Beaux Arts Ball. When the school closed from lack of money shortly thereafter, Dunham joined the white poet and dancer Mark Turbyfill to form the Negro Dance Group. Their idea was to stage a Negro ballet, a novel idea in the 1930s when there were no black ballerinas.

Dunham set her heart on becoming a ballerina, but two things changed the direction of her career. One was the lack of support in the field from such people as the white choreographer Agnes de Mille, who objected strenuously to the idea of black ballet dancers. The second influence was a professor of ethnology, who sparked Dunham's interest in ethnic dance to such an extent that she decided to major in anthropology. When she was chosen in 1933 for a part in *La Guiablesse,* a new ballet based on a West Indian legend, Dunham became eager to learn more about West Indian dance forms, to trace their African origins, and find out about their cultural origins. She decided to go to the West Indies and conduct her research directly in the villages.

Wrote about Haiti for her doctoral degree

After getting her bachelor's degree in anthropology from the University of Chicago (from which she also earned an M.S.) in 1936,

Dunham won a Julius Rosenwald travel fellowship to visit the West Indies and conduct anthropological studies on the local dance forms. Thus began a career that took her to Europe, Mexico, South America, Africa, Australia, and Japan. From three months of study in the Department of African Studies at Northwestern University, Dunham set off for Jamaica, where she based herself in an isolated village called Accompong. There she made friends with the people and studied their dances and rituals. She conducted similar studies in Martinique, Trinidad, and Haiti. And in Haiti, she was invited to be an initiate into voodoo.

On her return to New York, Dunham reported on her experiences to the Julius Rosenwald Foundation and was given another grant, allowing her to complete her studies for her master's degree. The Ph.D. Dunham earned from Northwestern University was based on her research in Haiti, and years later she published her dissertation in revised form as *Dances of Haiti* (1983). Her 1969 book *Island Possessed* also described her experiences in Haiti, while *Katherine Dunham's Journey to Accompong* (1946) was about her first trip to Jamaica.

Danced and choreographed to critical acclaim

Dunham's performances soon began to reflect the forms of dance she had witnessed on her research trips, and they drew approving notices from reviewers. One of her first successes was her fiery folk ballet, the "Ballet Fedre," staged in Chicago in 1938. The sets and costumes, which also drew great praise, were the work of the white Canadian designer John Pratt, whom she married in 1941. The couple had a long and successful career together, and in 1952 they adopted a five-year-old Martinique girl, Marie.

Dunham's new dance style first became widely known in 1940, when her Katherine Dunham Dance Company performed her own "Tropics and Le Jazz Hot" in New York. The production received rave reviews, as did her company's performance in the musical "Cabin in the Sky" later the same year. Dunham went on to star in several films, including *Stormy Weather* (1943), and she choreographed a number of movies as well as the opera "Aida." She also toured in the United States and in many parts of the world, returning often to Haiti, where she and her husband established a second home.

In 1966–67 Dunham visited Senegal, where she was invited to serve as technical adviser for the First World Festival of Negro Art. She retired from the stage soon afterwards but remained active in her field. In 1967 she opened the Katherine Dunham Center in East St. Louis, which includes a museum and a school, where she directed the annual Children's Workshop and the Dunham Technique Seminar well into her eighties.

Dunham received many honors over the years, notably the 1987 American Dance Theater tribute, "The Magic of Katherine Dunham." The *New York Times* summed up Dunham's genius in its review of this show, declaring, "Miss Dunham's shrewd mix of show business, art, and anthropology zings across the imaginary footlights like a thunderbolt."

Index

Volume number appears in **bold**.

Art

Hunter, Clementine **2**
Lawrence, Jacob **3**
Parks, Gordon **3**
Tanner, Henry Ossawa **4**

Business

Bing, Dave **1**
Eldridge, Elleanor **2**
Gaston, Arthur **2**
Gordy, Berry, Jr. **2**
Johnson, John H. **2**
Owens, Jesse **3**
Proctor, Barbara Gardner **3**
Randall, Dudley **3**
Sims, Naomi **4**
Walker, Madame C.J. **4**
Walker, Maggie L. **4**
Winfrey, Oprah **4**

Dance

Ailey, Alvin **1**
Dunham, Katherine **1**
Hines, Gregory **2**
Jones, Bill T. **2**

Education

Asante, Molefi Kete **1**
Baker, Augusta **1**
Baraka, Amiri **1**
Barnett, Marguerite Ross **1**
Bethune, Mary McLeod **1**

Chisholm, Shirley **1**
Clark, Joe **1**
Cobb, Jewel Plummer **1**
Cole, Johnnetta Betsch **1**
Collins, Marva **1**
Cooper, Anna J. **1**
Craft, Ellen **1**
Davis, Angela **1**
Derricotte, Juliette **1**
Diggs, Irene **1**
Du Bois, William Edward Burghardt (W.E.B.) **1**
Futrell, Mary Hatwood **2**
Gates, Henry Louis, Jr. **2**
Hill, Anita **2**
Lewis, Elma **3**
Madgett, Naomi Long **3**
McClellan, George Marion **3**
Robeson, Elsanda Goode **3**
Rollins, Charlemae Hill **3**
Scott, Gloria **4**
Steele, Shelby **4**
Sudarkasa, Niara **4**
Terrell, Mary Church **4**
Washington, Booker T. **4**
Woodson, Carter G. **4**

Exploration and adventure

Coleman, Bessie **1**
Henson, Matthew **2**

Fashion

Campbell, Naomi **1**
Houston, Whitney **2**
Johnson, Beverly **2**
Keckley, Elizabeth **3**
Kelly, Patrick **3**

Malone, Annie Turnbo **3**
Sims, Naomi **4**

Film

Belafonte, Harry **1**
Berry, Halle **1**
Campbell, Naomi **1**
Davis, Ossie **1**
Davis, Sammy, Jr. **1**
Givens, Robin **2**
Glover, Danny **2**
Goldberg, Whoopi **2**
Gregory, Dick **2**
Hall, Arsenio **2**
Hines, Gregory **2**
Horne, Lena **2**
Houston, Whitney **2**
Ice-T **2**
Jackson, Janet **2**
Johnson, Beverly **2**
Jones, James Earl **2**
Lee, Spike **3**
McDaniel, Hattie **3**
McQueen, Thelma "Butterfly" **3**
Murphy, Eddie **3**
Parks, Gordon **3**
Poitier, Sidney **3**
Pryor, Richard **3**
Robeson, Paul **3**
Ross, Diana **3**
Singleton, John **4**
Snipes, Wesley **4**
Townsend, Robert **4**
Van Peebles, Mario **4**
Washington, Denzel **4**
Wayans, Keenen Ivory **4**
Winfrey, Oprah **4**

Government and politics

Barry, Marion   1
Bethune, Mary McLeod   1
Bond, Julian   1
Braun, Carol Moseley   1
Brooke, Edward W., III   1
Brown, Ron   1
Bunche, Ralph   1
Burke, Yvonne Brathwaite   1
Chisholm, Shirley   1
Dinkins, David   1
Garvey, Marcus   2
George, Zelma Watson   2
Goode, W. Wilson   2
Harris, Patricia   2
Jackson, Jesse   2
Jordan, Barbara   2
Kelly, Sharon Pratt   3
Lafontant, Jewel Stradford   3
Motley, Constance Baker   3
O'Leary, Hazel   3
Powell, Adam Clayton, Jr.   3
Wilder, L. Douglas   4
Young, Coleman   4

Law

Braun, Carol Mosely   1
Burke, Yvonne Braithwaite   1
Edelman, Marian Wright   2
Harris, Patricia   2
Hill, Anita   2
Hooks, Benjamin L.   2
Jordan, Barbara   2
Jordan, Vernon E., Jr.   2
Kennedy, Flo   2
Lafontant, Jewel Stradford   3
Marshall, Thurgood   3

Motley, Constance Baker   3
Murray, Pauli   3
Sampson, Edith   4
Simmons, Althea T.L.   4
Stout, Juanita Kidd   4
Thomas, Clarence   4

Literature and journalism

Angelou, Maya   1
Asante, Molefi Kete   1
Baldwin, James   1
Baraka, Amiri   1
Barnett, Ida B. Wells   1
Bates, Daisy   1
Bontemps, Arna   1
Bradley, Ed   1
Brooks, Gwendolyn   1
Brown, Claude   1
Brown, H. Rap   1
Bullins, Ed   1
Butler, Octavia E.   1
Carmichael, Stokely   1
Chesnutt, Charles Waddell   1
Childress, Alice   1
Cleaver, Eldridge   1
Cooper, Anna J.   1
Cullin, Countee   1
Du Bois, William Edward
    Burghardt (W.E.B.)   1
Dunbar, Paul Laurence   1
Ellison, Ralph   2
Franklin, John Hope   2
Gaines, Ernest J.   2
Gates, Henry Louis, Jr.   2
Giovanni, Nikki   2
Gordone, Charles   2
Grimké, Angelina Weld   2

Haley, Alex   2
Hamilton, Virginia   2
Hansberry, Lorraine   2
Hayden, Robert, Jr.   2
Himes, Chester   2
Hughes, Langston   2
Hurston, Zora Neale   2
Johnson, James Weldon   2
Madgett, Naomi Long   3
Marshall, Paule   3
McClellan, George Marion   3
McKay, Claude   3
McMillan, Terry   3
Milner, Ron   3
Morrison, Toni   3
Motley, Willard   3
Naylor, Gloria   3
Newton, Huey   3
Parks, Gordon   3
Randall, Dudley   3
Raspberry, William   3
Reed, Ishmael   3
Rollins, Charlemae Hill   3
Rowan, Carl T.   3
Sanchez, Sonia   4
Seale, Bobby   4
Shange, Ntozake   4
Simpson, Carole   4
Steele, Shelby   4
Taylor, Mildred   4
Taylor, Susan   4
Toomer, Jean   4
Trotter, William Monroe   4
Van Peebles, Mario   4
Walker, Alice   4
Wheatley, Phillis   4
Williams, John A.   4
Williams, Sherley Anne   4